Black Girlhood in the Nineteenth Century

Black Girlhood in the Nineteenth Century

NAZERA SADIQ WRIGHT

University of Illinois Press

URBANA, CHICAGO, AND SPRINGFIELD

1 2 3 4 5 C P 5 4 3 2 1
∞ This book is printed on acid-free paper.

The Cataloging-in-Publication Data is available on the
Library of Congress website.

For my family, who sustains me

Contents

Acknowledgments ix

Introduction: Toward a Genealogy of Black Girlhood 1

1. Black Girlhood in the Early Black Press 23

2. Youthful Girls and Prematurely Knowing Girls: Antebellum Black Girlhood 60

3. "Teach Your Daughters": Black Girlhood and Mrs. N. F. Mossell's Advice Column in the *New York Freeman* 93

4. Moving the Boundaries: Black Girlhood and Public Careers in Frances E. W. Harper's *Trial and Triumph* 118

5. Black Girlhood in Early-Twentieth-Century Black Conduct Books 146

Epilogue: The Changing Same? Next-Generation Black Girlhood 179

Notes 187

Bibliography 219

Index 233

Acknowledgments

I KNEW I WANTED TO WRITE this book even before it was written. I thank faculty in the English Department at Howard University, where I earned my master's degree, for their incredible influence on my early intellectual and scholarly growth, which helped lay the groundwork for this study. They are A. Victoria Arana, Rosemarie Garland Thomson, Jennifer Jordan, and the late John Reilly. When I was a doctoral student at the University of Maryland at College Park, Mary Helen Washington encouraged me to take intellectual risks and to write with precision, nuance, and care. Carla L. Peterson's precise lessons in archival research are foundational to my scholarship today.

Several scholarly communities provided mentorship that aided significantly in the completion of the book. Heidi Ardizzone, Hugh Page, Richard Pierce, Dianne Pinderhughes, Al Tillery, and Ivy Wilson at Notre Dame taught me strategies that groomed me to succeed in the profession. I thank Rocio Magana and Jenny Tone-Pah-Hote, fellows in residence at Dartmouth College, for their companionship during our writing sessions, which I miss dearly. Your friendship made the wintry months in Hanover, New Hampshire, bearable and even fun. Ann duCille offered invaluable support, advice, and encouragement during my year as a visiting assistant professor at Wesleyan University. Participating in the Smitherman/Villanueva Summer Writing Retreat in 2013 under the direction of Adam Banks changed the way I view my contributions to the field. Core faculty in the African American and Africana Studies Department at the University of Kentucky offered community and family when I was miles away from home. I am fortunate to have colleagues in the English Department at the University of Kentucky whose scholarly rigor provided the model I needed to thrive. Special thanks goes to Jill Rappoport, whose mentorship and advice were instrumental in shepherding the book through its publication process.

Virginia Blum and Alan Nadel provided much-needed guidance throughout the tenure-track process.

I am grateful for financial support from the Ford Foundation, the National Endowment for the Humanities, the Thurgood Marshall Fellowship at Dartmouth College, and the Erskine Peters Fellowship at Notre Dame. The office of the vice president for institutional research and Dean Mark Kornbluh at the University of Kentucky generously supported my archival research with two Summer Faculty Research Fellowships.

This book is the result of the generosity of individuals who contributed to its successful completion. I thank colleagues who read carefully and commented on parts or all of the manuscript and book proposal. They include R. Victoria Arana, Robin Bernstein, Michael Chaney, Jeff Clymer, Christopher Cozier, Soyica Diggs Colbert, Anastasia Curwood, Rynetta Davis, Andy Doolen, Anna Mae Duane, Ann duCille, Daylanne English, John Ernest, Jan Fernheimer, Duncan Faherty, Eric Gardner, Ellen Gruber Garvey, David Ikard, Gene Andrew Jarrett, Peter Kalliney, Wayne Lewis, Deborah McDowell, Alyssa MacLean, Jeffrey McCune, Kristin Monroe, Joycelyn Moody, Amanda Moulder, Alan Nadel, Steven Thurston Oliver, Deirdre Cooper Owens, Robert Patterson, Simone Drake Poindexter, Melynda J. Price, Howard Rambsy, Jim Ridolfo, Marian Rust, Karen Sánchez-Eppler, Michelle Sizemore, Katharine Capshaw Smith, Greg Stump, Michael Trask, Rebecca Wanzo, and Andréa Williams.

I thank colleagues and friends who have enriched my life deeply through invaluable mentorship. Donald Pease's candid conversations early in my career were instrumental in helping me gain my footing in the field. I value still the scholarly acumen, sharp wit, and good cheer that Michael Chaney exhibited as my mentor for the Thurgood Marshall Fellowship at Dartmouth College. I continue to draw upon Gene Andrew Jarrett's genuine guidance and advice. Robin Bernstein, Eric Gardner, Karen Sánchez-Eppler, Ellen Gruber Garvey, John Ernest, P. Gabrielle Foreman, Joycelyn Moody, Kate Capshaw Smith, and Anna Mae Duane have included me in a scholarly network and community that I value deeply and that has nurtured my intellectual growth. I thank Trimiko Melancon for showing me that friendship and scholarly success are not mutually exclusive. I look forward to yearly dinner/dish sessions at ASA and C19 with Marlene Daut Zaka, who reminds me to "lean out" while doing the work of being a professor. I thank Melissa Stuckey for our sustaining friendship, which has thrived through many moves, moods, and miles. I am grateful to Michelle Sizemore for her friendship, trust, and daily texts that sustain me in more ways than she may ever realize.

My book has benefited from the brilliance of many archivists, curators, and librarians. I thank Krystal Appiah at the Library Company of Philadelphia for her genuine kindness, sharp intellect, and patience in answering my many questions. During my residence at the American Antiquarian Society as a Ford

Foundation postdoctoral fellow, Andrew Bourque, Paul Erickson, Kimberly Pelkey, Jackie Penny, Elizabeth Pope, and Laura Wasowicz provided me with access to materials that strengthened the book significantly. Jo Ellen El-Bashir of Howard University's Moorland-Spingarn Research Center is a treasure and a delight to work with.

I thank my editors at the University of Illinois Press: Larin McLaughlin, who solicited the project in its earliest stages, and Dawn Durante and Brigette Brown, who ushered the book to completion. Dawn's enthusiasm and dedication to my work throughout the publication process defined her as a true pleasure to work with. I thank Kate Babbitt, editor extraordinaire, for her historical acumen, keen insight, and, most important, her patience. Parts of the Introduction and Chapters 2 and 5 appeared previously as passages in "Maria W. Stewart's 'The First Stage of Life': Black Girlhood in the Repository of Religion and Literature, and of Science and Art," *MELUS: Multi-Ethnic Literature of the United States* 40.3 (2015): 150–175; and "Black Girls and Representative Citizenship," in *From Bourgeois to Boojie: Black Middle-Class Performances*, ed. Vershawn Ashanti Young and Bridget Harris Tsemo (Detroit: Wayne State University Press, 2011). I thank Oxford University Press and Wayne State University Press for permission to reprint portions of these articles.

It is rare to have lifelong friends who are like family and who continue to love me even when I retreat for months to complete a book. For their unfailing support, I am forever grateful to Morenike Kassim Miles, Vicky Beasley McPherson, Shawnta Totten and Jerilynne Ming. I thank Lisa Todd, Lakia Somerville, and Jerenze Campbell for always considering me their family.

My sisters and brothers, Jamillah, Bibi, Kala, Monique, Danielle, Karim, Ali, Abdullah, and Darrick, understand the importance of the work that I do even when it takes me far away to complete it. Visits to them in New York, D.C., and Portland are welcome reprieves that rejuvenate me with the energy I need to continue. I thank my nieces, Aliah, Naimah, and Ava, for their joyous spirits, which are daily reminders to take time to slow down and consider what is valuable in life. I thank Richard, Dottie, and Grandma for their continuous love and support. I thank Halima for her nurturing love over the years and Jamila and Latifah for their visit to Kentucky and our road trip to Nashville, which meant more to me than they can imagine.

I thank Keenan McGill for his endless support, love, and devotion, which provided me with the calm and balance to complete this book peacefully. He believes in me even when I do not believe in myself. I look forward to our next road trip and many more to come.

I thank my parents, Francine and Steven Wright—Mommy and Papa—for knowing my intellectual potential even before I did. Through their sacrifice, I gained educational opportunities that shaped me into a scholar. Through my father's example, I learned principles of discipline, determination, and drive. My mother taught me to read and write when I was three, planting the seeds of a true love of learning that continues to govern my intellectual and scholarly journey. She supports me by attending my lectures and joining me on many a research trip. Her elegance, grace, and wisdom are qualities I hope to emulate. I look forward to the day when we celebrate her own book.

Black Girlhood in the Nineteenth Century

Introduction

Toward a Genealogy of Black Girlhood

I WAS RAISED WITH THE BELIEF that with determination and drive, I could attain a future far beyond the limited scope that society held for black girls. I attended the illustrious Holton-Arms School for girls, where I learned that my intellectual curiosity, imagination, and self-expression were valued and permissible. The school's motto—*Inveniam viam aut faciam*, "I will find a way or make one"—taught me to be resourceful, resilient, and resolute. I was naturally drawn to black girls in African American literature who modeled these qualities. I admired the sassy and spirited voices of black girls in Toni Cade Bambara's 1970 collection of short stories, *Gorilla, My Love*, on whose subject I would later write a Master's thesis. Never before had I read about black girls who were outspoken, unafraid, and unmoved by society's gendered guidelines and institutional structures that sought to restrict them. These early impressions of brave, bold, black girls who battled injustices—when adults in their lives were unwilling to—primed me to recognize similar traits in the representations of nineteenth-century black girl characters that I examine in this book. I wanted to trace a literary tradition of irrepressible black girls from the earliest examples of writing on black girlhood by both men and women and in sources that had not been analyzed before.

My investigation led me to several key questions. Why did nineteenth-century black writers convey racial inequality, poverty, and discrimination through the prism of black girlhood? Why did black writers and activists emphasize certain types of girls? What tropes can we identify in the early literature of black girlhood? Where do these girlhood tropes originate?

Black Girlhood in the Nineteenth Century traces writing about black girlhood in early African American print sources in the nineteenth and very early twentieth centuries, a span of time that ranges from the early decades of the new republic to the eve of the New Negro Renaissance. I argue that during this period, black writers used black girls as tools to put forward their social and political agendas. Often these agendas touched upon national issues of concern to the black community, such as safety and survival during the decades when the Fugitive Slave Act was in effect, strategies for achieving full citizenship rights, working for the abolition of slavery, finding work in the post–Civil War industrialized North, and crafting strategies for educating the next generation. Just as often, writers relied upon black girls as emblems of home and family. Whatever stage they chose for their writing, the black girls they wrote about appeared to carry stories of warning and hope, concern and optimism, struggles and success.

Finding these literary girls was not always easy. I draw upon familiar representations of black girls such as Frado in Harriet Wilson's *Our Nig* (1859) and Linda Brent in Harriet Jacobs's *Incidents in the Life of a Slave Girl* (1861). Yet I wanted to identify and learn about other voices. The materials on black girlhood in this study derive from some of the earliest black newspapers and on fiction that has only recently been recovered, including an early short story by Maria W. Stewart; the newspaper advice columns of Gertrude Bustill Mossell; *Trial and Triumph*, an under-recognized serialized novel Frances E. W. Harper wrote in the late 1880s; and Silas X. Floyd's *Floyd's Flowers: Or, Duty and Beauty for Colored Children*, an early-twentieth-century conduct manual for black children. My analysis draws upon the writing of black men and black women. Some of the contributors to early black newspapers were anonymous. Each of them felt they had an important message to convey to and about black girls. Some writers wanted to control them. Others sought to empower them. All of them saw their potential power.

Through extensive archival research, I uncover tropes of black girlhood that provide an under-examined course for racial progress. In contrast to individual journeys to freedom that appeared in popular male-centered narratives such as Frederick Douglass's *The Narrative of the Life of Frederick Douglass* (1845) and Booker T. Washington's *Up from Slavery* (1901), the journey to adulthood of black girls in the literature examined in this book unfolds in the context of networks that include parents, extended family members, community members, and the reading public. These networks often nurture and shape the growth of black girls and help them gain access to the public sphere.

Most of the authors whose work I have chosen to analyze were members of a privileged middle class. In the decades before the Civil War, this group of community leaders was tiny, yet their influence through the printed word was great. They included editors, ministers, antislavery activists, journalists, and teachers. During this period, parents in this group sacrificed, often heavily, to ensure that their children obtained the best education available. As a result, after the Civil War, a new generation of men and women writers was ready to participate in the growing literary world of the black community. Black women journalists and novelists are prominent figures in this literary flowering. By the last decades of the nineteenth century, some black writers were focusing on childhood in book-length works.

Black Girlhood in the Nineteenth Century reveals a key difference in the writing of black men and black women in these decades. Although any generalization has its exceptions, a clear pattern emerged from my sources: black men tended to write the black girl as an *ideal* figure, or, more precisely, as *their* ideal figure. The black girls they wrote about were flat, two-dimensional figures that modeled the behaviors and attributes male authority figures believed were essential for the progress of the race. In contrast, black women writers tended to focus on the interiority of the girls. They wrote about their inner thoughts, their plans, their dreams and aspirations. They emphasized the determination and grit black girls exhibited as they formed successful strategies for fighting and rejecting oppression. They outlined trajectories that led to adulthoods that did not necessarily include wifehood and motherhood. Keeping this difference in mind is helpful when reading texts from the nineteenth and very early twentieth centuries. These differences help us focus on the agendas of men and women leaders of the black community for the girls who would be the next generation.

African American writers took great care in mentioning stages of girlhood and their journey to adulthood. Even in the earliest writings in the 1820s, when it seemed like editors of black newspapers were trying to impose a white value system on black families, they were also, perhaps, trying to insist on a period of childhood for black girls and boys. It is necessary to read deeply between the lines of the articles, speeches, and stories to understand how black writers and activists were using black girls politically.

Black girls emerge in the nineteenth century as exemplars apart from black male figures because they were considered more likely to carry out the aspirations and promises of racial progress. Black writer and journalist Mrs. N. F. Mossell (Gertrude Bustill Mossell) noted the capacity of black girls to act responsibly in matters of racial advancement. In "Only a Girl," published on February 13, 1886, in her weekly advice column in the *New York Freeman*, Mossell identified black girls as more likely to put into practice the teachings gained from early lessons, arguing that black boys were more apt to fall victim to vices of the "world":

> Girls are much more likely to remain what their mothers train them to be than boys. By the time a boy has reached his sixteenth year the world has begun its

> work on him, and often to a great extent undoes the primary training of the mother. Not so with a girl. She is always more or less subject to home influences. The old adage, "a son is a son until he gets him a wife; a daughter is a daughter all the days of her life," often, alas, contains more prose than poetry.[1]

Mossell's perspective relied on a separate spheres agenda, in which black girls would strengthen black homes if they were well educated in domestic habits. But this kind of education is civically oriented. In Mossell's view, black girls had options. They could use the early influences that they gained from an education in household management to prepare themselves for safe and successful entry into the workplace. One could see Mossell's dependence upon home influences as a view that curtailed black women's liberty. However, her view opposes a society made up solely of men who are granted entitlements and avenues of opportunity that black women are not.

We can better understand the lives of black girls in the contemporary moment by uncovering the power they wielded in the nineteenth century. In *Bone Black: Memories of Girlhood* (1996), bell hooks writes, "not enough is known about the experience of black girls in our society."[2] *Black Girlhood in the Nineteenth Century* responds to this call and contributes to recent scholarship in black girlhood studies that highlights the lives of black girls across history, region, and occupation.[3] Joyce Ladner's pioneering work, *Tomorrow's Tomorrow: The Black Woman* (1971), examines the process through which black girls discern the sociological factors that determine the kind of women they will become. Ladner argues that black girls are conditioned to survive in a hostile, oppressive society and become socialized into womanhood as early as seven or eight years old. Ladner's foundation for her analysis draws from nineteenth-century childhoods in slave histories, Sojourner Truth's autobiography, and the autobiographies of Fredrick Douglass and Booker T. Washington. I expand Ladner's work by contributing analysis of additional examples of black girlhoods in the nineteenth and early twentieth centuries. My research on the lives of black girls as seen through the writings of black men and women in the nineteenth century raises questions about black adults' expectations of children and the goals and aspirations of black girls during and after slavery. These same questions pertain to the lives of black boys. I hope that my work will inspire others to explore that history.

A study on nineteenth-century black boyhoods might explore whether African American authors constructed black boys to align with or depart from dominant ideals of nineteenth-century masculinities. Leadership is another issue that is relevant to the literature of black boyhood. Fictional and real-life representations of nineteenth-century black boyhoods such as in Frederick Douglass's *Narrative of the Life of Frederick Douglass* (1845), Sutton Griggs's

Imperium in Imperio: A Study of the Negro Race Problem: A Novel (1899), and Charles Chesnutt's *The House behind the Cedars* (1900) explore qualities that make black male figures capable leaders. These texts offered young readers a formula for reaching that goal.

"There Is Material in Them Well Worth Your While": Black Girlhood Studies

Literary scholar John Ernest has argued that "a complex understanding of racial history . . . is central to the cultural history that produced nineteenth-century American literature. This is the framework within which nineteenth-century African American literature and aesthetics can be most fully appreciated."[4] With this point in mind, I have assembled sources that reveal an evolving cultural and historical valuation of black girlhood in the nineteenth century.

The historical record of black girlhood tends to emphasize the victimization. In September 1832, Maria W. Stewart spoke to the New England Anti-Slavery Society at Franklin Hall in Boston. She documented how doors were closed to black girls in the labor force, even among women employers:

> I have asked several individuals of my sex, who transact business for themselves, if providing our girls were to give them the most satisfactory references, they would not be willing to grant them an equal opportunity with others? Their reply has been: for their own part they had no objection; but as it was not the custom, were they to take them into their employ, they would be in danger of losing the public patronage.[5]

Stewart was disheartened and outraged by the "powerful force of prejudice," even among (presumably white) women who should have been sisters and were unwilling to see the potential for change they held in their hands:

> Let our girls possess whatever amiable qualities of soul they may; let their characters be fair and spotless as innocence itself; let their natural taste and ingenuity be what they may; it is impossible for scarce an individual of them to rise above the condition of servants. Ah! Why is this cruel and unfeeling distinction?[6]

The seemingly immovable wall of prejudice harmed black females of all ages: "Most of our color have dragged out a miserable existence of servitude from cradle to grave." This prejudice stunted the development of black girls. "What literary acquirement can be made, or useful knowledge derived," Stewart asked, "from those who continually drudge from Monday morning until Sunday noon?" Boldly she challenged the white women in the audience to share the experience: "Oh, ye fairer sisters, whose hands are never soiled, and whose nerves and muscles are never strained, go learn from experience!"[7] Stewart aligns unjust acts against black girls to the denial of economic, social, and legislative gains African Americans needed to ensure the protection of their civil rights in the antebellum North. Stewart's speeches contribute to a trope of black girlhood in the nineteenth century in which black girls develop traits of early awareness, self-sufficiency, and resilient willfulness as preemptive weapons against their victimization. Through these actions, black girls become didactic figures who instruct readers about the unlawful society in which their images trafficked.

In his 1852 book *Condition, Elevation, Emigration and Destiny of the Colored People of the United States*, Martin Delany emphasized that black women were the key to the elevation and progress of the black race: "No people are ever elevated above the *condition* of their *females*. . . . To know the position of a people, it is only necessary to know the condition of their *females*; and despite themselves, they cannot rise above their level."[8] Developing black girls' minds through education was essential for racial progress, Delany argued. However, their lessons needed to be purposeful and well-guided: "Let our young women have education; let their minds be well formed; well stored with light and useful information and practical proficiency, rather than light superficial acquirements, popularly and fashionably called accomplishments. We desire accomplishments, but they must be *useful*."[9] Delany's emphasis on the "usefulness" of black women and girls' education suggests that he was not interested in their education for personal fulfillment or enrichment. Instead of educating black girls so they could fulfill individual potential, Delany insisted that their education had public, political ramifications. Delany supports the view that black women should become educated so they could be good examples to their children: "Our females must be qualified, because they are to be the mothers of our children. As mothers are the first nurses and instructors of children; from them children consequently get their first impressions, which being always the most lasting, should be the most correct."[10]

Almost half a century later, black girls were still a topic of great concern to leaders of the race. In 1883, Alexander Crummell, the rector of St. Luke's, the African Episcopal church he had founded in Washington, D.C., delivered a speech entitled "The Black Woman of the South: Her Neglects and Needs." The Woman's Home Missionary Society of his church published it, and Crummell donated the proceeds of the 500,000 copies that were sold to build a home for black women in Washington.[11] Crummell said that "since the day of emancipation hardly any one" had "lifted up a voice" on behalf of the "sisters and daughters of my race."[12] He raised an issue that any member of the black community knew but that whites were not ready to hear: during slavery, black women were not protected in their girlhood. He said, "In her girlhood all the delicate tenderness of her sex has been rudely outraged. . . . From her childhood she was the victim of the grossest passions."[13] Lest his audience (and his readers) think that this issue was part of the past, he reported that two decades after emancipation, white men of the South refused to recognize that any boundaries existed around black girls, even the young women who had prepared themselves for a career: "Of the fifteen thousand colored school teachers in the South, more than half are colored young women, educated since emancipation. But even these girls, as well as their more ignorant sisters in rude huts, are followed and tempted and insulted by the ruffianly element of Southern society, who think that black *men* have no rights which men should regard, and black *women* no virtue which white men should respect!"[14] Crummell's outrage over the failure of whites to respect the innocence of black girlhood and at the inability of the black community to protect its own daughters still sears the page.

Representations of black girls exposed disagreements and debates among black intellectuals about how best to tackle particular racial problems. Whereas Crummell described the industrial training of black girls as preparation for future domestic duties, Anna Julia Cooper, prominent spokeswoman for her race and Alexander Crummell's protégé, rewrites an image of the Southern black girl as a degraded, domesticated subject and encourages instead an image of black girlhood that is imbued with intellect. Her speeches emphasize the importance of the black woman's voice, which would in turn contribute to the strengthening of the black girl's mind as essential for racial progress. She promoted a feminist discourse that valued black girls' capabilities and protested against critical treatments of black girls that often emerged in black intellectual thought. In her 1886 speech "Womanhood: A Vital Element in the Regeneration and Progress of a Race," Cooper argued that black girls were an important component of nation formation:

> I . . . add my plea for the *Colored Girls* of the South: that large, bright, promising fatally beautiful class that stand shivering like a delicate plantlet before the fury of tempestuous elements, so full of promise and possibilities, yet so sure of destruction; often without a father to whom they dare apply the loving term, often without a stronger brother to espouse their cause and defend their honor with his life's blood; in the midst of pitfalls and snares, waylaid by the lower classes of white men, with no shelter, no protection. . . . There is material in them well worth your while, the hope in germ of a staunch, helpful, regenerating womanhood on which, primarily rests the foundation stones of our future as a race.[15]

Here, Cooper constructs black girls as unsheltered "plantlets," "often without a father," yet full of potential. "We need men who can let their interest and gallantry extend outside the circle of their aesthetic appreciation," she writes, and asks for "men who can be a father, a brother, a friend to every weak, struggling, unshielded girl." Cooper reverses the idea of black men as positioned solely in the public sphere. Her vision of the black community includes men who share the domestic responsibilities of parenting and nurturing their children and the children of others. The multiple relationships Cooper constructs for the black man as "a father, a brother, a friend" to black girls conveys a black feminist view of black manhood that counters Crummell's view.

These leaders of black intellectual thought saw mostly the obstacles that whites had placed in the paths of black girls. They believed that no matter how strong, how ambitious, how determined, how educated a black girl might become, she would face nearly insurmountable obstacles when she left her family home to make her way in the world. Despite every best effort, she would be placed in the position of victim against her will. These are not the only nineteenth-century voices about black girls, of course. But it is this mindset that seems to have traversed the centuries. I wondered if this was the whole story, if Stewart, Delany, Cooper, and Crummell, from their position as intellectual insiders, were telling us all we needed to know about the history of black girlhood in the nineteenth century.

Contemporary black feminist scholars center black female youthfulness as a fundamental component of nineteenth-century black civil rights struggles.[16] "Children were the wealth and future of the black nation," argues Ann duCille, who says that black women activists such as Mary Church Terrell and Anna Julia Cooper "defended . . . not only their own bodies but those of their daughters."[17] Mary Helen Washington addresses the void in black women's past experiences in an anthology of black women's writing. "Many of the stories in this collection look backward at the past," she writes, "because we believe it is necessary to understand the past in order to go forward, and there has, as yet, been no adequate investigation of the black woman's past."[18] *Black Girlhood in the Nineteenth Century* provides a long-overdue investigation of the black woman's past by analyzing the literature that explored her girlhood.

Literacy and Reading "Aright"

Literary scholar P. Gabrielle Foreman astutely notes that in Frances E. W. Harper's 1892 novel *Iola Leroy*, she cautioned whites that slavery had "so warped the consciences of men" that they failed to "read aright" the consequences, or what she called the "legible transcript of divine retribution." In other words, as Foreman writes, "reading script does not ensure literacy."[19] Reading representations of black girlhood in nineteenth-century texts requires an awareness of reading "aright." One must read very carefully, with the "eagle eyes" Harper and Foreman called for in order to uncover the intention of the writer. Texts must be read through and under the lines. In some cases they must be read for what is *not* being said as much as for what *is* being said. For example, a column Gertrude Bustill Mossell wrote in 1886 initially looks like a critique of how young black working girls behave in public. But when read "aright," it becomes a scathing critique of how privileged white women failed to extend even the most basic courtesies to black women in public spaces. A short story by a black minister that appears to validate education and public careers for young black women might in the end be a story about the importance of marriage, as in "Thanksgiving at Piney Grove" in Silas X. Floyd's *Floyd's Flowers* (1905). Each text must be read within and even against its social, political, and economic context.

One important question to ask when reading these texts on black girlhood is for whom they were written. The black newspapers of the pre–Civil War period were doubtless read aloud, especially in the 1820s and 1830s. The simple language of articles written for children must be read in this context. One can imagine an older child or an adult reading them to a circle of younger children. These texts were also written at a level that could be mastered by a new reader, regardless of age. The early newspaper columns for children promoted literacy in numerous ways.

Although black communities of the North put a very high premium on education, many schools were closed to black children in these decades, even after states passed laws requiring a common school education through the eighth grade. In these circumstances, the acquisition of literacy within the black community of the North demonstrates a determined commitment to education. We see this in the literacy rates of adults as they were measured by the U.S. census in 1850. These black community members were children in the difficult decades of the 1820s and 1830s, yet their literacy rates were surprisingly high. We can chart access to education by following geography: literacy rates were higher the further north one was and declined the closer one got to the slave states. In Boston and New York, it was 90 and 88 percent, respectively, but rates were lower in Philadelphia (67 percent), Baltimore (64 percent), and Washington, D. C. (65 percent).[20] In the absence of access to public schools for black children, the black newspapers I examine in this book likely contributed significantly to the acquisition of and desire for literacy.

However, access to formal education is not the only predictor of literacy or the knowledge that print sources could provide. Free blacks in the North began establishing literary societies at the beginning of the nineteenth century. In many of these societies, community members donated all forms of print material to build large libraries that were available to members. Literary societies did more than promote literacy; as Elizabeth McHenry has pointed out, they also functioned "to ensure that [blacks] would not be excluded from the benefits associated with reading and literary study."[21] She notes that these societies "offered [African Americans] a protected, collective environment in which to develop a literary background as well as the oral and written skills needed to express and represent themselves with confidence."[22] In 1841, James Willson, a southern black man who moved to Philadelphia and wrote an account of the city's class structure, counted six black literary societies in Philadelphia for both men and women, noting that membership in such societies promoted class aspirations: "The aspiring disposition that education imparts to its possessor . . . is of sufficient worth in fitting us for the high stations in the scale of being, designed by the Creator that we should occupy." The meetings of some literary societies incorporated formal debate, thus preparing members for participation in public life: "Many a young man of color in this community, who previous to the establishment of 'The Philadelphia Library of Colored Persons' never dreamed of rising before a public auditory to make an address, or engage in a debate, is now able to do so with little or no embarrassment, and in a manner highly creditable."[23] The class aspirations that accompanied literacy are visible in many of the sources I examine from the first half of the nineteenth century.

Age: Youthful and "Prematurely Knowing" Black Girlhood

Reading nineteenth-century black girlhood texts "aright" adds the variable of age to the familiar nexus of race, class, and gender. "Age offers an interesting corrective as a way of approaching cultural analysis," argues Karen Sánchez-Eppler, "because unlike gender, or race, or even class, age is inherently transitional."[24] Reading texts through the lens of age unveils specific developmental stages for black girls and the ways that slavery warped the timeline of maturity for them. The age markers that distinguish episodes in black girls' lives are remarkably similar. Black writers often introduce black girl characters at the age of six, which is a period that I call "youthful" girlhood. The age of fifteen or sixteen, what Harriet Jacobs in *Incidents in the Life of a Slave Girl* calls "prematurely knowing" girlhood, identifies a common stage of transition when black girls were forced to become aware of adult concerns in relation to their own lives.[25] These age markers convey that black girls did not have much time to be youthful before they arrived at the age when they needed to make mature decisions and take on adult roles. Black girls needed to find strategies to protect themselves and find a future at an early age. They had to find a way or make one.

As raced, gendered, and youthful figures, black girls occupy a space of in-betweenness, like the figures Hortense Spillers labels "not-yet" subjects: they are not yet citizens and not yet women.[26] In the nineteenth century, black girls possessed little social authority and virtually no property, insignia, rank, or role. Yet in the sources I explore, some of them rejected roles as victims and chose to view themselves as capable and committed to surviving their circumstances. Black girls in literary works convey the development of interiority, the pursuit of education, strategies for surviving abuse, and attempts to break down barriers in employment. Their ability to use their states of ambiguity and renewal to unsettle traditions and alter preconceived notions is but one example of their latent power.

In their literary productions, nineteenth-century African American writers identified clearly defined stages of girlhood. These writers tied youthfulness to moral behavior to contest negative representations of black female sexuality. As Deborah McDowell notes, "it is well known that during slavery the white slave master helped to construct an image of black female sexuality that shifted responsibility for his own sexual passions onto his female slaves. They, not he, had wanton, insatiable desires that he was powerless to resist."[27] Highlighting stages of girlhood challenged prevailing attitudes that black girls were valued solely for their future sexual roles, their economic potential, and their contributions to the slave populations on southern plantations. Identifying black girls as youthful and therefore childlike was a strategy designed to remove any suggestion of sexual objectification.

Phillis Wheatley's girlhood in the eighteenth century began a trope in African American literature that reveals how youthful black girls are gifted with survivalist tactics, which include learning languages and gaining other literacies that help them survive their hardships. In a letter to Wheatley's publisher, her owner, John Wheatley, connected Phillis's youthfulness to her literacy when he described her as a slave girl "between seven and eight years of age" who "in fifteen months time from her arrival, attained the English language, to which she was an utter stranger before, to such a degree, as to read any, the most difficult parts of the sacred writings, to the great astonishment of all who heard her."[28] An 1828 advertisement for a missing black girl in *Freedom's Journal*, a black newspaper, described "a colored girl named Eliza Pisco, about 11 years of age . . . [who] speaks the English and German languages" who was missing from her place of work.[29] Finally, a black girl learned language and writing at an early age in an article titled "The Little Black Girl," published in the *Liberator*, a primary organ of the antislavery movement. The article relates the story of "a good little black girl," named Sylvia, who is taken into a white family at "quite an early age—I think less than twelve." Similar to Wheatley, Sylvia is at first poor and wretched, but she is given religious instruction and learns "the principles of grammar, to apply them in her conversation and writing . . . so that very few grammarians knew more about it than Sylvia did."[30] The ages of these black girls—seven or eight, eleven, and in any case less than twelve—reveals them to be *youthful* girls. Still, they exhibit heightened intellectualism through their mastery of languages and their ability to read signs of danger, both legible and illegible.

African American writers identify the age of fifteen or sixteen as the endpoint of youthful girlhood, the time when black girls become knowingly aware of adult issues that include sexuality and sexual victimization. The concept of black girls' premature knowingness emerges from a girlhood model in Harriet Jacobs's *Incidents in the Life of a Slave Girl.* Enslaved Linda Brent offered age markers in her discussion of the sexual threats that many black girls endured at an early age on the plantation: "Even the little child, who is accustomed to wait on her mistress and her children, will learn, before she is twelve years old, why it is that her mistress hates such and such a one among the slaves. . . . She will become prematurely knowing in evil things. Soon she will learn to tremble when she hears her master's footfall. She will be compelled to realize she is no longer a child."[31] The repeated phrases ("will become prematurely knowing," "will learn," "will be compelled") reveal how enslaved black girls were forced into adulthood and motherhood too early. Purposely prim, the coded and biblical phrase, "prematurely knowing" may have shielded Brent's readers from the details of the sexual advances and rape that she experienced, but it clearly gestures toward the vile indecencies of slave masters and mistresses. Brent explained how she "entered on the fifteenth year—a sad epoch in the life of a slave girl. My master began to whisper foul words in my ear. Young as I was, I could not remain ignorant of their import."[32] Instead of receiving sweet messages as many girls might experience at fifteen, Brent was the unwilling receptor of forced, foul words whispered from her master. The phrase "prematurely knowing" carries an emotional, ethical appeal to readers.

In "Girlhood and Its Sorrows," a chapter published in the slave narrative *Behind the Scenes: Or, Thirty Years a Slave and Four Years in the White House* (1868), author Elizabeth Keckley described how her girlhood was "fraught with pain" because a white man who had "base designs . . . persecuted me for four years, and I—I—became a mother."[33] Keckley blames her repeated rapes on "the edicts of that society which deemed it no crime to undermine the virtue of girls in my then position."[34] The hesitation in Keckley's admission, presented linguistically through two dashes, is intended to omit explicit details of her sexual abuse. However, the dashes function as well to expose the sexual assaults to her readers. Both Jacobs and Keckley insisted on revealing the repeated sexual assaults that often befell enslaved black girls.

Black girls in the North gained premature knowledge when they faced hardships that forced them to think and act like adults. In the 1820s and 1830s, young black girls become prematurely knowing when they had to work because of economic disadvantages or incapacitated fathers. In Harriet Wilson's *Our Nig* (1859), the protagonist Frado becomes aware at an early age that although she lives in the North, she faces abandonment, violence, torture, and a complete betrayal of Christian values and must find the resolve to protect herself and survive. Letitia, Maria W. Stewart's black girl protagonist in "The First Stage of Life" (1861), and Annette in Frances E. W. Harper's *Trial and Triumph* (1888–1889) become prematurely aware when they experience betrayal from family members and must learn to accept the kindness of strangers who offer them nurturance and the space to develop their interior world and learn to govern their impulses. These literary girlhood experiences are mirrored in the lives of some nineteenth-century black women authors, who endured family instability, economic insecurity, servitude, violence, and betrayal by family members. They were forced to think about supporting themselves at a very young age as they looked for ways to escape their situations. These are all forms of premature knowledge. They are hardships that children were supposed to be shielded from.

Black writers and activists associate the trope of "prematurely knowing" black girls in the North with trying to survive a hostile northern landscape, follow expectations about moral behavior, and find ways to secure their futures. For authors who depicted the plight of enslaved black girls in the south, the trope of prematurely knowing black girlhood represented victimization, at once a critique of the unlawful actions of whites and a call for an end to the physical and sexual violence toward black girls in the South. On the one hand, Brent and Keckley's fortitude and rebelliousness function as strategies that prematurely knowing black girls deploy to survive hostile environments. The impulse to fight back rather than endure sexual abuse is a valid survivalist instinct. On the other hand, rebelliousness operates as a vice that renders black girls vulnerable to certain physical and sexual threats. Black girls' refusal to conform and acquiesce to dominant societal rules that dictate compliant behavior sometimes leads to their isolation, loneliness, and despair.

Reading these girlhood texts "aright," then, means paying close attention to clues about the meaning of age distinctions in these texts. Cues about age provide a deeper, more intimate understanding of black girlhood in the nineteenth century. Maria W. Stewart provides distinct age markers to convey the difficulties she experienced during her girlhood in Connecticut in the early nineteenth century:

> I was born in Hartford, Connecticut, in 1803; was left an orphan at five years of age; was bound out in a clergyman's family; had the seeds of piety and virtue early sown in my mind; but was deprived of the advantages of education, though my soul thirsted for knowledge. Left them at 15 years of age; attended Sabbath Schools until I was 20; in 1826, was married to James W. Stewart; was left a widow in 1829.[35]

The age markers show a strict division between Stewart's life as a child and her life as an adult, and indicate shifts in her maturity and development. She learns "the seeds of piety and virtue" at an early age but does not gain "the advantages" of a formal education until she attends Sabbath schools. Fifteen marks the end of Stewart's period of indenture. At this age, Stewart states that she "left them," an action that she attributes to *her will* rather than that of the people who indentured her. Her language conveys determined action, as do Stewart's next words, which show efforts to educate herself. While Stewart distinguishes her lack of choice when she "was left" an orphan and "was left" a widow, fifteen marks the stage in her life when she becomes a strategic thinker and planner. Through age markers, Stewart acknowledges stages of growth to convey that, similar to whites, black girls undergo shifts from youthfulness and dependence to maturity and independence.

Incidents in the Life of a Slave Girl participates in an ongoing tradition in which African American writers distinguish between youthful and prematurely knowing girls to show the unique diversity of black girls' experiences. After Emancipation, there are distinctions between the innocence of youthful black girls and prematurely knowing black girls who embrace their sexuality and view it as an impulse to leave their homes to discover life experiences. While knowingness may be sexual, it often includes a desire to gain worldly experiences and travel beyond the confinement of the home. In Zora Neale Hurston's *Their Eyes Were Watching God* (1937), the fictional protagonist Janie Crawford is six years old when she looks at a photograph of herself sitting among her white classmates and realizes she is black. Janie becomes "prematurely knowing" when she gains an awareness of herself as a sexual being and seeks worldliness. She longs for such experiences at the age of sixteen when she discovers both her sexuality and a yearning to travel and see the world while lying under a pear tree. Janie's impatience to experience the world suggests that her awareness of her sexuality opens her mind to the possibilities and opportunities for travel and experience.

In her 1928 novel, *Quicksand*, Nella Larsen provides distinct girlhood stages for her protagonist, Helga Crane, to explain the choices in men Helga will make as an adult. Through Helga's girlhood memories of her mother's unhappy marriage, we observe Helga's growth from youthful to prematurely knowing girlhood. At an early age, Helga witnesses her mother's damaging dependency on men because she relies on marriages to provide her with money. At fifteen, Helga finally gains fulfillment when she leaves her oppressive home. Unlike Linda Brent's persecution at fifteen, Helga's "prematurely knowing" girlhood at fifteen occurs when Helga's mother dies. Helga leaves her home, becomes educated, learns to accept her blackness, and is finally able to "breathe freely."[36]

In Gwendolyn Brooks's 1953 novel, *Maud Martha*, we meet Maud Martha at the youthful, unblemished age of seven when she is able to detect the beauty in an ordinary flower like a dandelion, which like herself is valued for its "demure prettiness" and "everydayness."[37] The endpoint of Maud Martha's youthful innocence occurs when she is "sixteen and very erect" and watches a performance at the Regal theater. Shocked to see people "parade themselves on a stage" and "exhibit their precious private identities," Maud Martha gains premature awareness that manifests in her staunch assuredness that such showiness is a quality that she would never seek to aspire.[38] Unable to see any other option for herself, Maud Martha retreats into rigid respectability and decides firmly to "keep herself to herself" and "donate to the world a good Maud Martha."[39] For Brooks, stages of black girlhood shift from a youthful place of imaginative acceptance to a rather restrictive outlook that is rooted in self-awareness.

Some representations of black girlhood are unbound by chronological age distinctions. In *Sula* (1973), Toni Morrison relies less on age and more on mood to define premature knowingness between her two black girl protagonists, Nel and Sula. At the end of the novel Nel laments the death of Sula, her dear childhood friend. Through colloquial idiom, Morrison captures their sisterly bond through Nel's intimate memory of their girlhoods: "'We was girls together,' she said as though explaining something. "O Lord, Sula," she cried, "girl, girl, girlgirlgirl.'" Nel's lament, which lifts upward in "circles and circles of sorrow" with "no beginning and no end" conveys how the cyclical nature of black girlhood is boundless, has no limits, and "no end."[40] For many black women, the length of their girlhoods is expansive, limitless, infinite, and capacious.

Reading the literature of black girlhood through the lens of the spaces black girls occupied and how they used those spaces is another way of reading "aright." On slave ships, black girls were often stored in cramped, rigid physical spaces that were often situated next to storage rooms, perhaps as an unconscious comment on the "storage" their wombs represented, the future fertility white owners would exploit for profit. When black girls were sold into slavery, they were defined in the space of the slave ledger. This accounting system identified black girls solely by their youth and future childbearing roles. The R. H. Dickinson & Brother daybook of slave auctions, for instance, documents the buying and selling of slaves in Richmond, Virginia, between 1846 and 1849. The columns in the slave ledger are another space with rigid borders that defined the space and value of black girlhood economically. "Girl Susan" is sold for $470, "girl Hally" is sold for $430, "girl Eliza" is sold for $530, and so on. The practice of buying, selling, and rearing black girls in the antebellum South was the surest, most remunerative way of increasing agricultural capital. The prices planters were willing to pay for black girls was high because they were prized for their economic potential as bearers of future slaves.[41]

African American women writers reconceived rigid spaces by showing their value. The attics and garrets in which Linda Brent in *Incidents in the Life of a Slave Girl* (1861) and Frado in *Our Nig* (1859) live are cramped, isolated, and at times oppressive spaces, yet these black girls used them as sources of mental freedom and places where they imagined and planned for a specific future. Black girls did not allow the physical barriers of narrowly defined spaces to become obstacles. They used them as sources of reprieve, where they could think, imagine, strategize solutions, and look forward.

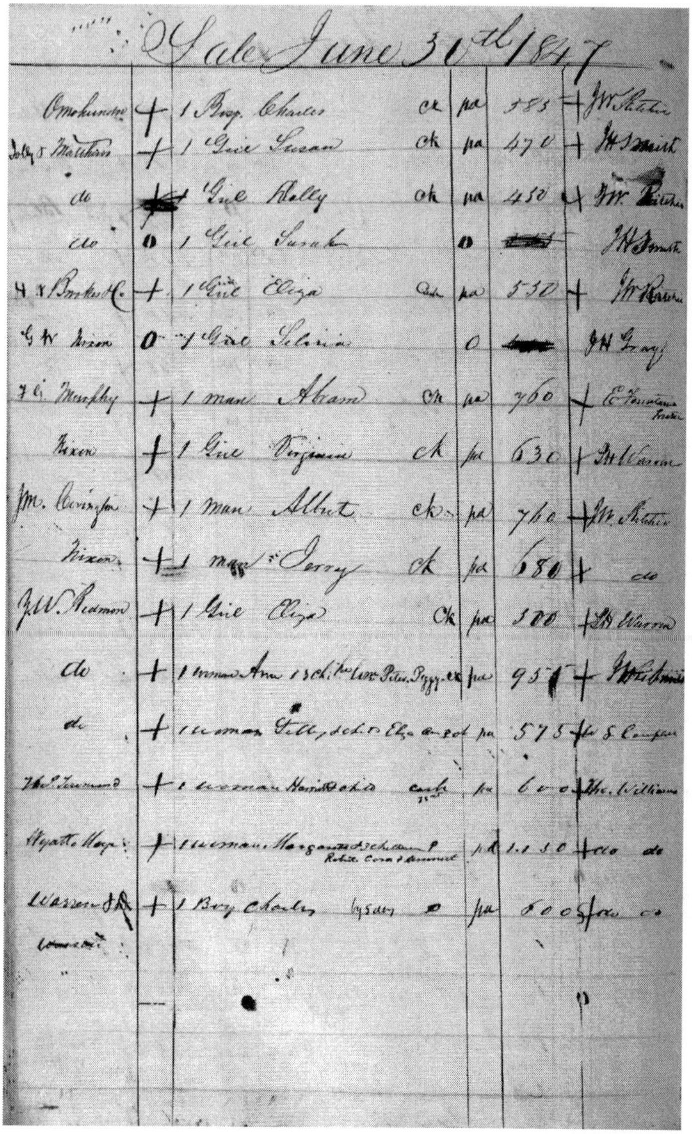

Sale June 30th 1847

Omohundro	+	1 Boy Charles	ck	pd	585	+ J.W. Ritchie
Joly & Matthews	+	1 Girl Susan	ck	pd	470	+ J.H. Smith
do	+	1 Girl Holly	ck	pd	450	+ J.W. Ritchie
do	0	1 Girl Sarah		0	—	J.H. Smith
H & Brooks & Co	+	1 Girl Eliza	cash	pd	550	+ J.W. Ritchie
G.W. Nixon	0	1 Girl Selina		0	—	J.H. Gray
F.C. Murphy	+	1 man Abram	ck	pd	760	+ E. Fountaine Trustee
Nixon	+	1 Girl Virginia	ck	pd	630	+ J.H. Warren
J.M. Covington	+	1 man Albert	ck	pd	760	+ J.W. Ritchie
Nixon	+	1 man Jerry	ck	pd	680	+ do
J.W. Redmon	+	1 Girl Eliza	ck	pd	500	+ J.H. Warren
do	+	1 woman Ann 3 ch. [illegible] Peter Peggy	ck	pd	955	+ [illegible]
do	+	1 woman [illegible] ch. Eliza [illegible]		pd	575	+ [illegible]
Thos. [illegible]	+	1 woman Harriet & ch.	cash	pd	600	+ Thos. Williams
Wyatt & Hays	+	1 woman Margaret & 3 children [illegible]		pd	1130	+ do do
Warren J.H.	+	1 Boy Charles	[illegible]	pd	600	[illegible]

FIGURE 0.1. Page from the daybook of R. H. Dickinson & Brother, Richmond, Virginia, for June 30, 1847. Photo Courtesy of the American Antiquarian Society.

After emancipation, although the advice columns and serialized novels published in the black press had boundaries on the pages of newspapers, they opened up spaces for black women and girls. Advice columns and serialized novels offered practical advice about negotiating the present and planning for the future through work and access to professional careers. They also offered black girls guides about how to occupy public spaces. Occupying public spaces boldly and bravely led black girls one step closer to using their bodies and their voices effectively for public service, and numerous advice givers in the black community, both male and female, wanted to ensure that black girls took their place in a way that would do credit to the race.

Black Girlhood in the Nineteenth Century unveils the possibilities for disciplinary intersections between African American literature, print culture, and black girlhood studies. Employing black girlhood as a critical analytic and methodological lens in early black print materials addresses Leon Jackson's assessment that there exists a "failure to communicate" or "cross-pollinate" between book historians and scholars of African American literature.[42] Reading black girlhood in nineteenth-century literary and visual texts broadens the boundaries of African American literary studies and connects disciplinary fissures in archival methods, girlhood studies, and African American literature in ways that expand our knowledge of African American representational practices and the methodologies we use to understand them.[43] Recent scholarship in African American print culture invites new paths of critical inquiry to expand the field. While critical genealogies of this field have arisen, black girlhood as an analytical index has yet to be fully theorized.[44] My use of black girlhood as a methodological practice responds to Eric Gardner's call for an expanded understanding of nineteenth-century African American literature through an awareness of literary enterprises in unexpected geographic spaces, and to consider "the importance of ideological, even metaphysical 'unexpected places.'"[45] Mapping black girlhood as a representational strategy in early African American literature serves as an "unexpected space" that advances understandings of the black female experience in the nineteenth century and reshapes the social relationship between African Americans and the culture of print.

My exploration of black girls in the nineteenth century contributes to foundational studies on childhood. Historians Dorothy Sterling and Wilma King have revealed how black parents on plantations taught their daughters certain strategies for survival within slave culture.[46] Katharine Capshaw Smith's examination of "the emblematic black child" in African American children's literature published during the Harlem Renaissance helped me understand the significance of periodicity, black authorship, black readership, and audience.[47] Considering the role of black children, including girls, as targeted readers of early black newspapers and periodicals led me to analyze ideas and motives in the primary source materials differently. Other scholars have focused on how new concepts of childhood that included innocence and dependence are grounded in the values of the new nation.[48] In Robin Bernstein's estimation, the relationship between childhood, race, and innocence is grounded historically in the nation's founding principles.[49] Indeed, this innocence is raced as white. African American children were not permitted the privilege of innocence in the nineteenth century. In the texts included in this book, African American authors often expose and undermine the purity associated with white childhood innocence. The constant vigilance black girls must maintain, often to protect themselves against mistreatment and violence, denies them privileged periods of ease or innocence. Instead of enjoying a period of innocence, black girls often suffer. Anna Mae Duane defines children's suffering in the nineteenth century as "powerful, social, political, and emotional resonances in early America," whose representations in literary works "provide[s] a key entry point into the messy processes of the era."[50] In the works included in this study, black girls suffer. Yet despite their suffering, black girls who survive demonstrate resiliency, hope, and triumph.

A Literary Genealogy of Black Girlhood

The texts I examine in this book reveal what I have come to understand as a genealogy of black girlhood. Starting from the earliest appearance of black girls in black publications in the late 1820s, representations of black girls changed over time to suit the purposes of various authors. In each "generation" of this genealogy, black writers conveyed strategies for moving forward that relied on certain behaviors and choices black girls might make. In the context of a nation that sought to restrict the progress, livelihoods, and free will of black people, these strategies were far more than mere musings. They were roadmaps for survival. In the 1820s and 1830s, black girls appeared in the first two known black newspapers as models of potential citizenship for black people. Fictionalized accounts and editorials in *Freedom's Journal* (1827–1829) and the *Colored American* (1837–1841) expose (sometimes unwittingly) the difficulties black men and women endured as they labored to sustain their households. In columns devoted to child readers, black girls exhibited adult behaviors in order to support their fathers both emotionally and morally and to perform the tasks that their working mothers were unable to do. The editors of these papers made it very clear that from the youngest age, black girls were expected to be exemplars of ideal behavior and provide clear moral guidance for other family members. This evidence reveals the struggles of black parents as they searched for work that would provide adequate food, shelter, and clothing for their families and the hopelessness that led some to turn to alcohol to dull their pain. The images of black girls in these early papers convey that, despite efforts to gain recognition as citizens, black families struggled economically and often the youngest, most unlikely members of the household had to assist in household management when parents were unable to do so. It is crucial to note that the black girls on these pages were written by black male editors. They created idealized figures who could encourage their families to adopt white middle-class values, a strategy black editors hoped would lead to greater acceptance in mainstream society.

The next generation I examine in this genealogy of black girlhood appeared in novels and newspapers published on the eve of the Civil War or soon after it began. This is when black women began telling their own stories in print. In Harriet Wilson's *Our Nig* (1859), Harriet Jacobs's *Incidents in the Life of a Slave Girl* (1861), and columns for children in black magazines, black women writers wrote about the struggles and strategies of black girls who did not have the nurturing care of their biological parents and who needed to find their own way to survive hardships. These writings reveal that the middle-class family, which male editors had urged the black community to aspire to a generation earlier, was not the experience of many black girls. Orphaned and unprotected, these girls lose their innocence when they must exhibit self-reliance, resistance, and resourcefulness at a very early age. They rise to the challenge. They are bold, they are vocal, and they refuse to acquiesce to abuse. They use their bodies physically to ward off sexual and physical threats. Although these black girls survive, the cost is high. Without family members to protect them, they must depend on the benevolence of extended kin or community members. Their loneliness and suffering expose both the hypocrisy of whites in the North, who see themselves as charitable abolitionists, and the violence of inhumane whites in the South.

The next generation I explore figured prominently in a growing body of literature produced after emancipation, largely in the late 1870s and 1880s. Some of this literature includes columns by black women journalists who advised black girls about how to move into the worlds of work and marriage. Novels by black women in this period frequently mentioned two-parent households and invariably featured a community surrounding black girls as they matured into adulthood. Literature featuring black girls advised parents on how to cultivate upright conduct in black girls. The texts of this period emphasize self-governing behavior in black girls so they can achieve their goals through their own actions. Formal education figures prominently in the strategies available to black girls. Another theme of this literature is racialization. Some black girl characters are described as dark-skinned while the racial categories of others remain indeterminate, reflecting the polarizing effects within the community of a class structure based on skin color. The literature on black girlhood published in the 1880s speaks openly about actual issues within black communities, such as the reunification of black families, difficulties in securing employment, ambivalent attitudes toward benevolent institutions (particularly white-run ones), and temperance.

The final generation in the literary genealogy of black girlhood that I present appeared at the turn of the twentieth century. Representations of black girls in black conduct books reflect a return to the domestic sphere and traditional values. The arc of racial progress returns to the ideals of the 1820s and 1830s, when black families were encouraged to establish stable homes, following a cultural script that seemed to mimic middle-class white values. Like the writings of black editors some eighty years earlier, black ministers at the turn of the twentieth century presented black girls whose sphere consisted solely of home life. Some between-the-lines evidence in texts such as *Floyd's Flowers* suggests that the social context of increasing racial violence may have informed this retrogressive move. Silas X. Floyd concedes that black girls should be educated, but he argues that that education should focus on home life and on raising children who will be good citizens. He actively discourages any indication of spirited, bold behavior among girls and seeks to rigorously discipline black girls' comportment, dress, and speech.

The genealogy of black girlhood that I present shows that throughout the nineteenth century girls used their wits and intelligence to fight against slavery, abuses as indentured servants, would-be rapists, and other obstacles that stood in the way of their plans for a better life. They rejected the constricting bonds of domesticity that editors laid out in the 1820s. As new opportunities for work, education, and careers emerged, black girls sought ways to take advantage of them. But by the turn of the twentieth century, the picture had changed as black people realized that many doors were still closed to them, which no amount of individual grit and determination could open. Structural obstacles and increasing racial violence turned the focus of the community toward sheer survival, and caution became the watchword of literature that included black girls. One of the interesting points my research revealed was the near silence of black women writers during the first years of the twentieth century. Scholarship to understand the reasons for that silence would doubtless reveal much about the hardships of daily and professional life for black women writers at the turn of the twentieth century. These years were a time when the community was gathering itself. *Floyd's Flowers* was published in 1905, the year W. E. B. Du Bois and his colleagues formed the Niagara Movement and the new strategies of the twentieth century for pursuing racial equality began to take shape. Thus, this book looks at a genealogy of black girlhood in the literary productions of black writers from the first years of the republic, through the difficult antebellum decades, through the initial hopeful decades after the Civil War, to the 1890s and early 1900s, as the community realized that despite emancipation, many doors were still firmly closed and black lives were still in danger. It precedes the flowering of the Harlem Renaissance and the rich body of literature black women produced from that time forward. The voices I analyze here are the voices of the literary foremothers of the black women authors who have shaped so many lives since the 1920s.

Chapter Outline

Black Girlhood in the Nineteenth Century begins with analyses of black girlhood in black newspapers in the 1820s and ends with examinations of literature published at the dawn of the twentieth century, before the Great Migration and before the Harlem Renaissance. Chapter 1 examines representations of black girls in the earliest extant examples of the black press. Looking at *Freedom's Journal* and the *Colored American*, the chapter analyzes the motives of early black editors for advocating roles for black girls in their families and communities that mirrored the idealized roles and perception of the dominant culture. I argue that despite the editors' focus on the ideal black family, the stories and columns they published reveal stress and struggle in black households in these early decades of the republic.

Chapter 2 examines the antebellum decades more broadly and looks at the first writings of black women about girlhood. In addition to the well-known work of Harriet Jacobs and Harriet Wilson, I consider a little-known short story by Maria W. Stewart and an abolitionist text imported from England. Several themes of the book are introduced in this chapter, including the differences in writing by black men and black women about girlhood and the stages of development women writers describe for black girls, which differed considerably from the developmental trajectory of white girls.

Chapter 3 moves past the Civil War and into the 1880s, when it was clear that Reconstruction had failed and blacks were left to shape their own futures. I analyze the life and writings of Gertrude Bustill Mossell in the mid-1880s, in particular her two-year editorship of the column, "Our Woman's Department" for T. Thomas Fortune's *New York Freeman*. This body of work is perhaps the first example of advice to black girls in the postwar industrialized North. The chapter explores the complex and multivalent views of the present and future prospects for black girls Mossell offered in her columns.

Chapter 4, which is set in the same decade, analyzes a novel by Frances E. W. Harper, *Trial and Triumph*, which was serialized in the *Christian Recorder* in 1888 and 1889. The novel is a departure in numerous ways, both from Harper's body of work and from the literature other writers were producing at the time. Harper's protagonist is a dark-skinned girl who rejects marriage and overcomes numerous losses in her early life. She charts her own course and becomes a professional woman who travels south to educate the black masses. The chapter ends with Harper's vision of the potential opportunities for black girls who establish themselves in activist careers before they marry.

Chapter 5 examines several selections from *Floyd's Flowers: Or, Duty and Beauty for Colored Children* (1905), a conduct manual for black children produced by a black minister, Silas X. Floyd. It explores Floyd's ideas about the purpose of education for black girls, how girls should behave in public, and the roles parents should be preparing girls for at the turn of the twentieth century. This chapter and the previous two chapters present a striking contrast between the ways black men and women imagined girlhood after emancipation, especially regarding the duty black girls had to the race, to their families, and to themselves. The epilogue to the book looks at how the knowledge gathered about girlhood in the nineteenth and very early twentieth centuries is relevant today.

In her 1905 essay "The Colored Girl," educator and activist Fannie Barrier Williams wrote: "What becomes of the colored girl? The muses of song, poetry and art do not woo and exalt her. . . . She has inspired no novels. Those who write for the press and magazines seldom think of this dark-skinned girl. . . . She is irrepressible. She is insulted, but she holds up her head; she is scorned, but she proudly demands respect. Thus, it has come to pass that the most interesting girl of this country is the colored girl. Upon her devolves the marvelous task of establishing the social status of the race."[51] This book challenges Williams's claims about the absence of black girls in literature and takes seriously her insistence that they were strong and powerful forces in their communities and in the nation. The lives and representations of black girls are often undocumented and noncatalogued. Yet, this book shows evidence of their presence in literary, historical, and archival records. Recovering a literary history of black girlhood in the nineteenth century will prove useful to the black girls of today and the people who care about them.

1. Black Girlhood in the Early Black Press

THE BLACK PRESS EMERGED in the second half of the 1820s, when the nation was still largely perceived as a new republic that had thrown off an oppressor. When the first black newspaper, *Freedom's Journal*, began publication in 1827, the values that historians refer to as republican ideology were part of everyday discourse. One of the main principles of this ideology was that the ideal republic was composed of citizens who practiced civic virtue—that is, citizens who made personal choices governed by considerations of what would benefit the greater society. Closely linked to this idea was the notion of independence: only free and independent citizens could make the choices that would enable the republic to remain free of tyranny. A man who was under the influence of another because he was in debt to that person, for example, could not say what he really thought, do the work he preferred, or even vote how he pleased. He was not truly free. Notions of freedom and independence were at the heart of the ideology that had led to the American Revolution and that shaped the ideals of the new republic.

The northern black community in the late 1820s was small in terms of proportion of the entire population, but it was large enough in a few cities to support a growing number of organizations, educational institutions, and, most significantly, a movement for the abolition of slavery. But the ideals of the new republic presented difficulties for free blacks. Most of them were pushed into low-skilled, low-status work that made it difficult for them to become property owners. Thus, their participation in the republic was challenged in two ways: their association with an enslaved race devalued them in the eyes of many whites and associated them with unfree people, and their inability to acquire property meant that they were excluded from the category of independent citizens who constituted an ideal republic.[1]

Leslie Harris details the difficulties work categories posed for black men in the context of republican ideology. Regardless of how many generations back a family's free status extended, most whites assumed that free blacks had been born in slavery. Most black men were underemployed and thus had to rely on the income of wives or other female family members.[2] Whites perceived free black men who worked in domestic service positions as dependents, not just in terms of work but also in terms of political guidance from employers. Each of these factors posed a challenge to free black men's sense of themselves as independent.[3]

Northern black men's sense of themselves as citizens was also attacked. In Pennsylvania, New York, and New Jersey—the northern states with the largest populations of free blacks—state officials moved to disenfranchise black men.[4] In New York in 1821 and in Pennsylvania in 1838, new state constitutions stipulated or retained property requirements for male voters that had the effect of excluding most black men. In New Jersey, a state law disenfranchised black voters in 1807.[5] Historian R. J. Young calculates that by 1840, 97 percent of free northern blacks lived in states that excluded them from voting.[6]

Excluded from most of the paths to masculinity that white men had access to, black men constructed their own versions of manhood. Young argues that the new definition emphasized an individual's humanity, control of his own body, freedom of movement, and search for knowledge.[7] Free blacks practiced these values in numerous ways. Choosing to live apart from whites was one strategy. In New York City, for example, free blacks settled their families in households in the 5th and 6th Wards, far from the tip of Manhattan, where former slaveholders lived. By the 1820s, an enclave of black households in what is now Central Park was known as Seneca Village, creating what Leslie Harris calls "a unique case of residential stability for black workers in New York City."[8]

Another strategy was choosing to do independent work. In New Haven, Connecticut, although most black men could find employment only as waiters, sailors, and general laborers, a tiny minority were able to establish themselves in skilled trades as shoemakers, blacksmiths, and bookmakers.[9] In New York City, most free blacks worked as domestic laborers or in other service occupations as the nineteenth century turned, but in the first decades of the century they sought work that gave them greater autonomy. Both men and women were self-employed as fruit peddlers, rag pickers, and day laborers. Washerwomen worked in their own homes. However, as Hillary J. Moss points out, "The price of such independence . . . could be unreliable income that threatened independence."[10] In Baltimore and Boston, free black men had all but abandoned work as domestic servants by 1850, choosing independent work instead.[11] For most free blacks in the North, practicing the republican virtues of independence, autonomy, and control over their bodies—in essence, practicing freedom—meant a daily balancing act between honoring their humanity and earning enough to put a roof over their heads and food on the table.

For black women, too, republican ideology posed difficulties. By the end of the eighteenth century, an ideal for white women had emerged that historian Linda Kerber has labeled *republican motherhood*. Women could not vote or govern and most could not own property; thus, they could not aspire to be the ideal citizens of a virtuous republic. But in their roles as mothers, they could school their children in the republican ideals of virtue, monitoring their acts so they would benefit the nation, independence, and self-control.[12] This ideal for women assumed the full-time presence of the wife and mother at home, which was not possible for most free black women. Most of them needed to work to supplement the low wages of male family members. Nevertheless, evidence from early newspapers shows that elite black males encouraged black women to adopt some of the behaviors of their white counterparts. Mothers were encouraged to use moral suasion, or reasoning, instead of corporal punishment as a means of shaping their children's behavior. Wives were expected to encourage their husbands and to create a home environment that was a refuge from the racism and proslavery ideology of the outside world. Newspaper editors assumed that all free black women had innate qualities of female influence that they could use to benefit their families and the entire black community, regardless of whether or not they worked for wages. As Erica Ball notes, "On a day-to-day basis, a wife could place her domesticity in the service of her family rather than a master or employer."[13]

Children do not figure prominently in republican ideology except as recipients of education and moral training that would prepare them to contribute to the republic: sons as future virtuous and independent voters and householders, and daughters as future mothers who would raise good citizens. However, in many free black households, neither parents nor children had much leisure time to focus on such ideals. Many free black children were forced to work for wages to supplement household income. Most of the chimney sweeps in New York City in the 1820s, for example, were black boys between the ages of four and ten. Black newspaper editors, aware that some children were unable to attend school, urged parents to be good examples because they were the only role models their children came into contact with.[14]

Despite the economic hardships created by a labor market that refused to provide adequate wages for black adults, many free black families gave their children every educational opportunity they could afford. Because most public schools in the North practiced a de facto form of segregation by the 1820s, black communities created alternative sources of education. Some black-run schools offered education that rivaled or surpassed what most white children received in public schools. For example, Watkins' Academy for Negro Youth, which opened in Philadelphia in the 1820s, offered a classical education and rigorous training in rhetoric.[15] But most black children attended schools that operated out of churches. Hilary J. Moss observes that "while white Sunday schools drifted away from teaching basic literacy after 1830 as public schools assumed that responsibility, black Sabbath schools continued to teach children to read and write throughout the antebellum period."[16] Census data makes clear that most black parents saw to it that their children learned to read and write. By 1850, over 85 percent of adults in the free black community in the Northeast were literate.[17] The vast majority of the free blacks who were adults in 1850 had attended enough school in earlier decades to acquire literacy. The rates differed by region, though. In the New England states, the literacy rate was over 90 percent. But in New York, New Jersey, and Pennsylvania, where slavery and indentured servitude for blacks persisted into the early decades of the century, the literacy rate was lower.[18]

This chapter argues that in articles published in the early black press, black male editors wrote and reprinted articles that assigned roles to black girls that suited their framework of adopting the values and mores of the white middle class as a route to greater participation in civic life. The early black press, which was managed by men, expressed the concerns of the free black communities in the North. In addition, black newspapers were a source of information that united scattered communities of free blacks. The messages articles conveyed were intended to mobilize and unite these communities by encouraging involvement in civic life, which included property ownership, voting rights, and working toward the abolition of slavery in the South.[19]

Articles about black girlhood in the early black press offer a lens through which to understand the everyday struggles of African Americans in the early nation. Articles that featured black girls who promoted temperance values and who aided black male figures suggest that black men faced obstacles that made it difficult to fulfill their roles as providers for and leaders of their families and that daughters were expected to take on adult roles when their fathers struggled. Articles that portray black girls receiving moral training or training in household management reveal that editors hoped that families could raise daughters to be model mothers and wives who could create homes for men and boys that were havens from a violent white society. In fact, the model family figured prominently in these newspapers. Articles in black newspapers encouraged black readers to be temperate, industrious, and pursue intellectual development through literacy and education. In this sense, early black newspapers served as conduct manuals. Editors clearly hoped that the articles they published would help readers strengthen their families and communities. They also believed that if white Americans could see blacks emulating their own values and behaviors, they would recognize them as worthy of democratic treatment regardless of their skin color.[20] Much of this literature was premised on a belief that republican values could be realized in the new nation. They believed (or hoped) that if free blacks demonstrated moral behavior, proper decorum, and correct behavior, whites would judge them on their merits and not by the color of their skin.

As early as the eighteenth century, black girls functioned in the writings of black men in relationship to the development of their masculinity. In *The Interesting Narrative of the Life of Olaudah Equiano: Or, Gustavus Vassa, the African* (1789), Olaudah Equiano explains how the memory of his sister's sexual victimization in the hands of slaveholders strengthened his resolve to embrace his manliness and pursue a future of prosperity. Equiano emphasized the connection between his sister's suffering and his budding masculinity: "Though you were early forced from my arms, your image has always riveted in my heart. While thoughts of your suffering have damped my prosperity, they have mingled with adversity and increased its bitterness."[21] Because Equiano could not protect his sister, he "commit[ed] the care of [her] innocence and virtue" to "that Heaven which protects the weak from the strong."[22] In this example, Equiano's inability to protect his sister from her suffering motivated his quest for independence and wealth.

The relationship between the victimized virtue of black girls and black men's roles as protectors is an ongoing trope in early African American protest literature. Scholars highlight the relationship between black manhood and men's role as protectors, particularly in slavery, by noting how difficult it was for enslaved men to achieve a sense of manhood when they were unable to protect their mothers, sisters, daughters, and lovers against abuse. The convention that dictated the inviolability of the white woman's body did not apply to black women. Literary historian Hazel Carby argues that the black female victim "was linked to a threat to, or denial of the manhood of the male slave. Black manhood . . . could not be achieved or maintained because of the inability of the slave to protect the black woman."[23] In the antebellum North, recurring representations of the physical exploitation of black girls in the black press reveal black men's awareness of their inability to fully protect their families and achieve or maintain full manhood.

Thirty years after the publication of Equiano's narrative, David Walker wrote *David Walker's Appeal to the Coloured Citizens of the World* (1829), which emphasized a more radical strategy that was distinctly different from the more cautious path that black editors advocated. Walker argued that black men should rely on rebellion instead of on Equiano's faith in heaven. Walker's fiery manifesto instilled fear throughout the nation and created a provocative image of black men who forcibly demanded civil rights from whites through violence. He wrote: "I do declare it, that one good black man can put to death six white men; and I give it as a fact, let twelve black men get well armed for battle, and they kill and put to flight fifty whites.—The reason is, the blacks, once you get them started, they glory in death."[24] However persuasive Walker's argument might have been, black men in the antebellum North could not rely on a dangerous stereotype that presented them as willing to pursue violence as a method of attaining rights. Black newspaper editors published articles that countered Walker's manifesto with advice for black men about how to attain a genteel character consistent with the middle-class values of self-improvement, temperance, and respectability. For example, "Formation of Character," published in 1829 in *Freedom's Journal*, advised that if a man wanted to attain "the invaluable boon" of prosperity, he need only "fix his eye upon the prize, and press toward it, in a course of virtuous and useful conduct, and it is his." The article presented the message that black men could achieve success and respectability "by resolution and effort," not violence, and the newspaper advised men to guard their steps toward success "with the utmost carefulness."[25] In her work on black conduct discourse in the antebellum North, Erica Ball argues that African American activists' linking of personal behavior to racial politics was informed by a belief that this strategy would lead to "the collective salvation of the entire race."[26] As "Formation of Character" indicates, editors of black newspapers promoted the notion that if black men developed the behaviors and character traits that belonged to the black masculine identities they promoted, they would be able to increase their participation in mainstream life.

Many articles in the early black press thus started from the idealized belief that black men could succeed economically, earning at least enough to support a wife and children. However, evidence peeks through and between the lines of this literature that reveals that this was not the case in most households. Articles about black girls in *Freedom's Journal*, which was published from 1827 to 1829, tacitly assumed that black mothers were often absent from their homes. Editors depicted many black girls as orphaned or bereft of the nurturance and guidance of a mother figure and as the frequent victims of violence. When *Freedom's Journal* folded in 1829, representations of black girls in abolitionist publications filled the gap in antebellum print culture. These publications presented black girls who were mothered and educated by a surrogate white female figure, thus staging black girlhood as a platform on which abolitionists could exalt the benevolence of white womanhood. The model of benevolence that paired black girls with white surrogate mother figures reinforced an ideology that emphasized the character of the white mother, the white household, and white religious and educational processes rather than the agency of black girls. In these abolitionist depictions, biological black parents were generally absent and black girls functioned as blank screens on which white activists projected their social agenda.

The second major black newspaper after *Freedom's Journal*, the *Colored American* (1837–1841), reinstated the black mother as the teacher of her children through intimate dialogues between mothers and daughters about household management, education, temperance, and other topics that would sustain black households. Articles offered representations of black girls who come of age with the aid of a black female figure, thus restoring black womanhood. Biological black mothers appear in nurturing roles to teach their daughters lessons on morality and decorum. This shift toward the presence of black mothers signaled a changing citizenship agenda for African Americans that was focused on improving black girls' minds through education and refining their outer appearance through dress and manners. Black maternal figures became republican mothers who instructed their daughters in matters of character and education.[27]

Freedom's Journal

After slavery was abolished in the northern states, African Americans married, created families, established residences, secured employment, purchased property, joined churches, and forged communities. They built a complex network of societies and institutions separate from the white power structure and engaged in practices that addressed the needs, interests, and aspirations of scattered and disparate northern black communities. Benevolent societies and literary clubs were at the center of black northern antebellum life in major cities. These institutions enabled people to organize across class, ethnic, and religious lines and adjust their activism to the changing social and political landscape.[28] Eventually, northern blacks created an institutional and intellectual public culture with an international reach that facilitated the movement of political ideals and political consensus within their community. *Freedom's Journal* was one resource through which black male editors constructed their civic identity as leaders of their communities.

Freedom's Journal was founded in 1827 in New York City, which at the time had the largest free educated black population of any northern city. In the 1820s, of the nearly 150,000 free people of color who lived in the North, 15,000 were located in New York City and 9,000 in Philadelphia.[29] The paper's mission statement announced that it would operate outside the control of whites. It was to be "strictly a Negro newspaper. It would be Negro speaking; it would be directed to the Negro's problems. Unlike abolitionist newspapers run by whites with black assistance, it would be Negro owned and Negro controlled."[30] As was the case with many later African American newspapers, its objective was to promote blacks' full realization of equality in American life. Its editors stressed to readers that personal responsibility, "the obligation to make it on their own," came with freedom and living in the North. Their intent was to provide a program of self-help and reform within the ranks of the free black population.[31]

Robert S. Levine argues that "the material act of the newspaper itself, circulating from country to country and state to state, can be regarded as a synecdoche for the black national body, which the editors imagined as a single body with 'a single voice.'"[32] In the first issue of *Freedom's Journal*, editors printed a list of black men who were "authorized agents" who disseminated the newspaper throughout the United States and abroad.[33] Able to reach further than the black church or meeting halls, black newspapers emerged as an effective means of communicating with readers who were scattered throughout the northern states. When they read black newspapers, black people became members of what Benedict Anderson has called "imagined communities" in which readers from one region felt instantly connected with those from other regions who were reading the same stories and working toward similar political goals. The newspaper allowed each reader to be "well aware that the ceremony he performs is being replicated simultaneously by thousands (or millions) of others of whose existence he is confident, yet of whose identity he has not the slightest notion."[34] The newspaper reported important meetings, coordinated the community's political work, facilitated the movement of information, and made black people's ideas, values, and politics accessible to a broader national audience. Black institutions such as the library of the Colored Reading Society of Philadelphia and the library of the African Free School maintained subscriptions to *Freedom's Journal*. The American Convention for Promoting the Abolition of Slavery had two subscriptions so it could circulate among those who were not subscribers.[35] *Freedom's Journal* also reached southern states and was even read by slaves, since it was a common practice in the South for literate slaves and free African Americans to read to others who could not read.[36]

Freedom's Journal acquired the characteristics, Frankie Hutton observes, of "a poor man's primer or practical guide for self-development and a provident life."[37] As Jacqueline Bacon argues, columns in *Freedom's Journal* connected independent action with moral, educational, and racial advancement for African Americans and advised readers to be "up and doing," that is, to budget time, conduct oneself discreetly, select friends carefully, elevate one's standing in life, realize the value of hard work, read the Bible regularly, and face problems squarely rather than run away from them.[38] As Susan Ryan notes, African Americans created institutions in response to forms of exclusion that "shifted the burden of citizenship of *who one is* to the more fluid register of *what one does*."[39] African American activism—"what one does"—contributed to the efforts of free blacks to attain full citizenship status in the antebellum era.

Servant Girls

A search on the word "girl" in *Freedom's Journal* using the *America's Historical Newspapers* database yields seventy-nine entries for articles that mention girls or girlhood.[40] Most pervasive in *Freedom's Journal* are articles that featured black girls who worked as housemaids or servants and were accused of crimes, grossly mistreated, and punished severely. For example, an 1828 article reprinted "Punishment of a Slave" from the *Commercial Advertiser*, a white newspaper.[41] The article portrayed the brutal whipping of "a housemaid; a neat, attentive, and orderly girl" who worked in a boarding house in New Orleans. It described a male guest, a Frenchman, who became outraged after the slave girl ignored his repeated requests for water, which he interpreted as insolence, when in fact she simply did not hear him. The Frenchman "struck her with his fist, so that the blood gushed down her face," while other white men stood by observing and demanding more violence. The girl, "excited by this undeserved treatment, put herself on the defensive and seized the aggressor by the throat." When the Frenchman packed his belongings and threatened to leave the boarding house, the landlady, Madame Herries, intervened. The author of the article, Saxe Weimer, described the violent scene that ensued:

> When [Madame Herries] heard this, in order to make her peace with the rascal, [she] had the infamy to order twenty-six strokes of a cow-skin to be inflicted upon the poor girl, and carried her cruelty so far, as to compel her lover, a young black slave who served in the family, to be the executioner. This was not all; the Frenchman, who was a clerk to a commercial house at Montpelier[,] was not satisfied with the punishment. He lodged a complaint against the girl at the Mayor's office, caused her to be arrested by two constables, and had her lashed again in his presence. I regret that I did not pay attention to the name of this wretch, in order to make his shameful conduct as public as it deserves to be.[42]

The "young black slave" in this story who was forced to beat the black girl was emasculated through his inability to protect his lover. It was the black girl, rather than the young male slave, who fought back against her aggressor in an act that displayed her courage and unwillingness to be a victim, yet the account did not celebrate her bravery. Instead, because the original source of the article was a white newspaper, the account focuses on her rebelliousness, for which she was punished severely. This story of a victimized black girl and her emasculated lover acquired different meanings when it was reprinted in a black newspaper. While the black girl's victimization and lack of protection from her lover or her employer reveals the lack of civil rights afforded to black persons and helped readers understand something about the lives of enslaved blacks in the South, the emasculation of the black man in this story was intended to elicit readers' sympathy, concern, and anger.

Protected by neither her lover nor the law, the black girl remains victimized. Through this reprinted article, black male editors removed the victimized black girl from the gaze of a white readership and redirected her image toward black readers. Representations of black girls' abused bodies held different meanings for different readerships. Although in this case, such a representation functioned for white readers to make the Frenchman's "shameful conduct as public as it deserves to be," for these readers, the black girl's aggression toward the Frenchman interfered with the order of the slave system. However, when this story of the girl's brutal treatment and a black male's emasculation was reprinted in a black newspaper, it may have mobilized readers to fight for the abolition of slavery.

The abused and scarred bodies of black girls also upheld the *potential* of black men as protectors. An article in *Freedom's Journal* reprinted from the *Boston Evening Bulletin* reported on the proceedings of a court case in which a white man was indicted after he had gouged out the eyes of a black servant girl "because she made the oath that he was the father of her illegitimate child." The article focused not on the servant girl, who during the trial was "present, in total blindness," but instead opened with a description of the attorney general who was "said to be more competent to the discharge of arduous duties of his highly honorable station than almost any practitioner at the bar." The article presented the testimony of the abused girl's brother, who ran to the attacker and "struck him with a pole, and broke his jaw." When the attorney general asked the brother why he did not "repeat the blow, and knock his d___d brains out!" the judge reminded the attorney that "profanity in court is a high offence punishable with imprisonment; but, in consequence of the unusual excitement of the case, it will, in this instance, be overlooked."[43]

In this article, the inhumane treatment of a black girl functions as an instructional scene. For editors of the *Boston Evening Bulletin*, the image of the abused black girl conveyed lessons on conduct and the misuse of profanity to its white readership. However, for readers of *Freedom's Journal*, the story of a black girl's abuse emphasized the valor of the brother who beat the attacker with a pole, doubtless reminding many black readers of the efforts of black men to protect their families. In both "Punishment of a Slave" and "Anecdote," official legal spaces (the mayor's office in the former and the courtroom in the latter) functioned to obstruct rather than provide full justice for victimized black girls. When such articles were reprinted in the black press, they offered a silent critique of a judicial system that obstructed African Americans' access to protection and civil rights.

As with "Punishment of a Slave" and "Anecdote," articles that featured girls in *Freedom's Journal* that are reprinted from white newspapers have important implications for black readers.[44] Although *Freedom's Journal* was aimed at a black readership and the editorial board was black, many articles in *Freedom's Journal* and later black newspapers were reprinted from mainstream newspapers with a largely white audience.[45] In these reprinted articles, representations of white characters become racialized as black. Reprinting in the early black press aligns with other forms of textual appropriation, such as borrowing, plagiarism, or what Geoffrey Sanborn labels the "lifting" of passages from other works.[46] This lifting was a common nineteenth-century practice in which writers "frequently and abruptly drop in . . . massive blocks of other people's language" and leave these passages "unmarked" or without attribution.[47] However, many reprinted materials in black newspapers are "marked" with a line that identifies the original source. Frances Smith Foster explains that "the nineteenth-century custom of periodicals exchanging complimentary subscriptions and then reprinting, excerpting, or summarizing articles of interest helped expand the range of articles and items."[48] As Foster notes, while reciprocity was less frequent, instances of Euro-American publications citing or endorsing black newspapers are not impossible to find.[49]

Print culture scholars have debated the implications of reprinting in black newspapers and its impact on black readers. Dalila Scruggs argues that a reprint unhinges authorial intent in order to recast the piece to serve another purpose.[50] "Reprinting had the potential," argues Scruggs, "to empty an article or a fictional story of its original intent and meaning to the point where they come to stand for the very inability to testify."[51] Instances of circulation and reprinting help us understand that editors encouraged a particular vision of conduct, ethics, and morality for black reading audiences. Reprinted articles and stories steeped in moral judgment suggested that cultivating black readers' conduct would provide alternative solutions for black families' disenfranchisement. Reprinting also supported a campaign among black activists to strengthen the reading habits of black readers of all ages, from children to adults. Holly Jackson labels reprinting a kind of "intertextual suturing" that contributed to an establishment of an African American print culture.[52] Joanna Brooks rightly argues that reprinting in black newspapers occurred as a result of the fast-paced publication schedule. Brooks notes, "highly motile, easily reprintable cheap print and pamphlets are better adapted to movement and thus have better chances at reaching more readers and staying in print longer. Longer, more substantial books are not adapted for mobility and thus truly depend on social movements to survive."[53] In addition, when black editors recruited reprinted articles for their own purposes, they "wrested authorial control" away from the original writers, thus "weakening [the authors'] own grasp on an original article's signification."[54] Eric Gardner argues that much of the material by writers long assumed to be African Americans was, in fact, reprinted material by white writers. He notes further that authors are identified in a range of ways in reprinted texts in black newspapers, including real names, initials, pseudonyms, and unsigned pieces. Thus, an "original" becomes a slippery category vis-à-vis these texts because "we can no longer assume when we come across a piece not marked a reprint . . . that such signed un-cited texts were original to the paper and/or were by African American authors."[55]

Freedom's Journal often reprinted sensationalist articles that featured abused black girls. For example, a notice for a missing black girl described "a colored girl named Eliza Pisco," an eleven-year-old with "large brown eyes, pretty well grown," who had " a scar a little above her forehead in the hair, speaks the English and German languages." As Eliza was most likely hired as an indentured servant working in the North, her family feared that she had been captured and transported to the South to be sold as a slave. The notice asked readers to keep a watchful eye for the lost servant girl: "The humane are earnestly requested to be on the look out, and whenever they meet with any person who may answer the description of the lost child, will please give information to the Mayor of [Baltimore]. Printers of papers, will serve the cause of humanity by giving this advertisement a place in their respective papers."[56]

The girl's knowledge of English and German and her visible scar highlighted a tension between the mind and the body, the exterior and interior, that heightened the critique of violence against an educated, enlightened person and underscored the inhumanity of slavery. The girl's scars reinforced in readers what Marianne Noble refers to as a "bodily experience of anguish caused by identification with the pain of another." Readers were meant to "feel the pain, an experience that awakens in them an intuitive recognition of the urgency of the antislavery cause and redoubles their commitment to it." Such a "transformation through feeling" when observing black girls' wounded and scarred bodies was meant to provoke a sentimental reaction against slavery.[57] Representations of victimized black girls who had gouged eyes, whipped bodies, and disfigured faces were permanent, painful reminders of black girls' lack of protection against slavery's cruelties.[58]

Black servant girls in *Freedom's Journal* offered black readers another perspective: equipped with keen eyes and a wise perspective that was deepened through their observations of the private actions and habits of the upper classes, they sometimes uncovered the unsavory lifestyles and actions of their employers. For example, in "The Ghost and Conjugal Affection" (June 29, 1827), a servant girl told readers of a widow who was so saddened and distraught by the recent death of her husband that she sought one last night of intimacy with the corpse. In this comical story, the servant girl's insight exposes the often-indecent practices of members of the higher classes. The servant girl's insider account teaches black readers to protect their family structure by refraining from indecent behaviors.

Black Girls and Marriage

Articles in *Freedom's Journal* also featured black men's attempts to protect the character of black girls. Editors printed articles featuring black girl figures who conformed to dominant mores regarding marriage in order to convey a morally upright image of the black race.[59] Articles on marriage in *Freedom's Journal* revealed how "contrary to popular belief, African American marriage, even in the antebellum times, was frequent, that family ties were strong, and that love was both an adolescent fantasy and a fulfilling reality."[60]

In her work on love and marriage in early African America, Frances Smith Foster argues that editors published articles about marriage and singlehood in early black newspapers to demonstrate what African Americans expected or desired and to reveal the "definitions and behaviors that African American[s] wanted to represent themselves and to guide their children and to protect their unions."[61] Articles on marriage in *Freedom's Journal* indicate that African Americans sought to define marriage expectations for their own communities.[62]

Writers for the black press promoted marriage for black girls as a route to respectability while consistently showing the consequences for young women who chose to remain unmarried. "An Unmarried Woman" and "The Old Maid's Diary" reveal that remaining unmarried was perceived to be an undesirable transgression.[63] In the poem "Lines Written on Hearing a Beautiful Young Lady Express a Determination to Live an Old Maid," the author states, "What! live an old maid! The idea is distressing, / Be banish'd for ever the thought—'tis unkind; / Remember great Natur's design, you're transgressing, / By leaving the pleasures of marriage behind."[64] To remain single was perceived an anomaly, a misbehavior, an act that disrupted the status quo. Yet the number of articles about singlehood demonstrated that some girls chose not to marry.[65]

Girls who talked too much were perceived as compromising their ability to attract a mate. "A Sketch of Comfort" featured a girl who was born with "the gift of tongues in the most exuberant manner you can conceive":

> The first thing she did when born was experimentalize on her lungs, and I think I may safely add that the experiment may stick by her to the last. As she grew up this amiable weakness grew with her; at six years old she would talk at you by the hour together, no matter to whom or to what, whether to a woman, a man, a pug dog, or a bed candlestick. She once talked her grandmother into fits, and when an apothecary was sent for, she chatted him into such confusion that the worthy man forgot to take his fee.[66]

The piece continues to ridicule her talkativeness, stating that a school might "possibly cure this distressing malady."[67] The girl eventually marries, but the talkativeness continues. The article ends on what is intended as a comical note, with the announcement that the woman described is actually the author's wife. Implicit throughout the piece is the idea that black girls should be mindful of using their voices sparingly so as not to disrupt the natural order of the household. The article suggests that black girls should be silenced in order to sustain a stable household.

An article that *Freedom's Journal* reprinted from the white press in 1827 emphasized that talking too much was the surest way to become an "old maid." The article asked readers how Tabitha Wilson, "the old maid of 45 . . . could be suffered to reach her 45th year, without being caught in the chains of wedlock." The author, Ned, told how Tabitha's "unruly member, the tongue," which she had put "to daily use and exercise," had prevented her from getting married. His assessment was that "a female wit is a dangerous thing." The article discouraged willful, vocal behavior in black women. It ended with a clear message to its young female readers: "Young ladies have you tongues? Beware how you conduct them. . . . You were made to soothe the toils, and cares, of man's laborious life; to be his partner in affliction, his comforter in trouble, not the destroyer of his happiness and the ruin of his hopes."[68] Tabitha's status as a single woman suggested that she has not quite learned the social codes, which is that her voice was to be used solely for the comfort of black men.

Articles in *Freedom's Journal* suggested that black girls who wanted to participate fully in the black community should aim for marriage, the younger the better. In an 1828 piece, "Girls 'Have at Ye All,'" "Dick Dashall" wrote to the editor that he "has been roaming about for the last two years, looking for a woman to fall in love with . . . but has not seen the girl yet that catches my eye." "Dashall" referred to a previous article in *Freedom's Journal* that identified a system for selecting a mate: "I observed, some time ago a communication in your worthy Journal, signed 'Benedick,' in which he wished to have a telegraphic system established for match-making" that would be based on "a combination of colours, the fortune, age, and connexions of the lady."[69] "Dick Dashall" also provided a list of desirable traits in potential wives. He offered female readers "a few salutary hints for their conduct in courtship" that would attract the right kind of husband:

> At fifteen affect vivacity: If you are in company with the man you would like for a husband, hold your breath long enough to blush when he speaks to you; be cautious at this age to wear your gowns made high in the neck, that your charms may be conceived to be greater than nature usually allots to you at this time of life. At sixteen, affect a great liking for little babies, and get the credit of being a good nurse. At seventeen, read the news of literature and fashion, and talk sentimentally of the happiness of retirement and domestic life; simper a little to put your lips into a pretty shape and kiss little children voluptuously. At eighteen, look out for a husband for yourself, and practice making baby linen

for a friend. At nineteen, go to routs and parties, but avoid "a general flirting"; if not naturally modest, affect it to such a degree as to seem blushing at your own shadow. At twenty, consider yourself in some danger of not getting a husband, and suit your conduct to your circumstances. At twenty-one, affect every thing, and marry any body that courts you. At twenty-two, make an expiring effort by going travelling. At twenty-three, advertise for a husband. I am undone—When you get to twenty-four you cease to be a young girl.[70]

Such literature advised black girls on how to create a proper public image. Although this article was presented in jest, its message was clear. It presented a rigid timeline for marriage in which only women in late adolescence were deemed desirable, and it warned those who were not chosen at that age to pay closer attention to exhibiting behavior that pleased men.

Black Girls in the Diaspora

Articles that feature abused black girls in an international context illustrated how citizenship pursuits took place beyond national borders. The editors of *Freedom's Journal* promoted a pan-African identity that connected the "fate and fortunes" of those living in the United States with others of the African diaspora.[71] The September 14, 1827, issue of *Freedom's Journal* featured a cluster of articles on the front page. The editors dedicated half of the page to an article about violence toward black girls in the West Indies. This story about a black girl's rape and murder was published alongside essays on colonization and missionary work. Together, these articles contributed to a debate on whether the inhumanity of the slave trade was equal in magnitude to pressing global matters of the era. In "West Indies," a soldier paid a slave girl a dollar for sexual services, but when he demanded his money back after the act, the girl "made an animated resistance," and the soldier "stabbed her with his bayonet, and left her bleeding on the ground." Although the girl was found "in a dying state," she spoke out and "gave [an] account" of the attack "before she expired."[72] In contrast to the silencing of black girls considering marriage, editors promoted stories about victimized but valiant black girls who spoke out against their abusers. As with this cluster of articles, the printing of articles about victimized black girls alongside other articles about religious work or national politics throughout *Freedom's Journal* aligned black girls' maltreatment with the historic denial of citizenship rights to the black race in American culture.

"Theresa—A Haytien Tale," featured a different sort of story about a black girl in the African diaspora. It is the story of a brave and heroic black girl. This short story, which was serialized in four installments in *Freedom's Journal* in January and February 1828, is set in the eighteenth century on the island of St. Domingo and details the trials of a mother, Madame Pauline, and her two daughters, Amanda and Theresa, who are left "unprotected, and exposed" when the girls' father and uncle die while fighting against the French in the Haitian Revolution.[73] To protect her daughters, Madame Pauline disguises herself "in the uniform of a French officer" and her daughters as Haitian prisoners in her charge when a French lieutenant and a party of French soldiers approach her. Because he accepts Madame Pauline's disguise, the French lieutenant discloses military intelligence, including the location of the French army's camp, and then leaves. Relieved about the outcome of their close call, Madame Pauline and Amanda rest, but Theresa, "the youngest of the adventurers, greeted not sleep. The vigour of her body was indeed much exhausted, but the emotions of her mind were more active than ever; she saw with the mind's eye the great services which might be rendered to her country." The author describes Theresa's savvy and intelligent listening skills when she overhears the conversation between her mother and the French lieutenant: "Seeming to be inattentive, she pensively bent her eyes towards the earth, listening the while as he unconsciously developed many military schemes, which were about to be executed, and if successful, would, in all probability, terminate in the destruction of the Revolutionists, and, in the final success of the French power in this island." After hearing this intelligence, Theresa decides to find the revolutionary leader Toussaint L'Ouverture and tell him the location and plans of the French army. "Like an heroine of the age of chivalry," Theresa left her mother and Amanda, who were still asleep, and "hastened on her way to the camp L'Ouverture" to save St. Domingo. She warns Toussaint L'Ouverture about an impending attack. Although Theresa's brave actions "prompted her disobedience, which induced her to overstep the bounds of modesty, and expose to immediate dangers her life and sex," Theresa "felt that her conduct was exculpated, and self-reproach was lost in the consciousness of her laudable efforts to save St. Domingo."[74] Her warning of the attack is what enables L'Ouverture and his army to eventually win the war.

When Theresa returns to the hiding place of her mother and sister and finds them gone, she worries that she no longer has a mother "to guide her in life, or affectionate sister, to whom to impart the sorrow of her soul, or participate with in innocent pleasure; friendless and disconsolate, she was now left exposed to many evils, and at a time when the assiduous care of a mother was most essential in the preservation of her well being." She returns to the camp of Toussaint L'Ouverture "to claim fatherly protection, and to seek a home in the bosom of those, to whom she had rendered herself dear by her wisdom and virtue." After Theresa witnesses the war between the French and the Haytiens and the French retreat, she is reunited with her mother and her sister, and "the lost ones are regained."[75] While Frances Smith Foster argues that Theresa's "gender is the single most important element that accentuates her heroism," youthfulness and bravery also contribute to her heroism and to the story's appeal.[76]

Foster speculates that the story, which was signed by "S," was written by Prince Saunders. Others have speculated that the "S" is Maria W. Stewart, although the writing style does not seem to be a good match for other writing by Stewart. I suggest the person who wrote this story was an anonymous woman writer. African American women writers, as we will see in later chapters, often created black girl characters who are heroic and sensitive, quick-thinking and courageous. The range of emotions and actions in the protagonist, Theresa, suggests that the author was deeply in tune with black girls and women's inner lives, thoughts, and motives, and with the interior spaces they inhabited as they moved across the landscape. The author describes Theresa's decision making, her trepidation about autonomous action, her sense of responsibility to her community, and her loyalty to her people with sensitivity and grace. Jacqueline Bacon suggests that "Theresa—A Haytien Tale" may be analyzed in terms of a reshaping of ideal roles for black women.[77] Although the story is about Toussaint L'Ouverture, the author focuses on the heroism and bravery of Theresa and her mother rather than on the heroism and bravery of black men.

While Deborah DeRosa locates Eva in *Uncle Tom's Cabin* (1852) as "the first girl to articulate abolitionist principles [and] the first female who takes center stage, talks, and tries to abolish slavery," Theresa's honorable actions demonstrate that fictional portrayals of black girls as vocal, resistant, and brave were published and circulating among black readers decades before the 1850s.[78] Furthermore, Madame Pauline's protective role as a single parent who cross-dresses and wears a soldier's uniform to save her daughters offers a highly unusual and revolutionary portrayal of black motherhood. Her costuming suggests that gender performance is a necessary tactic of resistance. The performance reveals further the slipperiness of gender identity, which teaches black readers that ideals of femininity and masculinity are neither fixed nor static.

Frances Smith Foster argues that articles that contained representations of children interacting with one parent show readers alternative versions of families alongside what was expected or desired. She asks whether a parent's absence in articles in the early black press "make this ideal family more possible for more people of African ancestry without commenting upon the rightness or wrongness, the existence, the reasons or excuses for single parent homes."[79] Whether black girls are protected by single parents, as in "Theresa—A Haytien Tale," or live in two-parent homes, editors emphasize nurturance as a key quality of family life.

Parenting was a common theme in *Freedom's Journal.* The influence parents have was the theme of an 1827 excerpt reprinted from *Dwight's Theology*: "Parents who read will have reading children. Industrious parents will have industrious children. Lying parents will have lying children."[80] Articles that mention young girls encouraged parents to cultivate righteous behavior in their children, as in "Honesty," an 1827 article that described how "a very little girl of eight or nine years of age" returned a man's pocketbook full of money to him when he dropped it.[81] In "Both Wrong," published in 1827, "a girl of about twelve years of age, who had given up attending a Sabbath School, on being reproved by her father for neglecting to commit to memory her questions, she said, 'Father, how can you make me get questions when you yourself neither pray, nor read, nor ask a blessing on your food when you take it?'"[82] This daughter no longer attends the Sabbath school, the alternative source of education that the black community created in the North, and her father does not put Christian customs and rituals into practice in his everyday life. Black elites such as newspaper editors believed that such choices posed a threat to the progress they were seeking for their community. However, one can imagine a black working-class household where both the child and the father would have found it a struggle to achieve the ideals black editors were promoting. If a child was working, attending school would have been almost impossible, and a father who did long hours of manual labor may well have been too tired to pray or read the Bible at the end of the day. Articles such as this one allow us to peek behind the curtain of normative ideals to glimpse the disjunction between what editors preached and how many members of the community actually lived.

Articles on proper parenting were often published alongside advertisements for black schools, work opportunities, and items about community involvement. "Both Wrong," for example, was published next to an advertisement for B. F. Hughes's School for Colored Children in the basement of St. Philips Episcopal Church in New York City. Hughes advertised "an evening school for persons of Colour," which "will be opened on the 15th of October next in the African School-room in Mulberry Street; where will be taught Reading, Writing, Arithmetic, English, Grammar, Geography, &c. Terms, Three Dollars per Quarter, payable in advance. Hours from 6 to half past 8'oclock."[83] Hughes's school was one of many attempts of black educators to establish black-run schools in New York. That city was the site of the African Free Schools operated by the Manumission Society, a group of white men who advocated colonization to Africa for free blacks.[84] This issue was a source of tension between the free black community and pro-colonization white reformers, and blacks in New York wanted schools where colonization would not enter the curriculum. They also wanted control over the education of their children.

Unlike the African Free Schools, which were subsidized by philanthropic donations and thus provided free education for the children of poor black families, Hughes was compelled to charge a fee. His alternative to the African Free Schools would have required considerable sacrifice for most black families: the comparative worth of those $3 in 2013 dollars is around $72.[85] Put in terms of the cost of living, that is roughly the cost of a week's food for one person. Parents who chose to enroll their children in his school would have had to make difficult choices about how to stretch the family income to pay for their children's education or possibly even about which child to send to the black-run school.

Hughes accepted the reality that many children worked for wages during the day and offered evening hours that made it possible for such children to have at least a few hours of education a day. His school presented a way around a major obstacle to education for many black families. Unfortunately, this school was short-lived. Headed by John Russwurm, the coeditor of *Freedom's Journal*, the school closed one year after it opened when Russwurm emigrated to Liberia.[86]

While *Freedom's Journal* was a strong supporter of the African Free Schools, it also supported black-run schools, as evidenced in this advertisement. Publishing the advertisement next to a cautionary tale of how difficult it was for children to keep up with their studies after they had dropped out of school tacitly but clearly informed mothers and fathers about which choices would have to be made so the next generation could have a better future, at least in the future black editors envisioned.

Black Girls and White Abolitionists

Abolitionist texts published by whites are another source of information about how black girls were viewed in the early decades of the republic. In some of these texts, white women provide education for black girls. As white women abolitionists entered further into the public sphere, abolitionist literature began to reflect their concerns vis-à-vis free black children. This presented a change in how black girls appeared in published literature; whereas the black press of the 1820s had often presented them as unprotected, they appeared in abolitionist texts as the object of white benevolence. This literature offers information about black girls that bridges the gap between the cessation of *Freedom's Journal* in 1829 and the birth of the *Colored American* in 1837. White abolitionist William Lloyd Garrison also filled this gap when he began publishing the *Liberator* on January 1, 1831.

In 1829, Samuel Wood and Sons published *Life and Adventures of Olaudah Equiano, or Gustavas Vassa, the African: From an Account Written by Himself, to Which Are Added Remarks on the Slave Trade, etc.*, an abridgement of Equiano's 1789 text, *Interesting Narrative of the Life of Olaudah Equiano: Or Gustavus Vassa, the African, from an Account Written by Himself.* The manuscript had been completed four years earlier by Quaker, educator, and abolitionist Abigail Mott Moore, who produced the abridged version of Equiano's text with the students of New York's Mulberry Street African Free School in mind. Abigail Moore was the mother of five children at the time and was herself an educator; she and her husband had run a profitable school for boys in Flushing since 1820.[87] She had often visited the Female Department of the African Free School as a member of the school's board of trustees, and she had noticed that the school used a ticket system to reward students for success. Tickets became "a sort of currency" that could be exchanged for various rewards or premiums. In her Preface to the volume, Mott observed that "there is scarcely any thing which can be given to a child as a premium for good behavior which has a better tendency than a book."[88]

When Mott's text was published in 1829, the African Free Schools were on the cusp of a major change in which black community members would wrest control of the schools from the Manumission Society, who had founded the first African Free School in 1789. Conflict was brewing over the issue of colonization; one year later, in 1830, Charles Andrews, a white teacher the Manumission Society had hired in 1809 to run the African Free School on Mulberry Street, became converted to the colonization views of his employers. His vocal support for the idea that free blacks should be transported to Africa put him in direct conflict with the leaders of the black community of New York City, and enrollment at his school abruptly declined. Soon after that, black community leaders demanded that all teachers in the city's three African Free Schools be black.[89]

Support for colonization was not the only reason blacks wanted control of their children's education. Andrews, and likely other white teachers in the three African Free Schools, exhibited a disdain for free blacks, children and their parents alike. In his history of the school, Andrews noted the curriculum for boys and girls. Boys were taught reading, writing, arithmetic, geography, map drawing, and the use of globes. Girls were taught reading, writing, arithmetic, English grammar, geography, sewing, knitting, and other needlework. This was very basic education that did not approach the level offered in most white public schools. Even so, Andrews seemed pleasantly surprised that the black students in his schools could grasp what they were being taught. He wrote, "The progress of the pupils is such as to warrant the conclusion, that they are as susceptible of mental cultivation as the children of white parents."[90] Although 600 students were enrolled in 1829, daily attendance averaged only around 350. Andrews estimated that there were about 1,800 free black children in New York City, and he could not understand why more did not attend his schools. He seemed blind to the reality that many of those children had to work and accused those who were not enrolled in an African Free School of "spending their time in idleness." He blamed parents, who, he said, lacked the capacity to "appreciate the benefits of an education, of which they themselves have not been partakers."[91] These attitudes glossed over worlds of context that included slavery, the crowding of free black men and women into the most menial and low-paying jobs, and his own racism and that of his employers in the Manumission Society. Parents clearly found it difficult to spare their children from work for wages every day. Andrews noted that only a "small proportion ever remain long enough to become proficient in the various branches of a common education."[92] Those who did complete their studies faced the dual obstacles of employers who refused to hire them and workers who refused to work alongside them when a friendly employer could be located.[93]

This environment of brewing racial conflict was the context in which Mott's abridgement of Equiano's autobiographical account of his escape from slavery was published and put into the classrooms of the African Free Schools as one of the "premiums" that could be exchanged for tickets for learning. Mott's belief that books were the best reward for "good behavior" is what "prompted me to attempt an abridgement of the Memoirs of Gustavus Vassa, the African; which, as they contain many interesting circumstances, may not be thought unsuitable for distribution in those schools."[94] What Mott does not say is that the text she abridged was an iconic text of the abolitionist movement and that she hoped that the text would help many young people decide to commit to antislavery. The story of an Igbo from Nigeria who was kidnapped by slave traders as a child, sold and resold numerous times, endured slavery in the harsh U.S. South, was forced to accompany an owner into battle during the Seven Years' War, bought his freedom as a young man, and became a leader of the British abolitionist movement certainly would have been a compelling one for young students of the African Free School.

Equiano's tale was decidedly not fodder for the colonization movement. As a free man, he chose to devote his life to the movement to free his fellow slaves. Returning to Africa was not part of that agenda. Instead, he married a white woman and settled in London, where he was a frequent contributor to debates that eventually led to the abolition of the slave trade in the British Empire in 1807 and the abolition of slavery itself in 1833. Clearly, Mott saw Equiano as a hero and a role model for young free blacks in the United States and hoped that her abridgement of his text would make his story more accessible to them. However, she was not certain how the white leadership structure of the African Free Schools would react to having the text put into the hands of its free black students. She hoped that regardless of the response of the trustees to her version of Equiano's memoir, it would find its way into the hands of schoolchildren: "Whether or not the design of these extracts meet the approbation of the Trustees of the African Schools, I think it will be an interesting little work for children of any class, and I have therefore placed it in the hands of the publisher."[95]

Mott's abridgement of Equiano's memoir included an addendum titled "Remarks on the Slave Trade," a broadside that was originally published by members of the Plymouth Committee for the Abolition of Slavery, a British group. It had been condensed by members of the Philadelphia Society for Promoting the Abolition of Slavery and republished in the *American Mercury* in 1789; this was the version that appeared at the end of Mott's abridgement of Equiano's memoir.[96] The broadside focused on the details of what the Middle Passage was like. Mott wrote a little paragraph to introduce the text in which she noted that it was the publisher's idea to include the broadside. She wrote that she hoped it would "not excite the indignation of any" and would instead "give the young and the uninformed a correct idea of what the poor inhabitants of Africa suffer."[97] "Remarks on the Slave Trade," with its focus on the horrors of slavery, seems to be at odds with Mott's agenda of sharing a story of empowerment and progress for free blacks. For example, in a paragraph that followed Equiano's text, she added an update about his family life after he achieved freedom: "About the time of writing his Narative [*sic*] he married and settled in London; and a son of his named Sancho, who received a good education, was assistant librarian to Sir Joseph Banks, and also secretary to the Committee for Vaccination."[98]

Mott's agenda was to put in the hands of black schoolchildren a shining example of success and productive citizenship. But somehow over the four years that elapsed between the time she submitted her text and the time of publication, her publisher, an ardent abolitionist, had decided to make her book something more than she intended: an antislavery text that might convince whites to support the abolitionist cause by reprinting a forty-year-old broadside that was designed to shock adults into realizing the horrors of slavery.

"Remarks on the Slave Trade" explained that Africans were transported in brutally cramped quarters that were only two feet, six inches tall. The men were crowded so tightly that each man's head was forced between the thighs of the man behind him. Black women were permitted "five feet ten inches by sixteen inches, and the black girls, four feet by twelve inches." Comments in the "Remarks" section of the text Mott abridged describe the lower deck of a slave ship as "one of the most horrible spectacles—a number of human creatures, packed, side by side, almost like herring in a barrel, and reduced nearly to the state of being buried alive, with just air enough to preserve a degree of life sufficient to make them sensible of all the horrors of their situation." When the weather permitted, the captives were allowed above decks for eight hours a day so their quarters could be cleaned. But when the weather was poor, this did not happen.[99] The broadside stated that 45,000 of 100,000 did not survive the Middle Passage and the seasoning process after they reached land. These gruesome details would have shocked the students at the African Free School into realizing what had happened to members of their race, perhaps their grandparents and great-grandparents. It would have forced them to confront knowledge they did not need to have to become abolitionists. They would already have had access to the level of information their parents and community elders deemed important for them to know. The broadside would have made them "prematurely knowing" about aspects of slavery and their history.

The broadside includes an image of a slave ship with captive Africans in their quarters that was reprinted with the broadside in Mott's abridgement of

Equiano's text. The space labeled "Girls' Room" separated black girls and women based on height and age and separated girls from their male and female kin. The location of the space allocated to girls in the back of the ship, next to a storage area indicated their low status. This was far from the message of empowerment that Abigail Mott hoped to convey with the text she had produced. The publication of this text illustrates the complexities of literary work by men and women at this time. Mott, whose goal was to empower free black children, may have been forced to accept a text that was inappropriate for schoolchildren as a condition of publication by Samuel Wood, whose goal was to reach as many whites as he could with an antislavery message. He apparently did not consider whether a forty-year-old text designed for adults was appropriate for children or whether it suited the goals of the text Mott had produced.

The image of the slave ship in Figure 1.1 shows the location of the "Girls' Room" and reveals that the literary genealogy of black girls began with their capture, enslavement, and forced confinement in a "room" that was so low there was not room to sit, much less stand. It would have been a harsh realization for the young black girls of the African Free School who were balancing learning to read, knit, and sew with the need to work to help support their families that their foremothers had endured such torture. It definitely would not have provided a model for their futures. That image and the text that accompanied it subverted the original intentions of the white female abolitionist.

The *Liberator*, another example of a white abolitionist publication, included a range of articles that feature black girl protagonists. Although the *Liberator* was controlled by a white editorial board, the majority of the paper's subscribers in its early years were black.[100] It ran for thirty-five years, from 1831 to January 1, 1866. It was an important publication outlet for black women writers, who published speeches and short or serialized fiction on its pages. Some of these texts challenged representations of black girls as victims. Sarah Forten, for example, a black woman and an active member of the Female Literary Association of Philadelphia, was a regular contributor to the *Liberator*. Forten used the pen names "Magawisca" and "Ada" in her publications.[101]

The *Liberator* also published articles that highlighted the dangers and hardships in the lives of black girls in the North. A small collection of articles on black girls touches on topics such as the eviction of a black girl from a white school after pressure from white parents ("Riot at Brookfield"), a poem by a black mother about the crushing of her girlhood dreams and her fears for her infant child ("The Colored Mother of New England to Her Infant"), and an article about a white couple who tried to transport a black child from the North to Baltimore (and apparently succeeded—"Kidnapping in Boston").[102]

This abolitionist newspaper also sometimes presented whites as benevolent and altruistic figures. In one article, "The Little Black Girl" (1834), the anony-

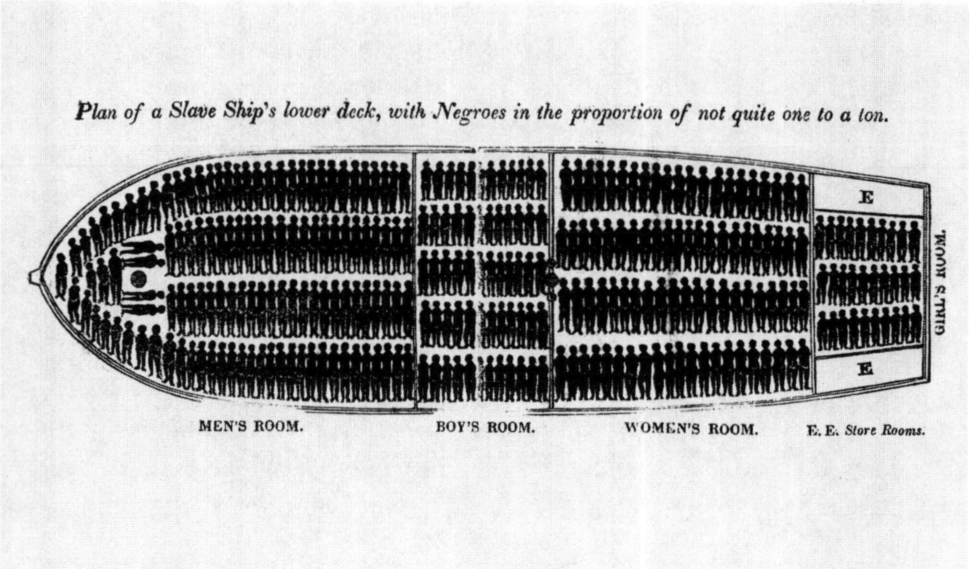

FIGURE 1.1. Slave ship with girls' room. Mott, *Olaudah Equiano, The Life and Adventures of Olaudah Equiano*. Courtesy, American Antiquarian Society.

mous author, presumably white, presents indentured servitude as beneficial for black girls. It tells the story of Sylvia, a poor twelve-year-old black girl, who is taken from her family and made to work as an indentured servant in a white family, of which Mrs. F. is the mistress.[103] This servitude is presented as a stroke of luck for the black girl. In addition to her work, Sylvia learns to read the Bible, converts to Christianity, and studies Latin and French. Through the white family's tutelage and her own perseverance, Sylvia lifts herself from despair and becomes an upstanding, educated young woman. The author informs readers that if poor, black, orphaned Sylvia can learn to read and cultivate a moral character, then surely anyone can follow her example and become a productive person. Sylvia's journey is translated into a set of practices that, if followed, will lead to the development of the ideal republican citizen. The author constructs Sylvia as a model for citizenship through a narrative formula that emphasizes three stages of development: she is a poor orphan, she becomes a dutiful "daughter" to a surrogate (white) mother, and she becomes an educated Christian. The article presumes that whites are benevolent masters who will improve the lives of poor uneducated black girls by giving them clothing, teaching them the Bible, and partnering them with their own white children, who will aid in their transformation. This was far from the strategy of the free black community, which desired to create educational institutions they controlled that would prepare their children for productive lives of self-supporting work.

The author of the article holds Mrs. F. in high regard for her performance of the role of nurturing female: she is "a kind and *good* lady, and loved to do *good*; and she wanted to make the little black girl *good* and happy too."[104] However, framing Mrs. F. as a surrogate mother draws attention to the absence of black women as nurturers and mothers, implicitly suggesting that black mothers were unable to or incapable of socializing their own children. The article also suggests that when biological mothers had died, no one in the black community was capable of stepping in to help the children who were left behind. Mrs. F. is the charitable, civilizing entity while the black girl, as a metonym of the black race, is reduced to playing the role of the mere recipient of the charity of whites.

Sylvia's trajectory is presented as a path the author instructs all readers to follow: "Remember what Sylvia was when she came into the family of Mrs. F. Poor, ignorant and wretched in the extreme; but consider what she is now, an enlightened, intelligent, and well-educated girl: her mind is stored with knowledge, and her heart filled with glowing love for her God." The author locates Sylvia in a particular home in a particular city to emphasize to youthful readers the reality of her transformation: "Children, this story of Sylvia is not a fiction: it is true, and she lives in a very respectable family in this city, and is, no doubt, growing up to be the most valuable member of society, beloved by Mrs. F. and respected by all who know her." The author emphasizes the reality of Sylvia's achievement and the capacity of readers to achieve similar enlightenment. The *Liberator* represents white employers of black, indentured servants as wholly gracious and overwhelmingly good-natured. The equation that being white meant being an innately good Christian and a savior of the black race left little room for any demonstrable action by black girls. This construction conflicted with the agenda of black newspapers, which promoted *self*-help, *self*-improvement, and the careful nurturance of children by black mothers and fathers.

Reuniting Black Girls with Black Mothers in the *Colored American*

The *Colored American* (1837–1841) is the second known black newspaper after *Freedom's Journal*. It began publication on January 7, 1837, in New York as the *Weekly Advocate* under managing editor Philip Alexander Bell and editorial board members James McCune Smith and Charles B. Ray. Bell was born in New York around 1808 and attended the New York City African Free School. Bell was a well-known community activist. He had previously worked as an agent for William Lloyd Garrison's *Liberator* and was a member of temperance, abolitionist, self-help, and charitable groups. He also founded the Philomethean Society, a self-improvement association for young people and was a participant in the Underground Railroad.[105] He wrote that the new paper's goals were to "serve the 'colored community' as a standard-bearer for the Black man's right and claims, and . . . foster emancipation, temperance, education, and universal suffrage."[106]

Three months after the *Weekly Advocate* began publication, it announced that Samuel Cornish, the former coeditor of *Freedom's Journal*, was its new editor.[107] Cornish changed the newspaper's name from the *Weekly Advocate* to the *Colored American*, claiming that an emphasis on "blood, nativity and complexion permitted [the black man] and his kind to be more exclusively American than our white brethren."[108] The *Colored American*'s mission was to promote the concept that African Americans were full members of the American nation. Benjamin Fagan explains that Cornish changed the newspaper's name to emphasize the importance of asserting a national identity. In "Title of This Journal," Cornish insisted on "the propriety of the name of our paper, COLORED AMERICAN, and of identifying the name with all our institutions, in spite of our enemies, who would rob us of our nationality and reproach us as exoticks [*sic*]."[109]

To promote an "exclusively American" identity, Cornish printed articles that instructed readers about the domestic habits and strict gender divisions that he believed would fortify black homes and contribute to middle-class identities. The *Colored American* also spoke out against slavery in the South; it was the "chief method" for communicating with the population of the free North scattered over 5,000 towns; it offered a venue to publicize wrongs toward African Americans and engender public sentiment on their behalf; and its articles sought to improve the public image and correct misconceptions of black men.[110] Throughout its run, the paper increased its readership from black people in the North to a more national base as black churches and organizations helped increase the number of subscribers.[111] A predominately black male editorial board operated the *Colored American* and solicited a wide range of subscribers—white and black, international and stateside, youthful and mature—for the paper through a corps of agents in the United States and southern Canada.[112] At the end of 1837, the newspaper had 1,650 subscribers, 800 of whom lived in New York City. By 1838, when the number of subscribers had increased to 1,800, the number of readers was estimated at 10,000.[113] In 1840, Charles B. Ray was installed as the paper's sole editor.

Preparing Black Girls to Be Household Managers

Articles in the *Colored American* presented gender-specific instructions about raising girls and boys designed to encourage black readers to adopt similar practices in their own households. They promoted lessons for boys that would lead to a profitable career while they encouraged girls to remain in the home. In "Education of Young Men," published in March 1837, the author encouraged readers to "teach our sons Commerce, Mechanism, and Agriculture, and make them the mechanics and producers of the land;—if possible, let us embody them with all the operations of the day. In this way, we shall succeed in their elevation, and in making them important and honorable constituents in society." The author's goals for black girls was not as ambitious: "As to our daughters, let us give them a solid education, and whatever else we neglect, let us not neglect to teach them the use of the needle, housework, and domestic economy in general."[114] While this article mentioned the role of black daughters in just one sentence, other articles focused exclusively on black girls' tutelage in decorum and domestic activities. "Female Education," which was also published in March 1837, explained how a daughter needed to be "taught to control her passion, and to cultivate an amiable and meek disposition." The author argued that a daughter "should be sent to school but four hours each day, for the first ten years of her life," emphasizing that mothers should not send their children to school simply "to get them out of the way, *especially* daughters." For the remainder of the day, a daughter "should be at home with her mother" to "follow her through all the departments of domestic life, and be taught in all the principles of domestic economy." Since "daughters are destined to be wives and mothers," they should be taught "to manage a house, and govern and instruct children" or they would become "lost, "destracted [*sic*]," and their homes "would be in disorder, and their children would grow up loose and without character." The author believed that if mothers followed these instructions, daughters would become "frugal house-[wives] and happy mother[s]."[115] These articles on household management may be read alongside Lydia Maria Child's *The American Frugal Housewife* (1829) and other books designed to teach women and girls to economize and to acquire an education that would prepare them for lives as wives and mothers with practical information. The material in black newspapers constitute what Erica Ball calls "black domestic literature," which was literature that "focused heavily on the roles and responsibilities of African American wives, urging them to act like proper dependents" in order to "help husbands shore up their status as independent heads of households."[116] Such literature appeared to assume that all black women, regardless of class, could follow these domestic ideals. "Rather than insisting on a limited domestic sphere for a small class of elite African American women," argues Ball, "black domestic writers instead praised a democratized version of female influence so that all respectable African American women—irrespective of their participation in the public world of wage labor—were deemed purveyors of qualities generally assumed to be reserved for middle-class whites alone."[117] Articles on household management in the *Colored American* offered encouragement to husbands, promoted the notion that the minds of sons should be trained, and emphasized that daughters should learn habits that would enable them to help their future husbands prosper and maintain economic independence.

Homemaking articles in the *Colored American* feature girls in dialogue with nurturing mothers who direct their daughters kindly and tenderly toward household management, family life, and moral codes. This message from black editors is actually quite a hopeful one. Editors were telling their community that they saw the goal of wife as household manager/mother to her children as achievable. They wanted black homes to be comforting spaces that provided what family members needed, and they saw black girls, the next generation of women, as key figures in that process. In "The Good Girl," a mother encourages her daughter to read her Bible so that she can understand "her obligation to obey its precepts." In "I Wish I Were a Kitten," "a very good girl" named Mary who would rather play all day than complete her chores learns the importance of obligation from her mother and becomes "an industrious little girl" who "feels very grateful to God for giving her a kind mother, that can direct her what to do."[118] "Order and Neatness," published in 1841, offers a similar lesson: a mother explains to her daughter "good habits" of order and neatness.[119] Other articles instructed black girls about how to act responsibly as household managers in training. For example, "Maternal Efforts," published in 1838, features a young daughter who offers financial assistance when her father loses his employment and the financial security of their household is threatened: "'I shall help,' said the youngest girl, hardly four years old. 'I will not have any new frock bought, and I shall sell my great wax doll.'" The black girl sacrifices her possessions as her contribution to restoring the economic health of the household and cheering her father, whose spirit "had sunk in his bosom like a stone" but was now "lifted up."[120] The behavior the *Colored American* taught black girls was intended to dispel negative images of the black race by foregrounding domestic habits that would enable girls to someday construct their own middle-class household. The reprinted article was written by Lydia H. Sigourney, a white poet and author of two conduct books for young women titled *Letters to Young Ladies* (1833) and *Letters to My Pupils* (1837). Sigourney encouraged girls to cultivate skills early in their lives that would contribute to a comfortable household later in their lives, such as strong reading and conversation skills.

The editors of the *Colored American* exchanged and reprinted articles from other early American newspapers to broaden the appeal of their newspaper. Benjamin Fagan notes that the *Colored American* maintained "an exchange list of fifty papers" and reprinted articles from a number of religious and political papers.[121] As long as the newspaper credited the source, reprinting and exchanging articles from other newspapers was encouraged. As they read reprinted articles, black subscribers learned to decipher whiteness and racially coded themes, characters, and words so they could incorporate certain lessons, maxims, and concepts into their daily lives. The articles the *Colored American* reprinted that featured girls taught black and white readers the character traits that whites would recognize as suitable for good citizens. For example, "The Little Hunch Back Girl," published in October 1837, educated readers about racial tolerance through a reprinted story about a disfigured girl named Ellen who wonders if she "might be loved, were I as beautiful as my cousin Mary." The article concludes with a section titled "Remarks" in which an editor compares Ellen's suffering due to her disfigurement to the prejudice black children experience "who feel and suffer . . . every day of their lives—just for the color God gave their skin. How cruel!"[122] This article offers an early example of how discrimination from physical disability might align with the injustices of racism.

According to the editors of the *Colored American*, formal education for African American children in the antebellum North was the surest way to attain a middle-class identity. However, articles on education expressed the vulnerabilities African American children experienced when they entered a new school and the resilience they needed to overcome obstacles. "The Shabby School Girl," which the *Colored American* reprinted from the *Christian Intelligencer* in October 1838, explains that "it is not [an] uncommon occurrence for colored youth, seeking the cultivation of their intellect, to be driven from our institutions of learning by the unkindness and cruelty of their fairer neighbors."[123] The editors were explicit about their disapproval of this intimidation of black schoolchildren. "Very Appropriate," an editorial that was published just above "The Shabby School Girl," stated, "The following narrative is very appropriate to frequent instances which occur within the field of our observation. It is no uncommon occurrence for colored youth, seeking the cultivation of their intellect, to be driven from our institutions of learning by the unkindness and cruelty of their fairer neighbors. Let the hard-hearted, thoughtless, cruel boys of Belleville read the following narrative. And let some of their parents and grandparents read it too."[124] In "Riot at Brookfield" published in September 1839, "a colored girl" accompanied by her mother attends Sabbath school for the first time. Although the teacher comes from a missionary family and thus does not expect mobs and riots in response to her mixed-race school, she encounters "a real scene" of barbarity against the girl.[125] Other white teachers in the North welcomed black girls in schools, as in "A Beautiful Illustration," published in June 1838, in which a black girl is distressed and fearful on her first day of school when she "looks upon trees, playgrounds, large rooms and the multitude of children and teachers." The teacher selects another student to be the "protector of the little stranger." The teacher encourages empathy between the two children, so that "if the stranger is injured, the protector grieve[s]; and kindness shown to one touches the other."[126] In contrast to the articles in *Freedom's Journal* in which black girls were forced to cope with persecution on their own, in the pages of the *Colored American*, black girls sometimes found protectors and supporters.

Temperance

In its articles on girlhood, the *Colored American* offered readers instruction on how to maintain morally upright households by embracing temperance values. The *Colored American* published original and reprinted articles that featured girls as storytellers who recounted sorrowful scenes of how intemperance had destroyed their families or how they had learned morally righteous behavior. These articles often reveal how a girl had come to an understanding of goodness by witnessing a form of mistreatment. Temperance stories told through the eyes of girls appeared repeatedly in the *Colored American*, often reprinted from other newspapers. For example, "The Jug" (June 1841) was reprinted from the *Reformed Family*, "My Cousin Mary, or the Inebriate" (July 1839) was reprinted from the *Maine Temperance Gazette*, and "An Affecting Story" (November 1839) was reprinted from the *Boston Mercantile Advertiser*. "Scenes in a Christian Family" (February 1839), reprinted from the *Christian Watchman*, is described as no "fancy sketch, but a true penciling from life" about a mother who dies and leaves her children orphaned after their drunkard father abandons his family. "A Heart-Moving Picture" is the conclusion of a story titled "Tale of Real Life" (November 1838), reprinted from the *Journal of the American Temperance Union*.[127] The story describes a drunkard father who loses the mortgage of his house and expresses his frustration by beating his wife and four children. They are forced out of their home and into the poorhouse. Because of their anguish, Mary, the wife, becomes ill, and "in a few days a fever set in, and she, too, rested from all her trials." The editors of the *Colored American* commented, "We believe the room occupied in our paper by this extract, could not be better occupied at this particular moment. In this representation of the horrid effects of the traffic of intoxication, touching to every feeling heart, as it must be, there is no over-drawing of the soul-sickening picture."[128] Temperance articles often featured mother figures whose presence was once felt but who suffer, become destitute, die, or are sometimes absent altogether as a result of the husband's drunkenness. In such cases, the daughter is often left to manage the family. "The End of the Drunkard," published in July 1839, describes a man "in a beastly state of intoxication" who is followed by "a young, beautiful interesting girl, not out of her teens" who is most likely his daughter. The man is witnessed abusing his daughter when "he . . . raise[s] his arm and [strikes] this lovely being to the earth." A crowd forms and would have pursued the "inebriated wretched," but "the same delicate form interposed to present the consummation of the deed."[129] The story reveals that the father "had once enjoyed a handsome property, but liquor ruined him." The black girl, whose mother had died from anguish and poverty, was left to support the household and feed her siblings. "The Deserted Children," published in September 1839, is an "affecting" story about how the eldest child of a poor family, "a girl of six years, but remarkably shrewd and acute for her age," saves her siblings from death when they are abandoned by their father, who drowns due to intoxication. Determined to save her family, the girl "set herself to examine her resources. She made them sleep together, and draw their feet under their clothes. She covered them with leaves and branches, and thus they passed the first night."[130] These articles characterize young black girls as valiant and strong. In these sorrowful stories, editors present an ideal world in which the heavy burden of family renewal is placed on tiny shoulders. Black daughters are expected to act in ways that will keep black families under stress together and protect the precious resource of private family life. When their fathers and mothers are struggling, black girls must become "prematurely knowing" and take on adult roles to help them.

Articles about temperance often depict black girls whose childlike wisdom induces men to be righteous. In "A Young Recruit to the Cold Water Army" (April 1840), reprinted from *Cold Water Army*, a little girl tells a group of adult men a simple rule for avoiding alcohol: keep their mouths shut.[131] As these articles reveal, black girls served as vocal, authoritative reminders of moral conduct and about how poor decisions might affect an entire family. Black girls in these stories functioned as moral arbiters and essential figures whose stories taught readers how to maintain healthy households. While young girls are incapable of or unlikely to convince an alcoholic to change his or her ways and the standards of "goodness" these articles set for black girls was well beyond their power to enact or achieve, their sentimental images were intended to encourage changes in poor behavior. These girlhood temperance tales are presented as universal regardless of race. Although black men would have many more stresses that might lead to alcohol as a refuge than most white men, the focus in all the temperance stories is the harm the alcoholic men inflict on their families. Regardless of the pressures and violence black men endured, they were presented as failures because they harmed their families. Although this was a well-known trope of the white temperance movement, the message suited black editors: weakened black families would weaken the black race as a whole. However, black editors did not see the black husbands and fathers who struggled with alcohol as irredeemably lost. They presented the love, loyalty, and gentle admonishments of daughters, even very young ones, as salvific influences that could rescue their parent.

The Youth's Department/Children's Department

The "Children's Department" was first titled the "Youth's Department," which issued five articles between April 5, 1836, and March 28, 1840, before the *Colored American* editors changed the column's name to the "Children's Department" in April 1840.[132] During that time, the forty-seven entries in the column included short stories, fairy tales, and maxims that promoted values consistent with middle-class life in the Northeast. The column reprinted widely from other publications, including the *Slave's Friend*, the *Juvenile Miscellany*, and the *Youth's Companion*.[133] The articles editors reprinted were often edifying tales from white publications that redirected lessons on moral growth toward youthful black readers. Frankie Hutton notes that with the inclusion of the "Youth's Department," the *Colored American* "devoted more column space to youth than did any other black newspaper in the antebellum period."[134] Topics included industriousness, temperance, reading, proper library usage, and thoughtfulness. The most significant category of messages was moral instruction and advice on good parenting.[135] The column's inaugural article, a brief editorial titled "Multiple News Items," makes explicit reference to the column's targeted audience of black child readers, noting the importance of training this "rising generation" of black children through "good moral lessons and correct habits":

> We commence this week a Youth's Department, which we intend to continue, and occupy with such matters as will be calculated to interest children, and at the same time teach them good moral lessons and correct habits. Our hope is in the rising generation, and if we can begin in season, and instruct them aright, we expect much of them, according to the maxim of Solomon—"Train up a child in the way he should go, and when he is old he will not depart from it." We hope this will interest parents to subscribe for our paper, for the sake of their children.[136]

The attention given to black children as readers was not focused on preserving their innocence; rather, articles in the "Youth's Department" and later in the "Children's Department" were intended to "instruct them aright," that is, to teach black children to grow into responsible, law-abiding citizens through edifying tales and moral lessons.[137] The *Colored American* editors described the "Youth's Department" as "an excellent little paper for children, and who always turns everything to anti-slavery account, or to reform mankind from their errors."[138] The newspaper sought to instill hope in black parents so they would properly prepare the "rising generation."

The "Youth's Department" portrayed black children as avid readers and argued that literacy was crucial to class advancement among free black populations living in the antebellum North. It imagined a generation of black children as full participants in their communities. Articles that featured girls encouraged youthful readers to find viable solutions to disfranchisement by channeling their literacy toward an engagement with political topics that were important to their immediate lives. Cultivating black children as sophisticated readers was crucial to the newspaper's promotion of a middle-class identity among black populations in the antebellum North. In an appeal titled "The Enlargement of Our Paper" published in September 1837, the editors asked their "brethren—especially the young" to subscribe to the paper in order to keep apace with the "transactions *of the civilized world*."[139] In their solicitation of youthful black readers, the editors recognized the importance of teaching black children how to acquire a worldly sophistication and become involved in national concerns. The column was invested in cultivating the literary taste and political awareness of black children and sought to groom the next generation of activists.

The "Youth's Department" column was often published in the middle of the page alongside political columns and articles about current events. This layout pattern was a deliberate practice that encouraged canny reading practices among black youth. A newspaper's layout patterns, or what Meredith McGill calls "formatting," is "the set of choices printers and publishers make in publishing a work."[140] The "Youth's Department's" formatting patterns connect to perceptions that black children needed to prepare for the dangers they might face by informing them about what was happening to blacks in the North and in the South. The placement of articles in the "Youth's Department" teaches young black readers to become "prematurely knowing," in this case about the political attitudes that influenced the lives of African Americans in the antebellum North. Black children learned at an early age about the political concerns that affected people of color.

Placing a children's column alongside articles about national concerns encouraged black children to become sophisticated readers. The placement of articles for or about children in proximity to articles of national concern was a clever strategy for enticing young readers to study and understand other articles in the newspaper. Printed alongside "Multiple News Items," for example, is "The Political Creed of Thomas Jefferson," reprinted from white journalist and historian Richard Hildreth's 1840 book *Despotism in America: Or, an Inquiry into the Nature and Results of the Slave-Holding System in the United States*, which analyzes the contradictions in Thomas Jefferson's ideals of liberty and justice. The article states that while Jefferson "was content to act the humble and comparatively inconsiderable part of a champion for equality among the aristocrats," he forgot that "the underprivileged class,—some of whom, to believe the voice of common report, were his own children—had any other capacities or rights than beasts of burden."[141] This critique of Jefferson, who was highly venerated as a founding father, was revolutionary, and printing this particular excerpt, with its mention of Jefferson's slave children, in a black newspaper gave it new layers of meaning. What was an aside for the white historian was the main point for the black community. The "Youth's Department's" cross-pollination layout strategy suggests that Cornish did not see domestic activities, the politics and history of the nation, and current events in the world as mutually exclusive. A young reader's eyes might have drifted from the "Youth's Department" column, over to the national news, and back to advice about how to navigate the local effects of national events. In the 1830s, the "Youth's Department" would have been an invaluable resource for African American families well versed in world events, politics, financial matters, and social concerns.

The "Youth's Department" reprinted articles from mainstream publications that taught lessons on conduct, politeness, and determination. Although characters in these stories might be white children, when reprinted in the *Colored American*, their actions conveyed to black children racialized lessons on appropriate behavior that, if followed, might lead to political change. The emphasis on polite, Christian behavior taught humility to youthful black readers.[142] Taking a nonviolent, peaceful approach to equality was, perhaps, Cornish's intention. For example, an article titled "Politeness," reprinted from the *Youth's Companion* in April 1837, explains the benefits of polite behavior among siblings, playmates, and adults, stating, "the little attentions which cost him nothing, and are so gratifying to those who receive them, will gain him many a friend."[143] Statements such as this encouraged children to follow the Golden Rule: "we should 'do unto others as we would that they should do unto us.'" Drawing upon a universal maxim, the article represented black children as capable of respect for others, an important aspect of a middle-class identity.

The "Youth's Department" ended its run on March 28, 1840, with an article on perseverance despite hardship, a theme that connects to the *Colored American*'s own financial hardships. "The Bishop and His Births," reprinted from "Banner and Pioneers," describes a poor white boy who longs to go to school, so he offers a schoolmaster a gift of two birds that he learns to catch on his own. Through representations of an impoverished white child, the article teaches black children that sheer pluck and commitment might lead to riches.[144] This message on perseverance despite poverty resonated with the newspaper's editors, who wrote candidly about the *Colored American*'s cash-flow problems and temporary suspension. In an article titled "Explanation," editors exposed the newspaper's financial struggles and reasssured subscribers that the paper will "make up for our suspension."[145] The *Colored American*'s "Youth's Department" established a clear investment in teaching young black readers varied forms of literacies that ranged from learning effective reading strategies to learning about piety and morality. This column is a good example of what black print culture scholars had in mind in their call for "a wider and more varied sense of black letters" that "moves beyond the bound book, beyond our disciplinary preference for novelistic narrative."[146] The "Youth's Department" reveals that newspaper editors viewed black children's literacies as important to early African American activism.

After the "Children's Department" replaced the "Youth's Department" on April 4, 1840, editors reprinted thirty-five of its forty-seven entries from other periodicals. The reprinted articles rendered white and black characters in the articles indistinguishable, thus endowing black children with the value and significance attached to white children. The didactic lessons in reprinted articles had different meanings for different readerships. While articles published in children's periodicals that targeted white children might teach about reformed behaviors, the same articles reprinted in the *Colored American*'s "Children's Department" taught a generation of young black readers racialized lessons about how to perform the type of behavioral practices that whites would identify as acceptable. Reprinted articles in the "Children's Department" provided a window into the everyday crises among free black populations in the antebellum North and offered solutions to remedy these concerns. Reprinted pieces conveyed the expectation that black children needed to learn to decipher whiteness and racially coded themes, characters, and words and to adopt certain lessons, maxims, and concepts in their daily lives.

In content (moral instruction) and hermeneutics (reading whiteness and racially coded themes), articles in the "Children's Department" offered training to potential citizens. Some articles discussed how young girls could best spend their leisure time. In "Winter Sports and Employments" (December 1841), reprinted from the *Christian Intelligencer*, the author emphasizes the importance of activities for girls that center on reading and domestic duties. The *Christian Intelligencer* was a publication of the Reformed Dutch Church. It was a white publication, so the author was talking about white girls. When the article is reprinted in a black newspaper, the intent of the article has a significant meaning for young black readers. The author suggests that rather than "dress their dolls anew," girls should "put their baby house in order." Instead of "spend[ing] ten or twelve hours in stupid sleep," a girl's time was best spent on reading "the whole library of story books." The article concludes with a reminder for girls to be "useful" and to "learn to knit and sew." Reading and usefulness are encouraged over playfulness and laziness. Other articles in the "Children's Department" reinforced gender conventions in order to warn black children against the violence that might result from indecorous behavior.[147] In "Patience and Resignation" (August 1841), reprinted from the *Sunday-School Monitor*, a mother makes her daughter Sally go without food for one day because Sally forgot to pick up a loaf of bread for dinner. Instead of complaining, Sally submits to her punishment and as a result, she "got the victory here, not by resistance, but by suffering."[148] Sally's mother was quite impressed and "fairly subdued by her daughter's quiet, patient submission." The editors reprinted this article to impart lessons to black girls that emphasized resignation over willfulness, duty over disobedience. Although Sally suffers because of her forgetful behavior, she learns fortitude and determination.

Conclusion

Black girls in the early black press are two-dimensional figures. Their images in articles are idealized figures that serve to instruct readers. Their role in the community, with the notable exception of the story of Theresa, is barely mentioned; most scenarios take place in the home. When they do venture forth, they are often portrayed in situations where they assist black men. Stories about girlhood were intended to show the black community what they should aspire to. These goals included secure, peaceful homes with male breadwinners and obedient children. The adoption of white middle-class values and beliefs included distinctly Christian teachings and literate children.

The early black press offered black girls who were willing helpers, virtuous and obedient, kind and concerned about the welfare of others, hard-working, and valiant. However, these articles also reveal actual realities in black homes when they are read carefully. The absence of black mothers in these articles is striking in the heyday of the ideal of republican motherhood, suggesting that many black mothers were working for wages outside the home. We know that many black men could not earn enough to support their families in the few jobs that were available to them. These stresses and strains on family life trickle down to the black girls in these stories. Daughters are sometimes called upon to shoulder the responsibility for the health and survival of the family, as when they are urged to do everything they can to prevent their fathers from drinking.

By the 1830s, black girls had also begun to appear in the literary productions of white abolitionists. This was much more tricky territory, for white writers often used black girls to promote their own agenda. They could appear in short stories or newspaper articles as pathetic figures designed to induce empathy among white children. They were sometimes presented in ways that presented a model of interracial interaction in which white children were the teachers and their black cohorts the learners; generally, such presentations expressed some surprise at the ability of the black girl to learn. This was also the attitude of the white male-dominated Manumission Society that operated the African Free Schools in New York City. Even the more enlightened abolitionists who were invested in presenting strong black heroes for black children, such as Abigail Mott Moore, were sometimes undermined when male publishers co-opted their project and inserted adult-level material about slavery that was inappropriate for children to read. It was for the black community to decide what details about slavery to share with their children and when to share it.

Thus, we must look hard between the lines of the literature of the early decades of the nineteenth century to see real black girls. The ones who appear on the page are there to serve the purposes of black editors, white educators, and white abolitionists. Even stories based on actual events place black girls in a framework that serves the didactic purposes of the author. The one exception during this period is the anonymously written story about the young, black girl, Theresa, who carries a crucial message to the leader of a revolution against white slave owners. The author of this story, I argue, was most likely a woman because of her attention to the interiority and decision-making process of her heroine.

The next chapters show how black girls developed their own scripts and strategies for surviving and moving ahead. The writings of black women in the next decades focused on fictionalized versions of the reality they had experienced as girls. Stories and autobiographies from the 1850s and 1860s described black families who were excluded from opportunities and torn apart by hardship. The daughters in these families must develop plans at a very young age that will enable them to move forward in life. The black girls who are the protagonists of these stories and narratives are so focused on survival that they have no time to focus on domestic ideology. Maria W. Stewart, Harriet Wilson, and Harriet Jacobs wrote narratives about girlhood that reveal what life was really like for many black women and girls living in the antebellum North and in the South during these decades.

2. Youthful Girls and Prematurely Knowing Girls

Antebellum Black Girlhood

THIS CHAPTER EXPLORES the trope of the self-reliant black girl in the face of adversity in the writing of African American women in the antebellum era. I argue that in contrast to the two-dimensional figures that appeared in the male-controlled black press, African American women writers drew upon their own experiences and presented black girls who faced situations that their real-life counterparts might encounter. The black girl characters that black women writers portrayed were much fuller and more complex than the models of decorum that appeared in much of the black press. Black women authors also depicted clearly defined stages of development to show that black girls deserved protection against cruel labor requirements or sexual victimization. Because the girls who appeared in black women's writing were based on real-life experiences, they had room to maneuver, to make decisions, to create paths for improvement in their life circumstances. The black girls these authors portrayed had physical endurance and demonstrated resilience and determination in the face of the most extreme circumstances. Black girls in this literature resisted and survived. In contrast to the morally perfect future wives and mothers the black press offered readers, black women writers presented black girls who engaged in indecorous conduct and nonvirtuous behavior as strategies for survival. These black girls defeated adversity with behavior that successfully combated the rampant unlawful actions of whites. African American women writers incorporated representations of black girls in narratives to expose how society sanctioned their victimization, failed to protect them, and violated their virtue.

To contest the prevailing attitude on southern plantations that black girls were valuable solely for their future fecundity and economic potential, African American women writers distinguished between *youthful* girlhood and *knowing* girlhood. In nineteenth-century African American literature, black women writers often introduced black girl characters when they were at a youthful age, usually less than twelve. This is a popular age in early African American literature because the youthful and *un*knowing girl represents a blank slate with the capacity to undergo transformation through intellectual agency and achievement. Two prominent examples are Frado in Harriet Wilson's *Our Nig* (1859) and Linda Brent in Harriet Jacobs's *Incidents in the Life of a Slave Girl* (1861), both of whom first appear at the age of six. Youthful black girls are sexually innocent. They are (as yet) untutored but capable of finding their way to the knowledge they need. When they are nurtured at this young age, youthful black girls acquire numerous types of literacy they will need to survive. They develop an ability to decipher potential signs of danger in addition to learning to read words, create poetry, and acquire an education. The malleable and regenerative state of youthfulness provides black girls with the mental and physical capacity to make them useful models of racial progress.

In this literature, extreme hardship and danger hasten the maturation of youthful girls, and the move from youthful to prematurely knowing girlhood occurs when black girls gain independence or a deepened awareness of their precarious positions and seek methods for survival. These methods involve strategies for protecting themselves when faced with threats and actual danger. Hostile whites did not deem black girls capable of innocence or worthy of protection, and the shift to knowledge about adult issues often took place much earlier for black girls than for many white girls. By the age of fifteen or sixteen (if not earlier), most black girls in the literature produced by black women writers had their first encounter with sexuality and sexual threat. They knew the pain of physical abuse, often from white mistresses. They were grappling with threats to family integrity in the form of the sale of parents, siblings, or other relatives (in the South) and (forced) abandonment or the early death of parents (in the North). The "prematurely knowing" black girl was contending with serious issues of survival and safety at an age when most middle-class white girls were being protected and carefully prepared for a successful marriage. The prematurely knowing black girl had already begun to look for ways of surviving. She had become alert and had experienced a shift in her consciousness. She had become aware of her power to do something about her situation. However, the transition from youthful to knowing girlhood need not always indicate growth in years. In the literature written by black women, black girls may gain a premature awareness—become prematurely knowing—when they are young. Young black girls may obtain a mature outlook through education in formal school structures or through informal observations, such as by witnessing the harmful actions of adults or overhearing adult conversation.

This chapter begins by exploring literature written by white authors that features black girl protagonists. These white-authored texts reveal the context in which African American women writers wrote. Black women began producing published writing at a time when children's print culture featuring black girl figures was growing. While African American children's literature was often published in serial form in black newspapers, white authors were publishing children's books for black children that relied heavily on sentimental appeal. Didactic story lines showed youthful readers how to be sympathetic to the needs of those who were living in poverty and introduced readers to the concept of a social conscience. The characters in these texts demonstrated altruism and steadfastness during adversity and moral attitudes marked by an unselfish concern for the welfare of others regardless of race or class. Often illustrated with vivid pictures and sketches, these texts contain plots that feature black girls who are orphaned or whose mothers are unavailable due to early death or extreme working conditions. Although young black protagonists in early children's literature written by white authors are nurtured by community members through acts that demonstrate goodwill, they often suffer. Rarely are there scenes of play, and if black children are described as engaging in play, the period of their lives when they are able to do so is usually short. The bulk of these narratives focus on grave life events, such as the death of one or both parents or the eventual death of the black girl herself.[1]

The chapter then moves from the didactic, two-dimensional figures of black girls that were a staple in the early black press to explore some of the first short stories and full-length books by black women that centered on the lives of black girls. In the 1830s–1850s, a difference emerged between the perspectives of black male editors in the early black press and the perspectives of black women writers that would persist through the rest of the century. Male editors focused on idealized black girls, the perfect black girls who could grow up to raise children who would advance the position of the race. In contrast, black women writers focused on the experiences of real girls, often writing from their own experience. They delved into the interior lives of the characters they wrote, showing their readers the thoughts, reasoning, and decision-making processes of black girls as they weighed complex moral issues and considered the impact of their actions on numerous others.

Black Girlhood in Early American Children's Print Culture

In the texts of African American women writers, black girls learn lessons in survival, self-reliance, fortitude, and determination. In contrast, in literature written by white authors, black girls suffer and/or die.[2] In these white-authored narratives, white women characters clothe, educate, and reform black girls by exposing them to teachings from the Bible, all acts that reinforced the image of the benevolent white female. This stereotype is presented in the most popular white-authored black girl figure, the enslaved black girl Topsy in Harriet Beecher Stowe's *Uncle Tom's Cabin* (1852). In the novel, when the white mistress, Miss Ophelia, asks Topsy where she originated from, Topsy replies that she "jes' growed," making no mention of parents. Miss Ophelia becomes the white surrogate mother figure that reforms Topsy. Through tutelage in religion and manners, Topsy matures from an untutored girl to a missionary who eventually leaves the United States to teach abroad in Africa. The writings of black women revised this mid-nineteenth-century narrative and created representations of black girls who learned to acquire an education through alternative means, sought reform movements that they chose on their own, found ways to become self-sufficient, and used their achievements to strengthen their own homes, attain freedom from danger, and ensure their survival.

The formula of white benevolence toward black girls exists in an earlier, lesser-known text, *The Tawny Girl: Or the History of Margaret Russel, Illustrating the Benefits of Education on the Most Degraded Classes of Society* (1823), by an anonymous author. Textual details point to white authorship: the book was published at a Quaker press that often published abolitionist literature. The use of the word "degraded" in the title is another clue. It would be hard to imagine a black writer using this word to describe his or her protagonist. But if we imagine a white writer, the word signals an idealized trajectory from poverty to a better state (whether the improvement is moral or economic is left ambiguous in this title). The title also suggests that behind the scenes is a white benefactor who will help the "degraded" black girl improve herself.

Although *The Tawny Girl* was first published in England by W. Alexander and Son in 1822, Samuel Wood, a Quaker teacher-turned-publisher and children's book author, reprinted *The Tawny Girl* in New York the next year at his publishing firm, Samuel Wood and Sons.[3] His company published children's books that were "seemingly devised to be instructive and moral."[4] Nearly all of them had a strong Christian message. The American primers and books Wood chose to reprint offered suitable reading for black children without traits of racial bias. Wood, who was greatly influenced by the children's books that were popular in England, decided that many children's books published in the United States were unsuitable for young readers. He installed a small printing press in the rear of his store and printed children's books of his own compilation and authorship. His first title, published in 1806, was *The Young Child's ABC, or, First Book*, which sold for three cents. By 1813, he had written and published over fifty books. Wood said that in making his selections, "he tried to avoid anything that would tend to corrupt the innocence of the youthful mind, and care was taken to void selections that would lead to a taste for the exhibitions of the stage."[5]

To our eyes today, the books Wood published might seem dull and didactic, but they were in high demand in the first quarter of the nineteenth century. Wood believed in moral suasion, the idea that children could be influenced by moral arguments and good examples to do right, in contrast to a reliance on punishment and threats of punishment that had characterized child rearing in the eighteenth century. Wood's books taught children that they should always make the good and useful choice. They also presented the uncomfortable issues of the times to youthful readers, including racial inequality and economic injustice. The portrayal of a mixed-raced girl in *The Tawny Girl* (1823) is an example of Wood's interest in publishing books with themes of social issues.

The Tawny Girl is a short novel that tells the story of an eight-year-old mulatto girl named Margaret Russel who is born in Ireland. Margaret eventually is forced to sell matches to care for her sickly white mother after her father, an African, dies and leaves his family impoverished.[6] *The Tawny Girl* opens when Margaret, her mother (an Irish servant), and her father (a servant to an Irish man) move from Ireland to Liverpool, England, to escape poverty. When the father falls ill and dies, Margaret's mother takes up residence in Warrington, England, where she obtains a basket and becomes a "tradeswoman" selling matches and "vending wares of small value, such as pins, tape, &C." Margaret and her mother move again, this time to York, where "as is customary with such wanderers, they put up at one of those places of wretchedness, a common lodging-house." Living in near poverty, the mother continues to sell matches while Margaret tries to sell her mother's goods from door to door. In her efforts to escape poverty, Margaret "range[s] the streets, only one step removed from a common beggar."[7]

Through the benevolence of a group of neighbors, Margaret is given a chance to enter school. She is at first rejected for fear that due to "her wandering life and probably dissolute habits, she might bring discredit on the school," but Margaret finally is admitted and is soon accepted by her classmates. Despite her hardships, Margaret learns her lessons and commits passages from the Bible to memory, which pleases her teacher. Mother and daughter eventually move to a crowded almshouse. However, concerned that her daughter's mind and body "might . . . be contaminated by the conversations and habits of the lodging-houses," Margaret's mother obtains "a wretched garret." Margaret tries to make friends but is ostracized when she must sell matches and obtain food to care for her sickly mother, who eventually dies. The daughter "bitterly lamented her destitute and forlorn situation;—she was left to struggle with the world, without any natural protector, at a dangerous age, being in her fourteenth year."[8] Margaret is relieved when benevolent neighbors in the community intervene to assist by housing her, clothing her, teaching her the Bible, and becoming surrogate parents. However, at the age of sixteen Margaret dies after a lengthy illness and much suffering. Margaret's suffering—the loss of both parents, extreme poverty, labor in the streets at fourteen, and death at sixteen—vividly describes for young readers the hardships of abject poverty, loneliness, and illness as a means of encouraging empathy for others. In the hands of an abolitionist publisher, those others included black people.

The wood-engraved frontispiece of *The Tawny Girl* features a black girl (Margaret) reading to a white woman (her mother), who is lying on a bed in a shabby garret. The artist, Dr. Alexander Anderson, was a white man who began his career as a doctor but left the field of medicine to become a wood engraver. The technique of wood engraving revolutionized book illustration. One of Anderson's contributions to American art was his illustrations of American scenes and people in the children's primers and tracts that were distributed across the nation.[9] Unlike expensive metal engraving, images created from wood engravings could be reproduced cheaply and made accessible to children. Through his wood engravings, Anderson captured intricate details of the lives of the working poor, drawing on observations from his medical career to relay the depth of poverty many early American families suffered.[10] The shading his wood engravings produced presented a nuanced depiction of subjects who lacked elegant dress or surroundings.

The frontispiece showcases sentimental props that heighten the appeal presented in the text (see figure 2.1). It depicts the domestic space of an impoverished family. The tiny garret's slanted roof, dim lighting, cracked window, and sparse furniture visually depict the family's poverty. A window with a missing pane is stuffed with rags to keep out the cold, and clothes hang from a post to dry. Opposite the dying mother, Margaret sits on a box with a slumped posture, holding a book and reading to her mother. The mother's face is turned toward the black girl.[11] An excerpt from Thomas Gray's "Elegy Written in a Country Churchyard" is reprinted on the title page, a poem designed to persuade readers to acknowledge the desires of the poor for education instead of regarding their ambitions with "disdain."[12] In the novel, although benevolent white members of Margaret's community step in to give her access to education, their assistance is futile. Although Margaret evolves from an uneducated beggar to a good, literate, Christian girl, this is not enough to save her. Despite her courage and determination to acquire an education, Margaret dies. Her efforts to become educated and adopt Christian moral values do not lead to resilience. Instead, as the frontispiece captures vividly, Margaret's fortitude serves primarily to point to the need for white benevolence and the good, charitable works of the white community. Her suffering and premature death are designed to elicit in white readers a desire to aid the poor and the "degraded."

The publication of *The Tawny Girl* in 1823 anticipated a cluster of antebellum children's literature by antislavery white authors in which black girl characters functioned as protagonists who addressed slavery and racial inequality. The suffering, alienation, loneliness, and premature death of black girls in this literature are designed to evoke empathy in young readers and deliver an antislavery message. Widely circulated early American children's texts that feature black girls include *Poems: Moral and Religious, for Children and Youth* (1821) and *Blessings in Disguise: Or, Pictures of Some of Miss Haydon's Girls*, by Caroline Chesebro.[13]

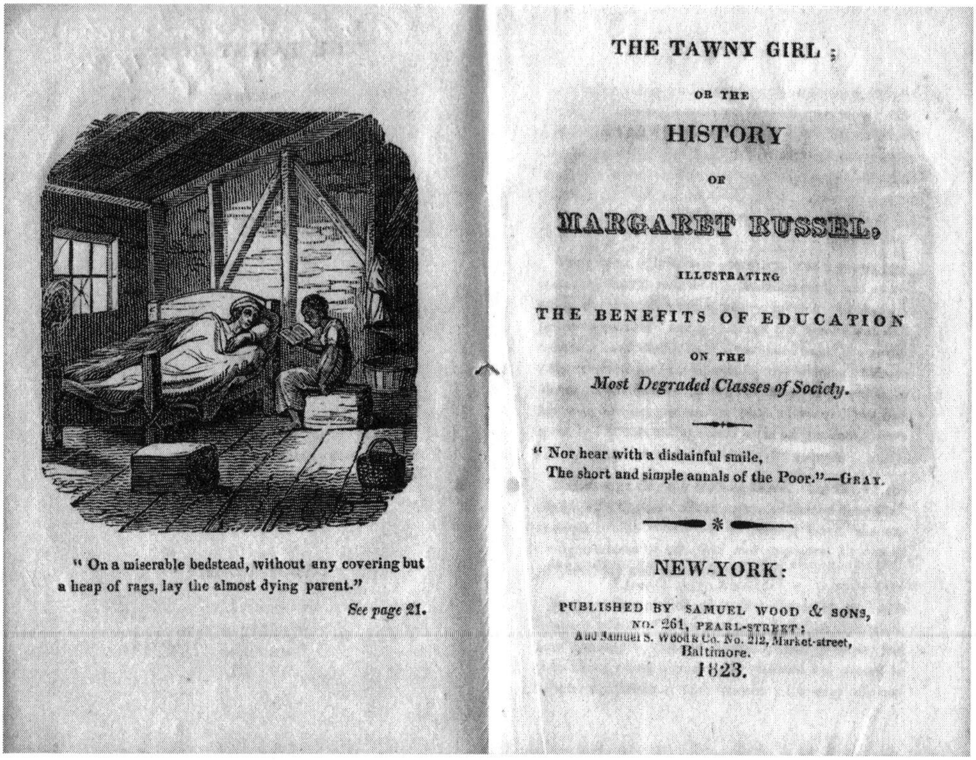

" On a miserable bedstead, without any covering but a heap of rags, lay the almost dying parent."

See page 21.

THE TAWNY GIRL;

OR THE

HISTORY

OF

MARGARET RUSSEL,

ILLUSTRATING

THE BENEFITS OF EDUCATION

ON THE

Most Degraded Classes of Society.

" Nor hear with a disdainful smile,
The short and simple annals of the Poor."—GRAY.

NEW-YORK:

PUBLISHED BY SAMUEL WOOD & SONS,
NO. 261, PEARL-STREET;
And Samuel S. Wood & Co. No. 212, Market-street,
Baltimore.
1823.

FIGURE 2.1. Frontispiece. *Tawny Girl*. Courtesy, American Antiquarian Society.

The Little Keepsake: Or Easy Lessons in Words of One Syllable (1825) contains four brief chapters that teach lessons to children using racial themes. "The Swing" illustrates the separation of the races when a group of white children who "have just come out of school" are playing on a swing while a group of black children, two boys and a black girl, lurk behind a tree and "wait for their turn to swing." The author tells readers: "Soon our white young friends will go home, and then these will take their turn."[14] The isolation of black children at school and at play is illustrated further by their labeling as "these" in this text, perhaps teaching young white readers less about tolerance and more about the hierarchical systems in place that separated the races.

A signature feature in early American children's literature that features black girls is what I call interracial playdates in which a black girl and a white girl play together as an illustration of racial harmony. The term *playdate* is intentionally unsettling because it is anachronistic. A playdate is a twentieth- and twenty-first-century activity commonly associated with innocence, yet these scenes of play in the nineteenth century evoke inequality, racial disharmony, danger, and conflict. The frontispiece image of an early issue of *Slave's Friend* (1837), an abolitionist periodical for children, features an illustration titled "Emma" that shows a white girl teaching a black girl how to read as a dog sits nearby (see figure 2.2).[15] The characters' hierarchical arrangement in the picture suggests imbalance. Emma, the white girl, is the tallest, most visible figure and is fully clothed. Grace sits in a crouching position under Emma's arm and has bare feet. The triangulation of a black girl, a white girl, and a dog might reinforce a sentimental scene of goodwill, togetherness, and acceptance, yet Grace's visually unequal position under Emma's arm conveys how her presence serves simply to support white benevolence.

The story "Emma," published in *Slave's Friend*, features "a neat little colored girl who used to come to the house of Emma's father every Saturday afternoon to see her mother[,] who lived with the family. Her name was Grace." Grace and Emma "used to play together; and sometimes they would work in the garden or sit down to read. Grace could tell her all the letters, A, B, C, and so on, but Emma wanted her to read without spelling, and so she would teach her, as you can see in the picture." The author encourages its young readers to look carefully at the picture: "Just look at them. Isn't it a pretty sight? How attentive Grace is. I dare say she loves to learn to read. Now do we see Emma, how animated and joyful she looks. She loves to be a little teacher, I guess. And how carefully they hold the book."[16] In this story, Grace is socialized through reading and learning with the aid of a white girl. The author's repeated request that readers "look carefully" at the "pretty sight" of Emma and Grace reading together suggests that the interracial pairing is instructive. In a similar way, *The Tawny Girl*'s frontispiece sought to attract early American readers with a rare display of a black girl reading to a white woman. In both of these illustrations, the pairing of literate black girls with white female figures supports the values of racial harmony, gratitude, and ideal households that all whites should aspire to.

Specific publishing houses were invested in publishing children's literature texts that featured black children. The American Tract Society, located in Boston, Massachusetts, published many antislavery titles and had an active publication program for children that competed with the literature of secular publishers. *Songs for My Children: With Memoirs with Numerous Illustrations* (1861), a popular publication by a white author, contained songs, rhymes, and miscellany for child readers such as "An Example to Children," "Aspirations," "Haste to School," "Calling Names," Deeds of Kindness," and "Don't Fret."[17] "The Little Black Girl" features a black girl named Susie who laments her loneliness when her mother, Chloe, must leave home daily to work as a domestic. Susie looks in a mirror and connects her loneliness with the color of her skin: "Susie to their tiny mirror, / Climbing, saw her ebon face; / But she hid it with her fingers, / As if 't were some deep disgrace."[18]

THE

SLAVE'S FRIEND.

VOL. II., NO. I. WHOLE NO. 13.

EMMA.

Emma was the little girl whose Papa once asked her, what made every body love her. She replied, you remember,

FIGURE 2.2. "Emma," frontispiece for *The Slave's Friend*, 2, no. 1 (1837). Courtesy, American Antiquarian Society.

"Oh why was it," sadly murmuring,
Susie asked herself aloud,
"When God made white children's faces,
Over mine he spread a cloud?"
"No one loves me; naughty children
Laugh when e'er I go along;
And rude boys are always singing
In my ear some negro song.
I don't love to sit at school,
With the children white and fair;
For it makes my face look blacker,

And more crisp my woolly hair.
Scrub and comb! And comb and scrub! I've
Tried to grow white many a day,
But my poor facc still is colored,
And my hair will knot this way![19]

The lines suggest that black skin is shameful and that black children understand that they are inferior because of it, a sentiment that conveys the racism of supposedly benevolent whites. This poem was designed to elicit sympathy in white children for black children. However, young black readers might have read it as a message to wait for salvation through divine intervention instead of relying on themselves or hoping for changes in the nation's legal system. When Chloe hears her daughter's cries, she urges Susie to rely on God's love to calm her worries: "Soon, my child, if we obey him, / We shall go to dwell above, / Where his own of every color / Share alike a father's love."[20] The image of Susie's forlorn face captures the loss and loneliness of racial isolation. Similar to the frontispiece in *The Tawny Girl*, the portrayal of the young girl Susie looking in the mirror depicts the intersection of race, poverty, and sorrow.

In *Lucy: Or, The Slave Girl of Kentucky*, published by the American Reform Tract and Book Society (1858), an enslaved black girl argues vehemently against the horrors of slavery. The story opens with a white boy named Arthur who receives "no black marks" on his reports in school. As a reward, his aunt tells him a story. She tells him about her travels to New Orleans as a young girl on a steamer headed to a slave market. The steamer stopped in Paducah, on the northwestern boundary of Kentucky, where she met a little slave girl named Lucy who was "about a dozen years old." In dialect, Lucy explains to the aunt how she cried and screamed when she was sold and separated from her mother and grandmother: "You see dey wouldn't nudder let me come wid mammy, nor take me back to granny, and so I couldn't do nothin' but scream."[21] Young Arthur learns about the plight of slaves, but he is relieved that he does not share their actual suffering: "I'll pray that I may continue to hate the whole thing with all my might, and I'll give thanks too, every day, that I was not born a colored child, to be sold away from all I love and to be taken down the Mississippi river."[22] The juxtaposition of the two sentimental scenes, in which an aunt tells a story to her nephew and an enslaved girl is separated from her family, serves to highlight the processes that contribute to a strong white family structure lest it be threatened by the influences of slavery.

Deborah C. De Rosa argues that white writers who delivered an antislavery message included representations of enslaved children primarily as a way to illustrate the impact of slavery's atrocities on the innocence of white children: "Ironically, while these works oppose the slave child's lost innocence and depict

THE LITTLE BLACK GIRL. 123

The Little Black Girl.

SUSIE'S home was neat and cleanly,
Though 't was poor, and plain, and small;
On the floor there was no carpet,
Not a picture on the wall.
In one corner stood the bedstead,
In another was the tub,
Where from morn till weary evening
Her poor mother, rub, dub, dub,
Toiled away with patient spirit,
Susie's daily bread to earn;
Teaching lessons of endurance,
Which more favored ones might learn.

FIGURE 2.3. "The Little Black Girl," in Dunbar, *Songs for My Children*. Courtesy, American Antiquarian Society.

individuals interceding to prevent the child's suffering, the domestic abolitionists nevertheless inflict lost innocence (through forced consciousness) onto the white child," writes De Rosa. "While these white children do not literally free the slave children, their promises of prayers set the groundwork for change."[23] In *Lucy: Or, The Slave Girl of Kentucky*, the white child's awareness of Lucy's suffering seems to be more about his lost innocence than it is about that child cultivating empathy for Lucy. In the hands of white writers, black girls were as flat and two-dimensional as they were in the hands of black newspaper editors. Their function was to support a didactic lesson, and the focus was on the moral value of their external actions. White writers were not concerned with the inner lives of the black children they wrote about; the main concern of these writers was to persuade white children that slavery was evil so they could adopt the proper moral attitude in childhood and (it was to be hoped) take proper action against slavery in adulthood. In other words, the children white writers were concerned about were their own.

"To Be a Good Girl": Youthful Girlhood in Maria W. Stewart's "The First Stage of Life"

Although Maria W. Stewart is primarily known as a lecturer, a journalist, and an abolitionist and women's rights activist, a recently recovered six-page short story she wrote, "The First Stage of Life" (1861), illuminates her contribution to children's print culture. In 1861, the *Repository of Religion and Literature, and of Science and Art* serialized Stewart's short story, "The First Stage of Life" in the April, July, and October issues.[24] The *Repository*, which was published from 1858 to 1863, was a black magazine administered by black men and designed for black readers.[25] Each issue of the magazine, which was published quarterly, included around twenty-two pages of poems, parables, and essays. The magazine attracted black households with rising amounts of disposable income and leisure time. Today, the *Repository* is available on microfilm only at the Indiana State Library. One extant issue is housed in Harvard University's Houghton Library.[26]

The moral rhetoric and small size of the *Repository* made the magazine inviting to youthful readers and their parents. In contrast to the large pages of *Freedom's Journal* and the *Colored American*, which were almost two feet in vertical length, the *Repository* was compact and portable like a book and small enough to fit in one's pocket.[27] Elizabeth McHenry argues that the *Repository*'s size and portability were intended to "expand the literary habits of black readers to include more attention to individual, solitary reading" and that this was "representative of notable changes taking place in the black community on the eve of the Civil War."[28] For black people, carrying a magazine that looked like a book contributed to the formation of bourgeois character that could be performed visibly on the street. The size and portability of the *Repository* allowed its editors to label the magazine an "intimate companion of all classes . . . capable of providing the individual reader with opportunities to engage in a communal model of literary activity even when away from the company of peers at the literary society meeting or in the lecture hall."[29] While the appeal of earlier newspapers such as *Freedom's Journal* and the *Colored American* was due to their nationalist mission as a newspaper for the people, the *Repository* focused on the morality and behavioral practices of the individual. Scholarly attention has turned toward this resource only recently.[30]

Stewart was a pioneer in creating literature for and about black children. She strongly supported the development of African American children's print culture and indicted white authors and publishers for excluding black children from their publications:

> I have taken a survey of the American people in my own mind, and I see them thriving in arts, and sciences, and in polite literature. Their highest aim is to excel in political, moral and religious improvement. They early consecrate their children to God, and their youth indeed are blushing on artless innocence. . . . But how very few are there among them that bestow one thought upon the benighted sons and daughters of Africa, who have enriched the soils of America with their tears and blood; few to promote their cause, none to encourage their talents.[31]

"The First Stage of Life" was published in "The Children's Room" column of the *Repository*, a literary space devoted to black children and their parents. In the issues in which Stewart's story was serialized, this column published religious selections for children such as the poems "All Fulness in Christ" and "Prayer for a Heathen."[32] Essays on parenting included "Sleeping without the Light," which explores "the treatment by [a] mother of [a] little boy's dread of sleeping in the dark," and "Bad Example," in which a boy reminds his father who is on the way to the distillery with fruit to make alcohol "that it would be a bad example for a member of the church to take peaches to a distillery."[33] Bishop Payne's essay on education, "The Duty of Children to Get Knowledge," asks readers, "Can children think? Can they learn to speak? Can they learn to read and write? Well, then, God made children to know." Payne tells young black readers how to be responsible for their own education: "How shall a child get knowledge? By thinking, thinking, thinking. By studying, studying, studying. By finding out the meaning of words; by comparing one word with another; and one thing to another, so as to find out their difference and their natures."[34] These selections reveal that the *Repository* editors were invested in ensuring that black children and their parents had access to a diverse range of children's texts.

The poems and parables printed in "The Children's Room" column were designed for African American children, parents, and community members who were engaged with public institutions such as schoolrooms and churches.[35] The conduct that the column promoted contributed to what historian Erica Ball calls "middle class self-fashioning," a set of behaviors and values that was "deemed crucial to the personal transformations required to become independent, virtuous, ideal men and women."[36] Through the articles, poems, and stories published in "The Children's Room" column, *Repository* editors described respectability, literary taste, and middle-class values to young black readers. "The Children's Room" functioned as a literary space where African

American writers could publish essays and create poems to be read and shared with parents and their children.

The selections published in "The Children's Room" encouraged black parents to teach their children ideals of honesty and perseverance that might protect them from the impact of hostile laws during the pre–Civil War era, such as the Fugitive Slave Act of 1850, which gave whites the right to repossess a slave even if the slave escaped to a free state. The act resulted in an increase of illegal capture and enslavement of black people, including already freed slaves. Black activists and writers countered acts of illegal seizure through stories that taught morals and didactic lessons designed to protect black families against increasing threats of violence. To combat this institutional terror, black families were advised to secure the strength and stability of their homes. Articles in sections devoted to children in the black press routinely centered the emotional and physical health of black children, particularly their girls, by instructing parents to prepare their daughters through care for the body, temperance, and feminine conventions through conversations between mothers and daughters.[37] "Keep Your Temper," published in July 1858, instructs black girls to maintain their equanimity even in frustrating and difficult circumstances. When a girl named Emma misplaces her sewing implements and cries, "I can never keep anything!" and stamps about "with vexation," Emma's mother replies with a simple instruction: "keep your temper; if you will only do that, perhaps, you will find it easy to keep other things."[38]

Black activists linked the management of black children's tempers to the futurity of the black race. In her speech titled "The Proper Training of Children," delivered November 21, 1860, at the Ladies Literary Festival in St. James' Protestant Episcopal Church in Baltimore, Maria W. Stewart denounced unfocused, impetuous impulses in black children, stating that it is "the parental duty of teaching children the first lessons of piety and obedience at home."[39] She identifies parental discipline of children as a religious duty:

> God has wisely arranged that the old and the middle-aged, by their wisdom and discretion, should counsel and guide the young. . . . The unruly tempers and passions of some children when let loose, are like the ragings of a *bear*; and unless children are taught self-government of temper at home, their tempers will govern them and become fastened upon them as iron bands. . . . Oh! Horrible! To allow children to posses ungovernable tempers and unbridled tongue to have the last word, to call ill-names, to wrangle, quarrel, and fight.[40]

Stewart places an emphasis on the lack of self-governing behavior and the duty of parents to teach their children "the first lessons of piety and obedience at home." However, many children in the antebellum era lacked parental figures to fill this educating role. Therefore, the black community fulfills the role of teacher, guide, and mentor to young black children. It is the responsibility of older and wiser adults to "counsel and guide the young" so that when the children grow, they do not "become the authors of their own misery and the misery of those around them."[41]

Articles also urged black girls to read in order to secure a profitable future. In "Young Ladies, Read!" the anonymous author denounces idle behavior in young women as detrimental to the good of the nation:

> They lounge or sleep their time in the morning. They never take hold of the drudgery, the repulsive toil, which each son and daughter of Adam should perform in the world. They know nothing of domestic duties, they have no habits of industry, no taste for the useful, no skill in any really useful art. They are in the streets, not in the performance of their duty, or for the acquisition of health, but to see and be seen.[42]

The author encourages parents to make sure their girls mastered domestic skills: "What a mistake is then made by our young girls and their parents when domestic education is unattended to! Our daughters should be taught practically to wash and iron, to arrange the table, to do every thing that pertains to the order and comfort of the household."[43] These articles intended to "hold the larger community together" through their moral instructions. The absence of fathers in these articles on conduct and behavior suggest that at this point, the instruction of children was seen as wholly the concern of mothers.[44]

Despite the attention the *Repository* gave to articles devoted to proper parenting in "The Children's Room" column, Stewart's short story emphasizes communal networks and suggests that the protection of a nuclear family was perhaps unattainable for many black girls in the antebellum period. Stewart's story reshaped the dominant narrative about the impoverished girl who eventually dies through a representation of a black girl who survives hardships and whose personal experiences illustrate strategic steps toward hopeful beginnings instead of an inevitable tragic ending. Stewart identifies an alternative support structure for black women and girls in the antebellum era when she reveals how her black girl protagonist gains awareness, education, and spiritual enlightenment outside of the protection of a nuclear family or a nurturing mother.

"The First Stage of Life" begins with a northern black mother's early death and the loneliness and isolation her daughter, the young girl protagonist, Letitia, experiences as a result. This conveys, perhaps, the hardships Stewart endured in her own childhood, who was orphaned at age five, was bound out to the home of a clergyman until age fifteen, and did not receive a formal education. Stewart seems to be describing the uneducated black child who perceives vividly through her senses. Stewart's description of Letitia's lonely wandering as a child perhaps mirrors the racial isolation that Stewart encountered in her work as a widowed public speaker and writer working in the American lecture circuit in the 1830s.[45]

"The First Stage of Life" tells the story of a six-year-old black girl named Letitia who is orphaned after her mother dies. Her father sends her to live with an uncaring aunt. Lacking nurturing parents and proper instruction, Letitia must discover the world on her own terms and make sense of her loneliness and unguided impressions. "A certain lady and gentleman" from the community eventually take in Letitia, raise her, and contribute to her survival. In her lecture "Prayer," presented in Boston in 1831, Stewart foregrounded the power of independent black communities and regeneration, noting especially how black women could cultivate traits to contribute to this communal growth: "Possess the spirit of independence. The Americans do, and why should not you? Possess the spirit of men, bold and enterprising, fearless and undaunted."[46] Stewart talked to her audience about ways to secure financial independence, which she felt was key to community building: "Do you ask, what can we do? Unite and build a store of your own, if you cannot procure a license. . . . Do you ask, where is the money? We have spent more than enough for nonsense to do what building we should want. We have never had an opportunity of displaying our talents; therefore the world thinks we know nothing."[47] In "The First Stage of Life," which was published thirty years after "Prayer," Stewart presented Letitia as a lonely, motherless girl without the care of a nurturing mother figure who is "cast upon the cold charities of the world"[48] at a young age but overcomes this challenge to become the kind of community member Stewart had envisioned nearly three decades before she wrote this story.

Several details of the story highlight Letitia's girlhood. We first meet Letitia when she is six years old. Instead of the innocence that often aligns children with youthfulness in antebellum literature, Letitia's youthful girlhood is laced with fear. Although she exhibits youthful curiosity, she is unaware and fearful of the world: "The first time Letitia ever noticed the blue sky, and the light of day, she was sent with another little girl to get a pail of water, she climbed upon a ledge of rocks, she fell, and then one of the rocks fell upon one of her limbs, she was wounded, she saw the blood flow. How she got home, or when she recovered, she knows not, she only knows that it was." Fear cloaks Letitia's first awareness of God: "The first time Letitia was ever out in the sable orb of night that she recollects[,] her attention [was] attracted by the light of the lamps. All was dark above, she saw no moon nor stars, she knew not what they were, and passing by a shop she saw a monstrous large boot, she was filled with fear, she thought it was God's boot, and walked away very softly. This was the first idea Letitia ever had of God."[49] The girlhood Stewart constructed for Letitia was full of fear and confusion.

Letitia's youthful girlhood is also characterized by playdates that result in physically and emotionally hurtful outcomes. When Letitia's mother and step-father take Letitia to a friend's house for a visit, the play introduces Letitia to the pain of disappointment and the fear associated with whiteness. Stewart describes the visit with a meandering sentence that linguistically signals Letitia's childlike confusion:

> And now the scene changes, and Letitia remembers that herself, her mother, and her step-father were all on their way, she knows not where, she knows not when this gentleman became her step-father, she only knew that he was her step-father, and when she comes again to her recollection, she finds herself in a strange place, surrounded by the beautiful light of pay [*sic*], the blue sky above her head, clouded with white, and herself disarranging a beautiful little baby house, the shelves all decorated with broken earthenware, her little playmate was absent, she returns, she reproves Letitia gently. She was white, the first white face, Letitia ever saw, that she knows off [*sic*].[50]

The passage mingles Letitia's uncertain feelings toward a new stepfather with an unruly act. Instead of playing politely with a "beautiful little baby house," Letitia breaks its earthenware and is chastised by "her little playmate." The broken dishes in the disordered dollhouse mirror Letitia's own disorganized home and the ambivalence she feels toward a new stepfather. While Robin Bernstein argues that "dolls offered one crucial way for parents to shape girls' imaginative play," Letitia's play involves neither imaginative escape nor glee but frustration, fear, and unease.[51] The earthenware's breakability suggests that Letitia is similarly fragile, breakable, and prone to pain. The emotional scene triangulates familial disruption, interracial play, and racial awareness to express Letitia's inability to articulate fully these interlocking systems of oppression. Stewart's pairing of a black and a white girl in an interracial play date dispels the assumption of racial harmony and benevolent intentions that prevailed in abolitionist literature by white authors and instead critiques the racial tension and inequalities black girls experienced in the antebellum North.

Letitia experiences physical violence when she becomes orphaned after her mother dies and she is sent to live with her uncaring Aunt Sally. Stewart decenters biological families as the sole nurturing protective body for black girls in the antebellum era by exposing the pain associated with this familial relationship: "The first time Letitia remembers of having her face and hands washed, was by her aunt Sally, but not without the threat of rubbing all the skin off from her arms, if she did not behave herself."[52] Threats of a brutal bath gave Letitia an early impression of uneasy and painful relations between children and extended family members.

Although Letitia's "intellect began to unfold and ripen" when she was barely six years old, she "did not yet know right from wrong," and her aunt was "incapable of training her up as she ought to have bee[n]." Her time with Aunt Sally initiated a period of wandering and loneliness. Aunt Sally "put her out" to another family, but "did not permit her to stay there long" and soon retrieved her. Under Aunt Sally's care, "The child became almost a wandering gypsy, for her aunt had no settled home, she taught Letititia [*sic*] all kinds of naughtiness, became very unkind and cruel to her, and went away and left her in the street without home and without friends." Letitia did not know how to resolve her solitude; she "did not cry unto God in her distress; she did not know [who] he was; she had never been taught anything about him."[53] Because of her lack of any conventional understanding or experience of regulation, religion, or restraint, Letitia found her joy outdoors.

After a period of lonely wandering, Letitia reached a low point in her girlhood and divine intervention led her to seek out members of the community for assistance: "But God knew who Letitia was, and directed her infant steps to an old man called Uncle Pete, and he told her to call on a certain lady and gentleman, and tell them, that her aunt had gone off and left her in the street, and that she had no father or mother." The unnamed "lady and gentleman" from the community stepped in to become Letitia's guardians and aid in her instruction because she "was almost a ruined child, she was so bad." The couple "took the little stranger under their charge; and when her Aunt Sally came after her, they would not let her go." Under the tutelage of her surrogate parents, Letitia "entered upon a new career. She was taught about God and how to read and pray. However, unable to retain her lessons and remain inside, Letitia found reprieve outdoors and was "always outdoors, robbing bird's nests, rambling in the woods, picking chestnuts and walnuts, and, in the winter, sliding on the ice." Her ramblings suggest that she lived outside the conventional structure of domesticity. Her disobedient disposition prevailed, as she "never liked to work very hard, and when she had to work harder than she felt disposed, she would cry, and make such a fuss, that they would send her to bed, or somewhere else, to get rid of her noise."[54] Letitia's surrogate parents at first proved unsuccessful in managing her unruly temperament. Letitia's time of roaming and living without a "settled home" happened at the time in her childhood when she would have been learning about social conventions if her parents had lived, and her physical movements outdoors transgressed the restrictive mores of decorum and domesticity.

Letitia eventually learns to restrain her youthful disobedience when she enters a home with the anonymous lady and gentleman. In this household, where Letitia is guided and taught, and where she "spent her summers" working in the house and the garden, Letitia evolves from a girlhood rooted in misconduct to a more mature outlook in which she became aware of changes she needed to make in her behavior in order to succeed and survive. Although Letitia was still young at this moment of awareness (she is sent to bed when she misbehaves), her growth is measured by her awareness that changing her unruly behavior will be to her benefit. Because her unruliness has contributed to her loneliness, Letitia developed a "religious desire to be a good girl." Her decision to change "from being one of the most abject and despised, [to] . . . one of the most caressed and admired among her associates" suggests that Stewart saw in Letitia's decision the exercise of individual will—in this case, the desire to acquire religious instruction, self-govern her temper, and live a moral life. Letitia channeled her naughtiness into a willful intention to know God and become good. Eric Gardner rightly argues that while Letitia decided to become good, the narrator "never tells *how*—never suggests any human agency much less the saving and symbiotic work of the itinerant minister and a group of settlers."[55] However, what is implicit about Letitia's decision is that she had matured. This growth was measured by her newfound awareness and acceptance of God, which led to her transformation: "The last time I heard from her she was like a tree planted in the house of my God, towering like some of the tall cedars of Lebanon, considering all things as loss compared to the excellency of Jesus Christ."[56] The seeds of religion, piety, and prayer that were planted in Letitia by members of the black community enabled her to grow morally. In turn, Letitia plants new seeds in the black community. The black community's investment in Letitia not only improved Letitia's station in life but also that of everyone around her. Letitia's feelings of loneliness and loss became the *necessary* emotional turmoil that led to her decision to become "good." By quelling her unruliness and deciding to become "good," Letitia managed herself: she read the Bible, returned from the outdoors, and lived in an actual home.

In contrast to the innocent childhood that white authors typically portrayed, the suffering that Stewart's protagonist Letitia experienced in the "The First Stage of Life" emphasized that childlike naïveté was attached to racialized privilege. Letitia's loneliness, her rambling in the woods, and her feelings of loss were the *necessary* events of physical and emotional turmoil that led her to reflect on her prospects, govern her behaviors, and arrive at her decision to evolve and become "a good girl." The path to enlightenment that Letitia demonstrates—from unruliness to focused determination—illustrates the steps Stewart felt black women in the antebellum era had to take to ensure their survival and that of their children. Letitia's growth in awareness through religious conversion and her desire to become "good" conveys that she understood that living a religious life and abiding by conventional understandings of goodness would ensure a better future for her. Stewart presented Letitia's time of wandering as a necessary stage in the journey to become aware, decisive, and knowing. In this process, Stewart emphasized the healing power of the community in forging relationships and nurturing black youth.

Stewart's story had an intergenerational appeal for a periodical invested in molding the literary habits of readers of every age. African American periodical literature that targeted black children broadens our understanding of the scope of nineteenth-century African American literature. It included writing that satisfied the diverse literary tastes of an increasingly literate black population of all ages. As Xiomara Santamarina argues, "the long-standing and almost exclusive emphasis on antebellum slavery in black literature has continually led many to overlook the dialogues that free blacks carried out within white publics and black counter-publics about topics beyond the scope of abolition."[57] Stewart's writing presented a black child who improved her mind through education and aspired to engage in refined behavior through acquiring literacy and demonstrating piety and good manners.

Maria W. Stewart's essays, speeches, and stories laid a foundation for black women writers to tell their *own* stories in which black girls were represented not as victims but as determined and victorious. Stewart's story about a black girl's coming of age broadens our knowledge of the contributions African American women made to nineteenth-century print culture. Her early emphasis on black girlhood invites further study of the methodologies, frameworks, and emerging trends that shaped this early literature and continue to shape the canon of early African American literature and print culture. Two other narratives by black women writers, Harriet Wilson's *Our Nig* and Harriet Jacobs's *Incidents in the Life of a Slave Girl*, demonstrate the black girl's growth from unruly child to educated and moral women. These works recognize the courses of action black women needed to pursue in order to ensure their survival. In these narratives, education occurs in both formal and informal ways. Representations of black girls in these narratives offered a new set of principles to assist both free and enslaved black women in their quest to acquire independence.

Survival Strategies in Harriet Wilson's *Our Nig* (1859)

In *Our Nig*, Harriet Wilson presented physical endurance and rebelliousness as essential survival skills for youthful black girls in the antebellum period. Although it is a novel, *Our Nig* is based on Harriet Wilson's youth and the extreme hardships she encountered while living and working in New Hampshire in the 1850s.[58] Wilson wrote the novel in the hope that she would earn enough from book sales to support herself and her son. In her preface, Wilson wrote that she "sincerely appeal[ed] to her colored brethren universally for patronage, hoping they [will] . . . rally around [her] a faithful band of supporters and defenders."[59]

Literary scholars P. Gabrielle Foreman and Reginald Pitts argue that Wilson had good reason to request patronage from black (male) readers: she wanted to request protection for her words and avoid negative reaction or treatment.[60] *Our Nig* was lost, forgotten, and out of print until 1984, when Henry Louis Gates Jr. recovered the text and introduced it to the public.

Our Nig tells the story of Frado, a six-year-old black girl who loses her family when her mother and stepfather abandon her to work as an indentured servant for a white family, the Bellmonts, where she endures physical and mental abuse. In response to her tribulations, Frado pursues alternative ways of finding protection and her eventual freedom, following paths that depart from mainstream ideals of decorum and convention for young girls.[61] Wilson takes Frado through iterations of subjecthood that signal her growth from youthful girlhood to prematurely knowing girlhood: the worker, the daredevil, the learner, and the sewer. During Frado's youthful girlhood at age six, playfulness and daring physical acts function as ways to survive in the face of torture. Frado becomes prematurely knowing at sixteen when she realizes that the Bellmont men's feeble attempts at protection will never fully prevent her physical abuse. Frado learns that she can decide to overcome her vulnerability, and she finally takes a stand against Mrs. Bellmont and refuses to be degraded. The pivotal and most memorable scene in the text is when Frado comes to realize her inner strength.

When we first meet Frado, she is six years old, a "wild, frolicky thing" with the ability to "do jest as she's mind to." Frado is engrossed in "her play" when she hears Seth, her mother's lover, discuss plans to hire her out at the Bellmont home. When Seth calls her, Frado runs away with "another little colored girl . . . a favorite playmate." The two girls "climb fences and walls." They "passed through thickets and marshes," and when it became dark, the two girls "selected a thick cluster of shrubbery as a covert for the night." The physical nature of Frado's play shows early signs of the survivalist instincts that distinguish her from her playmate, whose "childish fears she attempted to banish."[62] This playdate also reveals Frado's painful awareness that the paternal figure in her life offers her little protection.

Six is a pivotal age for Frado. It is the year she is abandoned at the Bellmont home and years of torture begin. The physical abuse Frado endures while working as an indentured servant mirror the experiences of many orphaned girls in the antebellum North who were forced to work as indentured servants from a young age. Historian Faye E. Dudden writes that "orphaned children were commonly bound out at about age ten or twelve to serve until they were eighteen."[63] R. J. Ellis argues that servitude often began even earlier, at age seven.[64] As a young girl and an isolated orphan in a white household, Frado stands outside of societal expectations and cannot connect to a larger black social structure.

Frado's room at the Bellmonts emphasizes her abject position in the household. When Frado arrives at the Bellmont home, Jack, one of the sons, takes her by the hand, and the two "ascended the stairs without any light."[65] Although they were "passing through nicely furnished rooms, which were a source of great amazement to the child," Frado's room was down "a dark, unfinished passageway." Jack leads Frado to her new "apartment,—an unfinished chamber over the kitchen, the roof slanting nearly to the floor, so that the bed could stand only in the middle of the room. A small half window furnished light and air." Frado's space is physically oppressive: "The hot sun had penetrated her room, and it was long before a cooling breeze reduced the temperature to that she could sleep." While the room is indeed cramped, hot, and uninviting, Frado is determined to survive. During that first night, Frado "lay, revolving in her little mind whether she would remain or not until her mother's return." She remembers when she ran away from her stepfather. We know from Frado's youth that she is "of [a] willful, determined nature, a stranger to fear, and would not hesitate to wander away should she decide to."[66] She remembers her resolve and reaches deep within herself to find the strength to survive.

Drawing on this strength, Frado comes to view her cramped chamber as a welcome reprieve from the torture she receives at the hands of Mrs. Bellmont. Wilson explains: "But there was one little spot seldom penetrated by her mistress' watchful eye: this was her room, uninviting and comfortless; but to herself a safe retreat. Here, she would listen to the pleadings of a Saviour, and try to penetrate the veil of doubt and sin which clouded her soul and long to cast off the fetters of sin, and rise to the communion of saints."[67] Frado reimagines her cramped living space as a place to gain physical and emotional self-care and spiritual uplift.

While Frado experiences emotional wounds from her tribulations, actual scars cover her youthful body. In his work on race and the home in the antebellum period, Robert Reid-Pharr describes how Mrs. Bellmont's violence toward Frado helps her make sense of Frado's black body in her white household.[68] Robin Bernstein argues that "in the second half of the nineteenth century, pain functioned as a wedge that split childhood innocence, as a cultural formation, into distinct black and white trajectories. White children became constructed as tender angels while black children were libeled as unfeeling, noninnocent nonchildren."[69] In *Our Nig*, Mrs. Bellmont's beatings "become the material markers of the very complex ideological structure that holds together slavery, domesticity, and American racialism. . . . Again and again, Mrs. Bellmont returns to Frado's body in order to assure herself that there is some reality to race that might be accessed through the corporeal."[70] In inflicting these scars on Frado, Mrs. Bellmont seeks to diminish her presence as a human and a child who deserves grace and understanding. The pain and suffering Frado endures and the scars on her body are intended to distance the black girl further from the white household by removing all traces of innocence from her abused body. The poem that begins Chapter VII, written by H. K. W. (likely Wilson herself), reveals the words of a shattered child and convey Frado's evolving awareness that northern households are not always safe havens and some northern mothers are cruel: "What are our joys but dreams? and what our hopes / But goodly shadows in the summer cloud?"

Wilson explains how the passing of time impacts those who suffer: "Some sufferer has counted the vibrations of the pendulum impatient for its dawn, who, now that it has arrived, is anxious for its close. The votary of pleasure, conscious of yesterday's void, wishes for power to arrest time's haste till a few more hours of mirth shall be enjoyed."[71] Wilson notes in particular the impact of time for the "innocent child, weary of its stay, [who] longs for another morrow."[72] Frado's youthful girlhood is marked by a long period of time that consists of an education in pain. Wilson highlights the idea of time and its connection to Frado's suffering. When Frado attended school, she "had rest from Mrs. Bellmont's tyranny" and she learned to "read and spell, and knew the elementary steps in grammar, arithmetic, and writing," but this education ended when "she was nine years old; time, her mistress said, such privileges would stop." Mrs. Bellmont insisted that Frado's "time and person belonged solely to her."[73] Mrs. Bellmont's possession of Frado's time increases Frado's suffering and prevents her from experiencing any youthful pleasure or joy.

Each time Mrs. Bellmont tortures Frado inside the house, Frado seeks brief moments of reprieve outdoors. She reclaims her body and learns lessons for survival through daring yet physically liberating acts outside the home and the schoolhouse. While the schoolhouse is intended as a place of formal education, Frado learns other forms of knowledge there—pranks and tricks that sharpen her mind and protect her from the abusive taunts she encounters in the schoolhouse. She is "ever at some sly prank" at school and often leaves the schoolhouse, "venturing far beyond propriety." Frado climbs to dangerous heights in a barn where she "mounted in high glee on the topmost board." She balances on the edge of a high bank near a stream and tricks an unruly ram into falling into the water.[74] After Frado receives a particularly brutal bout of torture from Mrs. Bellmont, she flees from the Bellmont home and runs across the landscape in a scene that parallels the earlier playful scene in which she wanders from her home with her first playmate.[75] This time, however, Frado's flight is not play; rather, it is provoked by violence. Frado escapes "far, far, into the fields, over the walls and through fences, into a piece of swampy land."[76] Frado's frantic venture "far, far" into the swamps contrasts sharply with her position in the Bellmont's restrictive household and reveals her unwillingness to remain wholly captive.

As was the case with Stewart's Letitia, Frado's movement across the landscape constitutes a survival strategy.

While her body accomplishes fearless physical acts, Frado's imagination remains restricted. Ultimately, Frado learns to channel her physical movement into strategic, calculated acts that retaliate against Mrs. Bellmont's torture. Frado's resistance takes the form of an inward determination to survive. Frado shifts from rambunctious, playful pranks to book learning and sewing—a path similar to the one Letitia followed—which suggests that refinement through formal education was as necessary as spirited resistance in order for black girls to survive in the antebellum North. Frado "strives to enrich her mind" through literacy and learning the Bible even as Mrs. Bellmont attempts to diminish her soul and her body through violence and work. Instead of the playmate of her youth, "school-books were her constant companions, and every leisure moment was applied to them." Frado always had a book nearby "where she could glance from toil to soul refreshment." Learning how to sew soon became a source of financial independence for the girl. When she finally left the Bellmont house, Frado supported herself by sewing clothes and weaving straw bonnets. With her newfound passion for sewing, Frado "felt herself capable of elevation": "Expert with the needle, Frado soon equaled her instructress." She felt so accomplished that she "sought also to teach [the instructress] the value of useful books."[77] Wilson characterized knowledge of sewing as an alternative form of education and a profitable source of income for poor black women. These shifts in education from pranks to book learning to sewing demonstrate the need for black girls to acquire the skills that would enable them to support themselves in the antebellum era.

When Frado is around sixteen years old, she awakens to the realization of her power and finally resists Mrs. Bellmont's beatings.[78] When Mrs. Bellmont orders Frado to retrieve wood from a woodpile outside the house, Mrs. Bellmont becomes angry because she feels Frado has not returned quickly enough. Mrs. Bellmont raises a piece of wood to hit her, but Frado "stood like one who feels the stirring of free and independent thoughts" and shouted "Stop!" In this pivotal scene, Frado realizes that "she did not know, before, that she had a power to ward off assaults."[79] Frado's knowledge of her power allows her this moment of "triumph." Frado refuses to carry the wood into the house, and seeing Mrs. Bellmont "enter the door with her burden, repaid her for much of her former suffering."[80] Frado's awareness of her resiliency arrived suddenly and prematurely. Her knowledge was based not on forced sexual awareness but on an increased awareness of her ability to protect her own body from physical harm. She learned at an early age to rely on herself. Frado's act of rebellion at sixteen can be distinguished from her youthful pranks. Instead of fleeing from Mrs. Bellmont, as she does in her youth, Frado stands her ground and refuses to be a victim.

The Prematurely Knowing Girl: Harriet Jacobs's *Incidents in the Life of a Slave Girl* (1861)

The chapters on girlhood in Harriet Jacobs's slave narrative *Incidents in the Life of a Slave Girl* (1861) function as a teaching apparatus that Jacobs uses to show her readers the horrors of slavery for black women through the lens of the black girl figure. These early chapters provide a point of entry into Jacobs's life on the plantation and offer shocking details of the experiences of enslaved black women and girls in the South. Jacobs creates a carefully constructed girlhood intended to deliver a political message to white women of the North by showing the specific stages of the growth and development of her protagonist, Linda Brent, on the plantation. Early chapters pay close attention to Linda's youthful age of six. At this age, Linda is innocent and unknowing yet acutely aware of her surroundings and of the loss she feels as an orphan when her mother dies. Linda is fifteen when she endures threats of sexual abuse and actual rape. The prematurely knowing Linda Brent is unwilling to become a victim of sexual assault and must intervene to prevent her victimization.

Harriet Jacobs published her account of her life in slavery and her escape to freedom with the aid of two white female abolitionists, Amy Post and Lydia Maria Child. Published twenty years after Jacobs's escape from slavery, the narrative, which Jacobs wrote under the pseudonym Linda Brent, is one of the few slave narratives written by a woman.[81] Scholarship on *Incidents* argues that Jacobs's narrative is unique because it details the sexual exploitation of enslaved girls and women and does not conform to the conventional rhetoric and form of slave narratives written by men.[82] Crucial to understanding Jacobs's narrative is an awareness of the generic literary conventions of the antebellum era, which she recruits for her text. Because the techniques and conventions of the slave narrative did not permit Jacobs to describe her sexual vulnerability, she employs but critiques the techniques of the sentimental novel to tell her own story.[83]

Recent scholarship on *Incidents* by P. Gabrielle Foreman, Aliyyah I. Abdur-Rahman, and Stephanie Li argue that it is necessary to carefully read single chapters or episodes in order to uncover the hidden and indelicate truths in Jacobs's narrative. P. Gabrielle Foreman notes that "distrust of audiences encouraged authors to gauge the distance between the strict truth that falls short and to undertell their stories to match what we might call delicate expectations, while simultaneously indicating to receptive readers that more is apparent for those who choose to look."[84] In this section, I argue that looking carefully at Linda Brent's girlhood subjectivity exposes Jacobs's "delicate" truths.

Jacobs's presentation of Linda's knowingness, which was cultivated early through forced sexual violence and impropriety, constructs enslaved black girls as outside the conventional rules and regulated practices of female maturation, sexual growth, and preparation for marriage that were circulated in the dominant culture and published in antebellum health manuals and medical books. In a chapter titled "Marriageable State," in *Ladies Physo Medical Companion* (1859), author J. X. Durham argued that girls during the impressionable ages of twelve to sixteen needed extra care: "Great attention and care is necessary to the young female from the age of twelve to that of sixteen. For by necessary information and careful management may be prevented irreparable mischief and injury to the constitution, arising from impudent conduct, in consequence of ignorance and a feeling of bashfulness. . . . Many, however, withhold this important knowledge, in consequence of a kind of bashfulness which they seem to possess."[85] Durham defines girls' maturation process based strictly on their preparation for marriage: "In many places young ladies are considered marriageable at the age of fifteen, which is, beyond doubt, in many instances, the cause of many broken down constitutions, and also, of many feeble and delicate children. In the southern states, young ladies are considered marriageable from sixteen to twenty years; and in the northern States from eighteen to twenty-five."[86] Many black girls who were living in the antebellum North or were enslaved in the South grew up without the protective care of parental figures and were often unable to uphold these conservative, feminine conventions. They broke from conventional understandings of feminine decorum and were forced to become prematurely aware of sexuality and danger despite their youth. The "great attention and care" that governed the girlhoods of many women in the antebellum era was never provided to Linda, so she developed strategies to escape her situation.

Jacobs assigned the young Linda the voice of an adult. Frances Smith Foster argues that "Jacobs recounts incidents in her life as a naïve slave girl but the narrative voice is clearly that of a free, informed woman. She not only intends to demonstrate the evils of slavery but to show her female readers the similarities to their situations and to convince them that as long as there are slave girls such as Linda Brent, no woman's freedom is secure."[87] Jacobs conveys how repeated threats of sexual assault make Linda's girlhood "a sad epoch in the life of a slave girl."[88] In acknowledging girlhood as an "epoch," a distinct stage in a female's development, Jacobs distinguishes between girlhood and womanhood, a rhetorical move that acknowledges the slave woman not as chattel but as human *and* female. Marking black girlhood as a stage of purity similar to that of white women was a strategy for encouraging white female readers to commiserate with slave girls who were beaten and raped and lend their support to the abolition movement.

Linda Brent's Youthful Girlhood

In "Childhood," the first chapter of Harriet Jacobs's narrative, Linda Brent offers a searing adult view of the triangulation of debt, broken promises, and utter loss incurred on the plantation among Mrs. Flint, Linda Brent's grandmother (Aunt Martha), and Linda. While the chapter title implies youthful scenes of Linda's childhood, readers are confronted instead with the child's clear awareness of the economics of slavery and familial loss through the language of debt, profits, and money. Readers learn about the death of Linda's biological mother, the backstory of Linda's grandmother's childhood and wrongful sale into slavery, and the grandmother's subsequent freedom. Linda explains how her father paid his female owner $200 a year for the privilege of being able to work as a carpenter who earned money so that he might be able to buy his own children, but "though he several times offered his hard earnings for that purpose, he never succeeded." Readers learn of the grandmother's business of baking and selling crackers in order to purchase clothing for herself and her children. It is the grandmother's hope that the income from her small enterprise would be "profitable" and she would be able to save enough to purchase her own children. When Mrs. Flint begs for $300 as a loan so she can buy a candelabra, "promising to pay her soon," the grandmother loses her hard-earned money. Well aware of the financial sacrifices her grandmother makes to ensure her safety, Jacobs explains how Linda is "indebted" to her grandmother "for many comforts" and how she continued to be "indebted to her for many more important services." This discussion of money, profits, and debts reveals that Linda is prematurely aware of the economics of slavery.

Jacobs reverses and undermines the power arrangement of money on the plantation by showing a more humane relationship between debt and gratitude. Although she is young, Linda thinks with the logic of a merchant. In describing Mrs. Flint's debt to Linda's grandmother (Aunt Martha) and acknowledging the debt that Linda, too, owes her grandmother for providing food and clothing, Linda explains to northern readers the system of debt in which she participates. Mrs. Flint owes Aunt Martha $300 and because debts are transferable, this debt implies that the mistress owes Linda, who is Aunt Martha's next of kin. Linda conveys subtly that although they are slaves, Mrs. Flint's unpaid debt makes Aunt Martha and Linda her creditors. Thus, they should be considered full members of society. Linda undermines a basic tenet of slavery by insisting that Mrs. Flint is in debt to her grandmother. Because she is not a full adult, Linda is able to carefully critique an economic system without fear of being attacked for her views and alienating readers. In her explanation of how the circulation of money functions on the plantation, Jacobs relies upon the naïveté of a youthful black girl to make her expressions of money and debt on the plantation palatable to readers.

Jacobs's depiction of Linda's youthful girlhood at age six in "Childhood" makes a political statement about slavery's violent impact on all women. For

Linda, this is an age when imagination and play are short-lived and are replaced with dismal thoughts about her condition as a slave. Linda describes how she experienced "unusually unfortunate circumstances" because "when [she] was six years old, [her] mother died; and then, for the first time, [she] learned, by the talk around [her], that [she] was a slave." Linda remembers how her "young mind was troubled with the thought who would now take care of me and my little brother."

The "Childhood" chapter recounts stories of interracial playdates on the plantation between Linda's mother and her white biological sister. When they became women, "my mother was a most faithful servant to her white foster sister." In "Trials of Girlhood," Linda witnesses another interracial playdate between an enslaved black girl and a white girl that foreshadows future misery instead of illustrating sentimental benevolence: "I once saw two children playing together. One was a fair white child; the other was her slave, and also her sister. When I saw them embracing each other, and heard their joyous laughter, I turned away sadly from the lovely sight. I foresaw the inevitable blight that would soon fall on the little slave's heart. I knew how soon her laughter would be changed to sighs."[89] The interracial playdate evokes the painful realization of familial disruption couched in fear of sexual assault. While the white and black girl play innocently, their painful pairing reveals the perverse sexual violence that often befalls enslaved black girls and disrupts black families. These depictions of the play of girls on southern plantations function as brief respites that magnify slavery's miseries. Enslaved black girls' play accentuates this ironic pairing: their vulnerability and resistance convey slavery's sadism.[90]

Scholars of nineteenth-century African American literature explore how slave narratives provided readers with titillating reading pleasures through spectacles of enforced jollity and slave performances.[91] Scenes of enslaved black girls' playfulness may be included in these performances. Acts of play between white and black girls on the plantation are rendered joyless due to the underlying implications of rape that the pairing reveals. As Saidiya Hartman argues, "The bucolic scenes of plantation life and the innocent amusements of the enslaved, contrary to our expectations, succeed not in mollifying terror but in assuring and sustaining its presence. . . . Behind the façade of innocent amusements lay the violence the master class assiduously denied." Scenes of black girls' playfulness are overshadowed by the ever-threatening exercise of the master's power and make it difficult to "discern domination from recreation."[92] The playfulness of black girls illuminates tensions between pleasure and punishment and reveals the quotidian nature of practices of dominance and violence.[93]

Antithetical pairing occurs in the first line of Jacobs's slave narrative: "I was born a slave; but I never knew it till six years of happy childhood had passed away." Jacobs pairs Linda's "happy childhood" with an early awareness of her condition as a slave. The two phrases separated by a semicolon oppose each other and serve to question whether an enslaved black girl could actually enjoy a "happy childhood." Antithetical pairing recurs when Linda's mother dies and Linda becomes an orphan. Linda remembers that "my home was now to be with her mistress; and I found it a happy one." Again, the pairing of two ironic opposites—becoming the surrogate daughter/slave to Mrs. Flint and the labeling of the home as "happy"—draws readers into the narrative by critiquing the systemic violent injustice enslaved girls endured. Linda explains that while she was living with Mrs. Flint, "no toilsome duties were imposed upon [her]." Instead, as a young girl, "she would sit with her mistress sewing diligently," and "when she thought I was tired, she would send me out to run and jump" or "gather berries or flowers to decorate her room." Linda calls these youthful moments "happy days—too happy to last." Linda remembers her youth as initially filled with play, and these childhood memories appear to be joyous and sincere. Upon closer scrutiny, however, it becomes clear that the mistress demands that the young enslaved girl do chores and sew "diligently." Instead of allowing her to rest, she orders Linda to continue working. The repeated mentioning of Linda's "happiness" in slavery unsettles readers. Jacobs distinguishes between the carefree state of happiness and the slave girl's obligation to exhibit good behavior: "We, who are slave-children, without father or mother, could not expect to be happy. We must be good; perhaps that would bring us contentment."[94] This correlation of pleasure and duty foregrounds a tangled, masochistic relationship between girlhood, pleasure, and pain.

Linda Brent's Deliberate Calculation

When Linda turns fifteen, she transitions from youthful girlhood to "prematurely knowing" girlhood, a time when her mind is filled "with unclean images, such as only a vile monster would think of." Her master is the one who is responsible for "peopling her mind" with such thoughts. Linda replaces these unclean images with plans to orchestrate her safe escape and that of her children. While these calculated and strategic thoughts, which Linda refers to as her "meditations," may be devoid of childlike wonder and were often "very sad," Linda expresses imagination when she thinks of another kind of life for herself in freedom.[95] This new way of thinking departs from Letitia's and Frado's youthful girlhood experience; for Linda, play and wandering are replaced with keen awareness and calculated, imaginative thought. For enslaved girls, "knowing" girlhood critiques lawlessness—the physical and sexual violence toward black girls in the South. Linda's resistance takes the form of active *knowingness* of her danger, and she absorbs her lessons simply by being attuned to her environment—as she must to survive.

Linda's awareness of the vile indecencies that occur on the plantation and the strategic steps she takes to protect her family from abuse contributes to her growth into prematurely knowing girlhood. Despite the pure principles she learns from her grandmother, before she is twelve, Linda learns about the violent abuse of enslaved black women and how she, too, might fall victim to it:

> Even the little child, who is accustomed to wait on her mistress and her children, *will learn*, before she is twelve years old, why it is that her mistress hates such and such a one among the slaves. Perhaps the child's own mother is among those hated ones. She *listens* to violent outbreaks of jealous passion, and cannot help understanding what is the cause. She *will become prematurely knowing* in evil things. Soon she *will learn* to tremble when she hears her master's footfall. She *will be compelled to realize* that she is no longer a child.[96]

The repeated phrase of emphasis (*will* learn, *will* become prematurely knowing, *will* be compelled) suggests that Linda's experiences are the routine, likely consequences for many black girls who came of age in the antebellum South. The predicament of youthful black girls as unwilling receivers of dangerous knowledge—as evidenced in Jacobs's image of Linda as the unwilling recipient of Dr. Flint's whispered advances—contrasts with "knowing" black girls' conscious recognition of their danger. Linda comes to the realization, finally, that she must be shrewd and deliberate in developing her scheme for survival. Linda's realization of sexual threats is at first laced with the wonder of a young girl but is quickly replaced by a determined *adult* insistence on fighting back. Linda Brent's torture fuels her desire to seek protection by orchestrating an escape from slavery. Her reaction to assault is characterized by a language of power, a perceptive wit, and the full awareness that she needs to escape her danger. She becomes aware that "the influences of slavery had had the same effect on me that they had on other young girls; they made me prematurely knowing, concerning the ways of the world. I knew what I did, and I did it with deliberate calculation." Jacobs contrasts Linda's forced "premature knowingness" of sexual assault and the deliberateness she conveys when she admits that she "knew what she did" when she had two children with another white man, Mr. Sands, to avoid sexual insult from Dr. Flint. Linda's testimony is couched in two levels of knowingness. Admitting to being prematurely knowing evokes sympathy from readers. Admitting that she "knew what she did" reclaims her body on her own terms.

Linda Brent's testimony of her sexual assault and the deliberate use of her sexuality to devise an escape from slavery challenges a republican model in which men attempt to protect their families and uphold the ideals of republican motherhood. Jacobs reveals how in the South, black men were unable to protect their families and black girls had to protect themselves. Linda's father is unable to offer her any form of protection against sexual abuse. Jacobs describes the endemic inability of enslaved black men to protect their families:

> Some poor creatures have been so brutalized by the lash that they will sneak out of the way to give their masters free access to their wives and daughters. Do you think this proves the black man to belong to an inferior order of beings? What would *you* be, if you had been born and brought up a slave, with generations of slaves as ancestors? I admit that the black man *is* inferior. But what makes him so? It is the ignorance in which white men compel him to live; it is the torturing whip that lashes manhood out of him, it is the fierce bloodhounds of the South, and the scarcely less cruel human bloodhounds of the north, who enforce the Fugitive Slave Law. *They* do the work.[97]

Linda becomes prematurely knowing when she realizes the need to develop "bonds of affection" with her aunt and grandmother and with her Uncle Phillip and friend Peter, all of whom offer protection and nurturance throughout her childhood and as she prepares for escape.[98] Linda realizes that her escape will not be something she will experience alone; members of a network of kin and friends will work together to aid her. Linda's Uncle Phillip is a carpenter who makes the concealed trap door to the garret that allows Linda to hide safely and provides access to another part of the house, the storeroom, where she can communicate with her family. The storeroom serves a significant role in Linda's captivity. Jacobs reinterprets storerooms and tight spaces such as those on slave ships as useful for black girls' survival.

Conclusion

By revealing the qualities and behaviors black girls exhibited across literary genres, black women writers uncovered the power and potential of black girls as seekers of their own fate. In their narratives, black girl figures knowingly break laws of conventionality and feminine virtue. They take on active roles and revolutionary stances that reject their objectification as victims of violence or as models for marriage and reform. Black women writers wrote stories about black girls who demonstrated strategic and brave acts of rebellion. These stories offer a *new* set of laws to assist black women, free and enslaved, in their efforts to address the unlawful violations of their bodies.

The work of African American women writers in the antebellum era illustrates the difference between what black male newspaper editors and white abolitionists were imagining and what black women and girls were experiencing. Black male editors presented black girls as idealized, almost static two-dimensional figures who served their didactic goals. For black male newspaper editors, girlhood figures were symbols that they used to convey the type of racial roles that would bolster efforts among African Americans in the antebellum North to become more full participants in civic life and to strengthen their families. White abolitionist writers also used the figure of the black girl for their own purposes. The suffering of black girls in the literature they produced was a tool of moral suasion that was designed to elicit empathy among white children and socialize them into antislavery attitudes.

In contrast, African American women writers insisted on telling their own stories. Black women writers' depictions of black girls' suffering exposed the inaccuracies of the ways black men and white abolitionists portrayed black girls. In the hands of women writers, black girls were three-dimensional figures whose varied experiences demanded the genres of long fiction and autobiography to accommodate fuller explorations. Although they depicted the suffering of girls living in slavery in the South or working as servants in the North in great detail, they emphasized the determined will of black girls to survive. They focused on the types of education their protagonists needed that were very different from the education white children received in public schools. Although formal education was essential in the stories they told, the girls they wrote about also needed wit, cunning, patience, long-term strategies, and the ability to protect their bodies. They also needed assistance from the black community around them. The girls who could draw upon all these resources not only survived but were able to escape into better lives as they entered adulthood. Black women writers rejected the trope of the suffering black girl who dies for want of resources or sympathy. They emphasized instead how black girls learned to draw on their own inner resources and then gather resources from the environment and the community around them.

Black women writers reimagined the tight, torturous spaces of attics, garrets, and storerooms as regenerative. In these spaces, black girls can think, imagine, and plan. They could strategize escapes. They could reinvigorate their spirits. Although physically cramped, black girls in the literature black women produced widened these restrictive walls and pushed against boundaries through determined willpower strengthened by connecting to their minds. They sewed clothes, mastered multiple types of literacy, and read books. In essence, these black girls built an arsenal of tactics to engage in the necessary warfare to secure their survival. In a similar way, sections devoted to children's literature in black magazines such as the *Repository*'s "Children's Room" column offered Maria W. Stewart and other black women writers literary spaces to discuss concerns for their children and teach them the skills they needed to ensure better futures. The different literary genres present in the "Children's Room" column, from poems to essays to short fiction, conveyed that black editors and writers were invested in reaching audiences using diverse modes of communication. The "Children's Room" column offered burgeoning writers, many of whom were black women, a literary space they could use to write creatively and directly to an audience. Whether the lives of black girls unfolded in cramped attics and garrets or in a section of a black magazine, these spaces, both physically and figuratively, revealed the potential of black girls. Black girls in this literature were visible, valiant, and valuable, and they maintained the will to survive against all odds.

3. "Teach Your Daughters"

Black Girlhood and Mrs. N. F. Mossell's Advice Column in the New York Freeman

IN "THE FATE OF THE NEWSPAPER THAT HAD NOTHING IN IT," an 1886 article published in the *Christian Recorder*, African American writer Gertrude Bustill Mossell took her readers through a day in the life of an issue of a black newspaper. Tom, the eldest child of the family, who "belonged to the race, but took pleasure and pride in disparaging all efforts made by any individual of the race," finds it first. He intends to discard it but discovers an article titled "Before Using Anti-Curl. After Using Anti-Curl" that complements his "dudish" ways. Tom saves the article and throws away the rest of the paper, but "soon his sister Nellie, in her tour of straightening up the room, came across the despised object." She glances over its contents until a poem titled "Last Poem by H.H." meets her eye. "Just what I have been looking for!" she cries. "'I will keep it for my scrapbook.' Snip go the scissors, and once more the paper has been under the dissecting knife." Every member of the family clips an article from the paper. The father selects an editorial and the mother cuts out an article on tips for managing a household. The newspaper eventually reaches the youngest daughter, who takes it to school, where her teacher clips out an article. A schoolmate is so impressed with the remaining contents of the paper that he purchases a subscription. The youngest daughter determines the newspaper's "fate" by extending its reach outside her home and into the community to perform "good work."[1]

Mossell's snapshot had a second, less overt, agenda: she described a day in the life of a middle-class black family whose members were consumers, students, and participants in community life. Each family member had his or her own concerns, yet they all worked together to cultivate family life from a stable home base. This is the idealized family black newspaper editors had been describing for decades, translated into the new consumer economy of the industrial era.

Mossell's article also highlights two representations of young black women as forward-thinking figures in the postbellum era. The oldest daughter who clips articles for her scrapbook and the youngest daughter who takes the remainder of the newspaper into her school serve as two models for a new generation of black girls. In the first model, a black girl contributes to the domesticity and order of the family home when she creates scrapbooks and "straightens the room"; in the second model, a black girl is actively involved in her education. The curiosity and pluck Mossell ascribes to the two black girls in the article defines them as participants in an emerging model of familial and civic participation for black women.

In this chapter, I argue that Mossell used her platform as the editor of an advice column, "Our Woman's Department," published between 1886 and 1887 in the *New York Freeman*, to promote models of public citizenship that widened the boundaries of black female purposefulness in the postbellum period. She offered solutions to the everyday problems of black families who were working to maintain their households amid the social and political pressures of disenfranchisement, denial of public services, and threats of white mob violence. Mossell's columns combine a no-nonsense tone with direct instructions that depart from the Christian-centered sentimental prose of the girlhood stories of earlier black newspapers, such as the *Repository of Religion and Literature, and of Science and Art* and the *Christian Recorder* in the Civil War and Reconstruction era.

In "The Fate of the Newspaper That Had Nothing in It," Mossell presented roles for black females that highlighted themes she touched on often during her two-year tenure as editor of "Our Woman's Department." Nellie, one daughter in the family, chronicles her culture by creating a scrapbook. She creates a record of what she deems the best expressions of African American life and arts. Ellen Gruber Garvey cogently argues that African American scrapbook makers created an "alternative record" of "unwritten histories" that could "fill gaps in mainstream accounts and assert African American importance in the nation's history."[2] Elsewhere, Mossell wrote that the black race needed to "produce its own delineators of Negro life," and Nellie was doing just that.[3] As a scrapbook maker, Nellie imagined herself as a reader, a writer, and a recorder of history. On an individual level, Nellie's scrapbook created a resource of the accomplishments of black men and women that mirrored the resource Mossell would create several years later with *The Work of the Afro-American Woman* (1894). Nellie illustrated a second theme that was dear to Mossell's heart: she demonstrated the value of thrift. For her, the newspaper had value even after her brother had discarded it. Finally, the youngest daughter illustrated the virtues of engagement with public life and sharing resources with other community members. The actions of the two daughters illustrated the importance of the print record, a stable family life and well-ordered household, and involvement in the public sector for black women and girls in the postbellum period.

During its two-year span, "Our Woman's Department" was published biweekly. The articles in the column ranged from such topics as child care and education to securing work and aiding the poor. Mossell encouraged parents to view their daughters as useful members of the household by preparing them for household management and for working safely outside the home as domestics or in other professions. She advised black girls to negotiate equal relationships with employers, to protect their bodies and their incomes, and to avoid the dangers of men with bad intentions and overindulgence in saloons. She explained how to discipline children and marry wisely. Mossell's columns appealed to a wide readership that was engaged with issues such as looking for gainful employment, raising healthy families, and seeking suitable education for children. This assemblage of advice contains an underlying tone of self-sufficiency that subverts the idea that women needed to rely solely on men to bring stability, income, and knowledge into their lives. Mossell's columns may be placed alongside literary genres that are representative of post-Reconstruction uplift efforts, such as Pauline Hopkins's historical fiction, Anna Julia Cooper's speeches, and Ida B. Wells's antilynching treatises. Mossell's advice columns also anticipated future black institutions such as female training schools, black suffragist societies, temperance unions, and black women's clubs.[4]

In the 1880s and 1890s, black men and women began to take stock of where their community was a generation after emancipation. It was clear that Reconstruction had failed. Industrialization was not delivering new employment opportunities to black men and women in the North, and in the South many families were trapped in the vicious sharecropper system that kept them on the bottom rung of the so-called agricultural ladder. Many wondered what hopes and dreams were possible for the next generation, and opinion was divided about whether to push to remove structural obstacles or advise young people how best to cope with a society and economy that was closing many doors. This chapter presents several snapshots of the views of one woman leader in print media who promoted both of these strategies. In an era when the path forward was being vigorously debated among many prominent African Americans, Gertrude Mossell had plenty to say.

The Bustill and Mossell Family Histories

Gertrude Bustill was born in 1855 into a Philadelphia family that had been politically active community builders for decades. The free status of the Bustill family dated back to the Revolutionary War era. Bustill's great-grandfather Cyrus

Bustill, a baker, had provisioned George Washington's troops during the war. He was a member of the Free African Society, the first mutual aid society for blacks in the United States.[5] He also started a school for black children in Philadelphia.[6] Her grandfather, David Bustill, wrote in his diary that he felt that God had called him to help free the slaves.[7] Her uncle, Joseph Bustill, was a leader in the Pennsylvania branch of the National Equal Rights League, an organization that was formed in 1864 to oppose segregation and fight for the political rights of blacks, including full suffrage for both men and women. He was also active in the Underground Railroad before the war.[8] Like his brother, Gertrude's father, Charles Hicks Bustill (ca. 1815–1890), worked in the Underground Railroad.[9] In 1852, he was also one of the founding members of Philadelphia's newly reorganized Vigilance Committee, the clandestine fund-raising organization for the Vigilant Association, the group founded in 1837 in Philadelphia to assist escaping slaves.[10] Although Charles Bustill was a manual laborer, a plasterer, for his entire working life, his most significant work was done on behalf of his race.[11]

In 1850, thirty-year-old Charles was living with his father David and his mother Mary, his younger brother Joseph (26), and his three sisters, Esther (22), Mary (20), and Rebecca (18). Two other young men, both plasterers like Charles, Joseph, and David, also lived with the family.[12] The household must have been full of energy and careful strategizing as two generations of Bustills worked to both support the household and help conduct slaves north to freedom. Ten years later, in 1860, Charles was a widower with two small daughters, Louisa, age six, and Gertrude, age five. His mother had died the year before, and his father would die six years later.[13] When Charles lost his young wife, he was not able to turn to his parents for help raising his small daughters. These losses meant that Gertrude grew up without a mother and without paternal grandparents. In 1860, a thirty-seven-year-old woman, Sarah Fisher, was living in Charles's household with her two children, likely to provide housekeeping and child care.[14] Charles must have been away from home a lot in that decade of the Civil War as he supported his daughters, continued his work in the Underground Railroad, and likely participated in forming strategies for the future of the race.

Despite the national turmoil, Charles Bustill provided his two daughters with the best education available to black students in Philadelphia. Both attended the Institute for Colored Youth, which had been founded in 1837 with money from a bequest from a wealthy Quaker. By the 1860s and early 1870s, when Gertrude attended, the entire staff was comprised of black women teachers and the focus of education had shifted from industrial education to the training of teachers.[15] One of her teachers there was her second cousin, Sarah Mapps Douglass.[16] The institute was a hub of black community life in Philadelphia; in 1868, almost 3,000 people attended the graduation ceremony—for a class of just nine students. After the war, the Institute for Colored Youth sent more graduates to teach in the South than any other school.[17] Gertrude may not have had a mother, but she was surrounded by black women leaders as she grew up, and her education prepared her to be a leader herself.

When she completed her education shortly after 1870, Gertrude taught school for seven years in Philadelphia and Trenton, New Jersey. At the same time, she began her career in journalism through part-time work for the *Philadelphia Echo* and the *Philadelphia Independent*, both black newspapers.[18] While she was teaching in Philadelphia, she saw firsthand what could happen when young girls could not complete their education. She boarded in the household of Anna Hilton—likely a widow—and her seventeen-year-old son, Edward Hilton, and fourteen-year-old daughter, Anna. Both of Anna Hilton's children contributed to the household, Edward as a barber and Anna as a mill hand. For young Anna, the days of education had ended in her early teens and her chance to prepare herself for a trade or work as a teacher or nurse was over.[19] This was not the kind of future Gertrude Bustill and many other black community members envisioned for black children in the 1870s.

In 1881, Gertrude married Nathan Mossell, who was still studying at the University of Pennsylvania Medical School.[20] Like Charles Bustill, Nathan's parents Aaron and Elizabeth Mossell valued education highly, so much so that they were willing to disrupt family networks and leave the country to ensure that their children had access to it. In 1850, while Charles Bustill was working to help enslaved blacks reach freedom, Aaron and Elizabeth Mossell were living in freedom in Maryland. Deeply dissatisfied with the prospects for the education of their two young children, they migrated to Hamilton, Ontario, Canada, so their children could have access to a good education. Aaron, a brick maker, was able to support his family with his trade, and Elizabeth Mossell was a full-time homemaker. They had seven more children while in Canada, including a set of female triplets who apparently did not survive.[21] Nathan was born in Canada in 1856.

After the Civil War, the Mossell family moved to Lockport, New York. Aaron had saved enough money to build a house for his family and began to invest in property. He built a successful brickworks that employed between fifteen and twenty people of all nationalities and supplied the bricks for many of the buildings of Lockport, including a new city school. He and other members of the black community protested vigorously when black children were shut out of the new school. They won their campaign, and the schools of Lockport were integrated in 1876.[22]

From her own family history and that of the Mossells, Gertrude observed that large community goals could be accomplished even when the work that family members did for wages was not considered prestigious in mainstream society. Thrifty monitoring of resources, the presence of a mother in the home full time, a strong focus on education for children, and fierce devotion to important political and social goals for the black community was the recipe families could use to battle prejudice and obstacles. These were the values Gertrude Bustill Mossell carried into her work as the editor of a woman's column for a national black newspaper.

The *New York Freeman*

Five years after her marriage, in 1886, Gertrude Mossell began editing the woman's column of the *New York Freeman*. The paper had begun in 1884, when the publisher, T. Thomas Fortune, bought out his partner in the paper's predecessor, the *New York Globe*.[23] Fortune offered a new voice to the black community that was independent and, most important, secular. He refused to identify with one camp or another in debates within the community, and he insisted that secular black newspaper editors had as much power to shape opinion as religious leaders. Within a short time, the *New York Freeman* was a highly respected paper that was distributed throughout the North and West.[24] Brian L. Johnson notes that the *Freeman* "gained the highest respect among African American newspapers appearing in the 1880s," and historian John Hope Franklin, noting that the "editors of the Afro-American press were almost as influential as the religious leaders," felt that T. Thomas Fortune "was surely preeminent among the secular black leaders of his time."[25]

Her new position at the newspaper gave Mossell a national voice. It also made her the highest-paid black newspaperwoman at the time; her annual salary of $500 a year was a measure of the value T. Thomas Fortune placed on explorations of black women's issues. This income enabled her to contribute to her household at a time when her husband was building his medical practice in Philadelphia. None of the city's white hospitals would admit blacks as attending physicians, so the small handful of black doctors had no alternative but private practice.[26]

Mossell introduced a model of civic engagement to her readers that she embodied in her own life as a wife, mother, and journalist. As Joanne Braxton notes, Mossell worked as a regular reporter and correspondent for mainstream white and black newspapers and contributed to magazines such as *Our Women and Children*, the *Ladies Home Journal*, and the *Inquirer*. After her marriage to Nathan Mossell and the birth of her two children, Gertrude worked as a syndicated columnist for newspapers such as the *AME Church Review*, the *Philadelphia Times*, the *Philadelphia Echo*, the *Independent*, and the *Press Republican*, where she wrote articles on political and social issues emphasizing women's rights and responsibilities. Mossell also edited the "Woman's Department" of the *New York Age*, the *Indianapolis World*, and the *New York Freeman*.[27]

Mossell's professional name—Mrs. N. F. Mossell—referenced her identity as a married black woman with a public career. This self-fashioning suggests that Mossell's identity as a wife was as important to her as her love of writing and civic participation. Claudia Tate argues that Mossell's use of her husband's name "referenced proper feminine posture for a middle-class woman."[28] Such public modesty signaled what Joanne Braxton calls Mossell's intention to "defend and celebrate black womanhood without disrupting the delicate balance of black male-female relations or challenging masculine authority."[29] At the same time, Mossell's matter-of-fact advice encouraged her readers to maintain control over their lives and be responsible for their own careers in the public sphere. Her professional name also suggests an allegiance to the Mossells, a prominent family from upstate New York.

The location of "Our Woman's Department" in the *New York Freeman* underpinned Mossell's status as a public woman. The arrangement of "Our Woman's Department" alongside politically charged articles suggests that the newspaper's agenda included encouraging women readers to be aware of political issues impacting their lives. Mossell's column was consistently easy to find on the page; it was either on the edge or in the middle alongside political columns and articles about current events. This placement was a deliberate editorial practice intended to encourage canny reading practices and influence readers' opinions. The cross-pollination layout strategy suggests that domestic activities, the politics of the nation, and current events of the world would not have been viewed as mutually exclusive. A reader's eyes might have drifted over to the national news and back to advice about how to navigate the local effects of national events from the hearth. In the 1880s, Mossell's advice column would have been an invaluable resource for African American women well versed in world events, politics, financial matters, and social matters.

Mossell's advice columns in the black press offered important information to the reading public, promoted literary exchange, and encouraged readers to participate in civic life. Biweekly installments increased the chances that readers would come to every issue primed and eager to engage with the material, building on the column they had read two weeks before. The length of Mossell's written advice—which rarely exceeded a single column—was amenable to a black reading public that was rapidly gaining literacy.

Although Gertrude Bustill Mossell is regarded as one of the first black female journalists to write her own column, "Our Woman's Department" has received little critical attention.[30] Literary scholars Claudia Tate and Ann duCille discuss Mossell's dedication to black women's political involvement in her collection of essays and articles, *The Work of the Afro-American Woman* (1894), yet neither scholar addresses Mossell's advice column. Of *The Work*, Claudia Tate notes that

Mossell "defined the liberated black American not in the conceptual framework of black manhood, but of black womanhood instead, focusing on the responsibilities of feminine citizenship to represent the body politic."[31] DuCille argues that essays and articles published in *The Work* "offered a critical assessment of the sexist directives with which black women were bombarded."[32] P. Gabrielle Foreman situates Mossell alongside black women activists of the 1880s such as Amelia E. Johnson and Frances E. W. Harper in an assessment of Mossell's rarely discussed book, *Little Dansie's One Day at Sabbath School*.[33] Joanne Braxton argues that Mossell's smart, sharp voice gave readers "instruction and inspiration" that made a "powerful and progressive" contribution to American cultural and intellectual work at the turn of the century. Mossell's rarely read and rarely studied columns contain "the wellsprings of black feminist literary expression" and reflect the impulse to document, share, inspire, and instruct that informed black women's writing in the postbellum era.[34]

The recurrent voice of the columnist participated in national dialogues and responded to social and political events. Readers were drawn into and able to respond to discussions. Ritualized reading of each advice column throughout the calendar year created anticipation among readers and encouraged conversation and reflection at home and in the street. Such conversations sought to build community among black readers. Mossell's advice columns showed a wide readership how to educate their daughters so they could participate in civic life, become efficient household managers, and engage safely in work outside the home. While her columns championed chastity and standards of sexual modesty, two of her favorite topics were the value of women and girls who worked outside the home and how to navigate the public sphere safely.

Audiences and Advice Columns

Mossell's public image as an advice columnist for black women and girls aligned with the *New York Freeman*'s mission of protecting and properly defending the people it served. In doing so, the newspaper reinforced its place at the center of the black community. The word *Our* in the title of the column "Our Woman's Department" coupled with the aim of Mossell's column "to promote true womanhood, especially that of the African race," reinforces an intimate, communal, gendered space within a national black newspaper. The title suggests that while columns for white women might exist in other publications, her column was a space devoted specifically to black women and girls.

Mossell's advice columns were published alongside other articles on black girls in the *New York Freeman* in the 1880s. In "A Chapter on Our Girls: Their Position in the World—How to Educate Them," published in March 1886 and reprinted from the *Louisiana Standard*, a black newspaper, the author, Ivy, disclosed the "unknown power" in a society that reduced girls to stereotypes: "Somehow or other, Providence, fate, chance, or whatever you choose to call it, does not seem to take note of the various adjectives by which we are wont to characterize girls. Indeed, this unknown power seems to take particular delight in defeating our pet projects in regard to shaping the destiny of girls."[35] The sharing of material among black newspapers through reprinting articles from other regions is evidence of the attempts of editors to foster a national black culture. Mossell's columns rebuked the "unknown power" that reduced black girls to stereotypes by offering solutions intended to shape black girls' futures. The possessive word *Our* shifted to register black girls when the article was reprinted in a black newspaper.

Individuals listed in the Acknowledgments section of her column revealed the network of people with whom Mossell associated.[36] In February 1886, Mossell wrote in this section of her column, "We desire to return thanks to those who by their valuable hints, comments, and suggestions have added to the future usefulness of this column. . . . Mrs. F. E. W. Harper has kindly extended the use of her private library, and the use of [her] Mercantile Library ticket." The gratitude Mossell expressed to Frances E. W. Harper highlighted Mossell's friendship with another black woman writer. Users of the Mercantile Library in Philadelphia were shareholders of the library. Each user had to purchase a share in the library each year to use its resources. The "library ticket," then, was proof that Harper was a paid subscriber. This relationship between Mossell and Harper signals important connections between reading, self-improvement, and access to public institutions as markers of social aspiration for African American women and girls. By reading the acknowledgments, readers might learn the value of widening their own networks. By mentioning the Mercantile Library, a largely white and predominately male institution, Mossell made the point that public institutions are for all, regardless of race, and she encouraged her readers to go where the knowledge is and learn. She also modeled for aspiring writers that journalists need to do research. Finally, she showed that women can and should use public resources that were created for men only and that professional women could help each other by sharing resources.[37]

Black girls were likely part of Mossell's readership. In her analysis of child readers and periodicals, Courtney Weikle-Mills notes that "children and youth were part of the readership for such texts, including those that are usually studied with respect to adult audiences."[38] Mossell's rare attention to black girls as central subjects in her advice column joined the focus on children's literacy development that appeared in other periodicals of the period, such as those devoted to boys' education and children's epistolary writing in the *Boys' and Girls' Magazine*.[39] Similar to these periodicals, Mossell's dedication to black girls' literacy suggests that her columns attracted a diverse readership of adults and their daughters.

Mossell's columns belong to a continuum of advice columns written by African Americans and designed for an African American readership. This genre of communication reached back to the early black press. Readers of the nation's first black newspaper, *Freedom's Journal* (1827–1829), wrote letters to an anonymous "Mr. Observer" to seek advice about such issues as marriage and singlehood. Mr. Observer's columns ran from August to November 1827. As Frances Smith Foster notes, the columns were published under the heading "For the Freedom's Journal," a designation that the column was written "expressly for *Freedom's Journal*" and that "Mr. Observer was indeed an African American writing to and about African Americans." Foster notes that advice columns "serve us today as mirrors upon our cultural past. . . . They reflect versions of and precedents for our present concerns with and authority of popular media." Readers expected the columnist to "take a stance, to declare what should or must be done."[40] In a February 1886 column, written shortly after Mossell began editing "Our Woman's Department," she used a conversational, reassuring tone to invite readers to participate with her in a literary exchange: "All those desiring to gain further information on any subject spoken of in this column will receive a prompt reply by making a request and enclosing a stamp. The great motive of this column is to do the greatest good to the largest number, and no one need fear that they will be giving the editor too much trouble."[41] As with Mr. Observer's columns, black readers and subscribers to the *New York Freeman* knew Mossell's columns were original contributions, not selections cobbled together from reprints, and that a black journalist welcomed exchanges with and input from them.

Advice about Nurturing Black Girls

Mossell felt that parents, teachers, and training schools could provide support for black girls as they entered public forms of womanhood. She encouraged parents to reexamine how they were raising their children, specifically black girls, and to recognize their daughters' contributions to the household. In her articles "Only a Girl," "Domestic Training for Girls," and "Teach Your Daughters," Mossell conceptualized the black home as a well-organized, industrious, and egalitarian space in which black fathers, mothers, and children all had something to offer the community.[42]

In "Only a Girl," Mossell argued that girls should be viewed as an asset to their families. Mossell noted that because girls had greater opportunities in the 1880s than they once had, fathers could expect their daughters to contribute economically to the family: "In these days a father can gratify his ambition in that his daughter can often succeed him in his business, or profession, or take another equally lucrative and honorable.'"[43] Here, Mossell was quietly advocating economic self-sufficiency in the black community. "What opening is there for them?" was a question the black community was asking about the young people who each year were "thrown upon their own resources after graduating from the schools." One southern editor concluded that "the only way for our educated ones to be provided for, is for those of us who are able, to establish various kinds of businesses and give them employment."[44] Mossell was aware of the protection and racial pride that employment in a black-owned business could provide young people; her husband, Nathan Mossell, had worked in his father's brickyard in Hamilton, Ontario, before attending college. Nathan Mossell later recalled, "The only man I ever worked for was father. I had no opportunity to become a white man's 'boy.'" He believed that such a background had prepared him to have a "manly outlook on life."[45] Gertrude Mossell suggested that girls could also benefit from employment in family businesses, where they would be protected from racial prejudice, just as her husband had.

In her 1886 article "Care of Children," Mossell noted that teachers and community members could have a significant impact on young girls: "Parents and teachers should cooperate in an attempt to keep the minds of the little ones filled with pure thoughts, and see that they are not led into bad habits and temptations by evil association, or too much liberty in going and coming."[46] Her focus on "purity of mind" anticipated the ideology of later conduct discourse by African American writers of the early twentieth century such as Silas X. Floyd, author of *Floyd's Flowers: Or Duty and Beauty for Colored Children* (1905) and Azalia Hackley, author of *The Colored Girl Beautiful* (1916). Mossell acknowledged that community members outside the nuclear black family could aid in the project of racial uplift.

Mossell's advice to female readers on household management and effective housekeeping practices portrayed efficient domesticity as vital to harmoniously structured black households. Mossell drew upon examples from other countries to reinforce her recommendations to parents about raising girls: "In Germany the children of noblemen as well as day laborers learn to do all the manner of domestic work and do it well. In France the children are taught the strictest economy, and every meal is prepared with the utmost care and skill. Most nations teach their girls carefully that which will be required of them."[47] She advised American parents that "if we would have competent housekeeping, we must train our girls more carefully to habits of economy."[48] Here, early in her first year as editor of the column, Mossell introduced a theme she returned to again and again: the importance of thrift and avoiding debt. She was well aware of the many temptations of the new industrial consumer economy, especially for a generation of young girls for whom earning an income was a new experience. Working girls who spent their earnings on impractical clothing would lack savings if they were laid off; they also would not have a nest egg to bring to a marriage when they set up their own households. She wrote, "In our large cities, the growth of the installment system . . . has largely encouraged extravagance in dress."[49] She printed the contribution of a reader from Livonia Station, New York, who wrote, "Girls work, earn[,] and spend their money . . . mostly on themselves, and mainly for dress, for they have nowhere else to invest it, and the body becomes 'their world.'" These girls, who "with few exceptions" would marry "young men of modest means," were unprepared for home life in two ways: they brought no contribution to their marriage and had no experience of thrift. Mossell added, "We return thanks to the writer . . . for the good advice to young women of the race."[50]

Mossell advised black parents to groom their daughters to be well-informed about men and marriage. She encouraged black girls to learn to make wise choices when selecting their mates. "Teach Your Daughters" advised parents to teach daughters to look at a man's honesty, compassion, and trustworthiness rather than his economic status: "Teach them that an honest mechanic in his working dress is a better object of esteem than a dozen haughty, finely dressed idlers."[51] The daughter of a plasterer and the daughter-in-law of a brick maker knew well that occupation did not determine status; character and actions were the qualities that were potential assets to black families and the black community. A black girl's selection of a suitable mate would promote the public image of the black family as stable, productive, and law-abiding.

Advice to Working Girls

Mossell plunged into the issues that concerned working girls in the first issue of her tenure as the editor of "Our Woman's Department." Her first article on the topic was a call for domestic workers to cultivate self-respect and insist on working conditions that allowed them to have a full private life. At first glance, it might seem that tackling this topic in a first foray on women's issues was a conservative move that promoted a lowering of horizons for young working girls. But Mossell was responding to a harsh reality that was unfolding before her eyes in Philadelphia and in other major cities of the North. While industrialization was beginning to open new doors for white women, black female workers were being crowded into the lowest-paying and lowest-status work. New technology led to new opportunities for white female workers; in the 1880s, women typists moved into clerical work. They also replaced males as the dominant workforce in the telephone industry.[52] Even though conditions were poor and work was seasonal, many white women, especially immigrants, entered the garment industry in that decade.[53]

For black women in northern cities, the story was very different. In New York City, the center of the garment industry, black women were shut out of the outwork system and new manufacturing jobs were closed to them.[54] Janet Dabel, who has compiled a picture of black women workers in New York from 9,000 census records and other sources, writes that city legislation dating back to 1825 barred black female workers from some occupations and racism closed other doors. "Black women," Dabel writes, "therefore, were relegated to positions as servants, washerwomen, and cooks, the first, second, and third most common black female occupations . . . in 1880." Dabel also found that black women's working careers began at a young age, around sixteen. And because black men were also being crowded into low-paying service occupations, over 60 percent of the city's black women and girls were in the labor force.[55]

Black people were migrating from the South to Philadelphia, where Mossell lived, in the 1880s. The city's black population doubled between 1870 and 1890, from just over 22,000 to just under 40,000, and young black women were a key component of this population shift.[56] In 1890, young black women migrants in their twenties significantly outnumbered male migrants in the same age group. The migration of young black women to Philadelphia in the 1880s was what Kali N. Gross calls "both a literal and symbolic refusal to accept the wholesale disregard of their humanity and self-worth."[57] Thus, when Mossell wrote about domestic work, she was writing to multiple audiences. Philadelphia was the home of the largest community of free blacks before the Civil War, and women in that community had been crowded into domestic work for decades.[58] The black women who were newcomers to the city had come looking for higher wages than they would have received in the South doing similar work. Both groups of women were doubtless looking for better opportunities than domestic work, but in the meantime, they wanted to be respected in the workplace.

Mossell's first piece on women workers exposed the often unspoken inequities and indignities that occurred between black female domestic workers and their employers. She advised black domestic workers about communication styles that would help them earn respect and keep their jobs. Mossell insisted that these workers had the same rights and privileges as any American. She identified several reasons why many domestic workers left places of employment for better working conditions and why "wealthy employers are at their wits end how to secure good servants and to succeed in retaining them." Mossell noted the tendency of white employers to insist on class distinctions and subordination by requiring domestic workers to wear uniforms and using demeaning language. She identified such practices as primary reasons for the absence of harmony between domestic workers and their employers. She wrote that "Americans do not like to wear a badge of servitude; no class distinction is one of their aims. So many girls leave good places if required to wear the nurses cap and apron."[59] Mossell very carefully planted evidence in her article that black women and girls doing domestic work rejected certain conditions and would leave an employer if those conditions were not met. She encouraged women in this labor force sector to maintain those standards and to take them to a higher level.

Mossell critiqued the use of the word "servant" in relation to black domestic workers:

> "Servant" is a term desired by no one. "Servant of the people" may not offend the ears of the president of the United States, but a servant in Mr. or Mrs. So and So's family is a very different matter. I heard one woman say "I am not a servant; I am simply help." To be helping, you see, was not considered in the same light as serving. Americans do not like to wear a badge of servitude; no class distinction is one of their aims.[60]

Mossell characterizes domestic workers as citizens who, like any other person, wanted to make independent choices. She wrote: "We all desire independence of action. The rag picker in our large cities is certainly more independent than a woman serving in a private family—though much less comfortable. The customary Thursday afternoon and every other Sunday may satisfy the desires of the mistress, but rarely that of the maid, who may desire to go out oftener, or attend service each Sabbath." Here, Mossell emphasized that domestic workers and their mistresses had equal desires for independent action and that the former needed more time away from work to engage in civic life.

Again very carefully, Mossell encouraged white employers to make working conditions amenable to black girls. Her advice is clearly directed at white women, but she presented it as advice for both black female workers and their white employers. Her list of recommendations anticipated the working conditions unions would demand in future decades and insisted on the personhood and human rights of black women and girls:

> Have a right estimate of each other's rights and privileges and have them well-defined; having a high degree of efficiency. Stop inducing other people's servants to leave; stop calling servants away from work on slight provocation, and sending them on unnecessary errands; treat servants more as if they are human beings and less like brutes; help girls to feel benefitted by remaining in one place; have a definite time to give notice of a discharge; give references as well as receive them; let girls content themselves for time being with the station they occupy; let each one put herself in the others place, observe the golden rule, and each treat the other as she would desire to be treated of occupying the opposite position. But with all of these precautions taken, with every inducement held out it will always remain almost a matter of impossibility to secure good servants or retain a servant for any great length of time.[61]

Mossell's advice to working girls was important for practical reasons: black working girls needed safe, secure, and stable jobs so they could contribute financially to their own households, either as daughters or as wives. But the list was also a manifesto that affirmed the rights of black girls and women and encouraged them to cultivate pride and self-respect, regardless of the status of the work they did.

The careful reader would understand that this was not the only horizon Mossell envisioned for black girls. Directly under the article on domestic service, without even a header to separate the two pieces, she offered a list of young women who were pursuing education and doing work in the field of education for girls. Talent and success were the watchwords of this paragraph. She reported that Verena Harris, a "talented young lady," was in her first year at the Woman's Medical College of Philadelphia. A Miss Bennett from Massachusetts was in her second year at the same college. Mossell described her as "a faithful student" and commented that "to such a one success is assured." Bridging the gap between those who advocated education for professional work and those who promoted education in industrial schools, Mossell reported on the "successful efforts" of Fannie Jackson Coppin, the principal of Philadelphia's Institute for Colored Youth, in the field of industrial education.[62] Her article announced to black girls that she had practical advice to offer for the present-day realities of most working girls but that she also refused to accept the limitations the current economy presented. Quietly and without fanfare, she pointed to other possible futures, drawing on the successes of women she knew in Philadelphia.[63]

Working girls also needed to protect their money. In "A Woman's Pocket-Book," Mossell relates "the good old days of . . . our grandmothers," who "made capacious pockets and tied them with stout tapes around their waists under the dresses," to modern black girls who enter the workforce and become targets of crime due to their "pocket-books." [64] Mossell connects black women readers to a time in their girlhoods when they sat in church during long sermons and were relieved when "their grandmothers turned up their dresses and dived into the recess of the pocket" to "receive a portion of the contents." [65] Mossell remembers how the hidden pockets contained "cake or apple" or "jingled with its weight of silver coin."[66] While stitching hidden pockets inside dresses to hold money and other items might be "a thing of the past," Mossell chides working girls for their lack of attention to these early models of safety, security, and sensible thinking. Rather than hold onto their grandmothers' seemingly archaic methods of resourcefulness, the pockets of the "modern belle . . . are picked . . . chatelaines are pulled from the hand, [and] leaded pockets [are] cut from the dress."[67] Mockingly, Mossell explains how men who work do not participate in careless behaviors: "What man would swing his wallet to his side from a quarter yard of chain and push through a crowd and expect to find it when he looked for it? Or what man would stand on a street car, pay his fare, close his purse with a snap, drop it in the back pocket of his coat, and float gracefully through the crowd and then raise a hue and cry because it was stolen, or put fifty dollars in a small bag and swing it lightly in the hand through a crowded thoroughfare. And each and all of these things the most sensible women are guilty of."[68] This column exposes Mossell's privileged childhood in comparison to that of most black women and girls. Although Mossell's tone is disapproving as she scolds working girls for their lack of urban savvy, her advice is crucial and clear.

Advice for a Stable Future

Because black men in northern cities were pushed into the lowest-paying occupations, Mossell knew that for black girls on the cusp of womanhood, choosing a husband was a complex task. In many (if not most) working-class black households, both partners in a couple had to work to support a household. When men refused to accept this economic equation, the burden that fell on the shoulders of their female partners was doubly heavy. Mossell frequently advised young girls to be very careful when they took the first steps toward courtship. She was especially aware of the vulnerability of girls who were new to city life. She writes: "Many young girls reared in the country are tempted by the promise of higher wages and a brighter life into leaving their safe and sheltered homes, crowding into large cities where they meet with a class of men stylish in their appearance, fluent talkers and apparently with a large amount of unoccupied time on their hands. Many girls, dazzled by their seeming superiority, willingly accept their attentions."[69] Mossell presented a character study of men who took advantage of young girls, offering them detailed information that would enable them to quickly identify poor potential partners:

> These men are, in the majority of the cases, totally unprincipled, without moral character; often their entire existence is eked out by gambling, policy playing, free lunches, &c. They stand around saloons and cigar shops part of the day, and in the evening they call on two or three girls, take tea with one, go to the theatre or the opera with another at her expense, and borrow a small sum of money from another, and so they manage to live an easy idle life at the expense of hard working parents and foolish girls.[70]

Mossell warned her young readers to be wise about the men with whom they socialized and to avoid "city dandies." Such men, Mossell advised, were "not fit company for fit-minded women," and she warned that if a young girl chose to marry one, "only misery untold [would] follow." She offered as an alternative the "honest, sturdy country man, willing to work and win subsistence for his family" even if he did not have a "stylish appearance."[71]

Mossell also cautioned young women about what could happen if they hurried into marriage without enough forethought. Girls who rejected the "independent farmer" who looked "so uncouth" next to "city men" who depended on wages for everything a household needed might come to regret a decision to marry a "barber or waiter who works for eighteen or twenty-five dollars a month." Especially when the young wife decided that marriage meant that she "won't have to work," Mossell claimed, the straitened circumstances of the household would put great strain on the relationship. With "only the necessities of life" and not enough money to "beautify" the home, the home would soon "lose its attraction." The wife would become "cross" and wish she was single. The husband would eventually "leave in disgust," and the young woman, with "no trade, no knowledge of housework" might be forced to consider prostitution, the "wide [door] leading straight to destruction." Mossell abjured mothers to teach their daughters when they were young that "God made them for a purpose; that they were put here to make the world better by their coming in it." Equally important, she claimed, mothers should teach their daughters to "earn an honest living" and that money and personal appearance were not everything. "Many a time under a cheap suit of clothing beats a true heart, and under an unfashionably cut crop of hair rests a good supply of brains."[72] Mossell conveyed a principle that she had learned from her abolitionist working-class family: what people did with their hearts and minds was much more significant than what clothes they wore or other aspects of outward appearance. She also emphasized that each young black woman had value and a particular purpose in her community. These girls should value themselves and make wise choices so they could find their purpose and fulfill it.

Another decision that a young woman in the mid-Atlantic might confront was whether to earn some easy money in seaside resort towns in the summertime. Mossell offered useful information and practical advice about this issue. She advised mothers not to allow daughters to pursue such work because "unprincipled characters are there in large numbers" and "restraints seem removed." Away from the protection of her family and community, black girls were especially vulnerable, Mossell pointed out. While hotel owners typically prohibited white male employees from talking to white female employees after dark, "no employer guards the colored girl." Mossell acknowledged the attraction of a break from the routine of winter work, but she cautioned that reputations could be injured and that "in many cases it is money earned at a sad loss."[73]

Mossell also wrote about how black girls could protect themselves against sexual violence. Mossell advised black girls and women to be equally wary of potential black male suitors and white employers who sought to victimize them:

> A woman's safeguard is to keep a man's hands off her. If you need his assistance in walking take his arm instead of his taking yours. Just tell him in plain English to keep his "hands off." He may not like it at first, but he will respect you ten fold

> more. Men do just what the women allow them to do. Keep your girls off the street, except when they have to do business. Teach them it is unnecessary to go to the Post Office every time they go out. Your girls can go home alone just as well as your boys. If possible, instill in their very nature that they are safer in their own hands than they are in the hands of any man—preachers not excepted.[74]

Here is another quiet warning to young women that even male authority figures in the black community, even preachers, were potential threats. Her statement that girls were "safer in their own hands than they are in the hands of any man" was a quietly radical bombshell that had many layers of meaning for the girl who read her words right.

In another article titled "Home," Mossell revised the long-standing meaning of that word as a haven for the black family. Instead, the homes she wrote about were the homes of single, self-supporting women. She began the article by acknowledging that the "orthodox opinion" was that "a woman should have a home and she should stay in it." But Mossell "went further" and stated that she believed that women "belonged in the home and in other places also," even though that opinion might make some people "cry unorthodox." Although she was careful to state that the "best homes" were those with fathers, mothers, and children, she insisted that a woman without a husband or children could make a good home for herself. She recounted examples of single older women she had known who had made cozy, inviting homes. One was the home of her "maiden aunt," who served as a surrogate mother to her in her childhood. Aunt Ruth taught her to sew and encouraged her to read. Her home offered a high standard of housekeeping. As a girl, she dreamed that her visits to Aunt Ruth would "last forever."[75] Although she did not mention how Aunt Ruth supported herself, if she was her father's relative, she may have had a stall in downtown Philadelphia, as her father's sisters did in 1847.[76] Her great-aunt, Grace Bustill Douglass, had a millinery shop next to the family's bakery in the antebellum decades.[77] Her second cousin, Sarah Mapps Douglass, who never married, supported herself as an educator.[78] Whether they were married or single, the women in Mossell's extended family found meaningful ways to earn income.

But Mossell was not satisfied with looking to the past. She was interested in chronicling wage-earning opportunities for black girls and women in the present of the post–Civil War, post-Reconstruction, postindustrialization North of the 1880s. She frequently mentioned careers that women she knew were pursuing.[79] In addition, she offered innovative suggestions for businesses for black women, including operating a circulating library, "conducting an intelligence office" (an information bureau, perhaps a service for newspaper editors), and running a boardinghouse.[80] Mossell drew deeply from her own life experiences and those of women in her family; these experiences illustrated what was possible. She also looked at the present with a very practical eye and sought new economic paths for women. And she never stopped envisioning a better future.

Education for Girls

In the article "Training School for Girls," Mossell published a report that Rev. Raymond Rice of Bordentown, New Jersey, had sent her. Rice, who had begun his life as a slave in North Carolina, had made his way north and fought for a Union company in the Civil War. After the war, he had pursued an education in New Jersey and become a minister in the A. M. E. church. He had started an industrial school for girls in his home in New Brunswick in 1886. By August of 1886, the school had outgrown his home, and classes were being held in Mt. Zion Church temporarily while fund-raising took place to build in Bordentown.[81] That month, Rev. Rice and two other ministers—one from Trenton and the other from Lincoln University, where Nathan Mossell took his undergraduate degree—and a committee of "colored ladies, school teachers, and friends of education" approached New Jersey governor Leon Abbett for support for the school. After carefully considering their proposal, the governor "gave his approval and . . . promised to do all in his power to make the school a success." The governor believed the school was "a blessing to the now more than twenty-two thousand colored women in this state and perhaps adjoining states, as there is no such school in any of the Middle States where colored girls have access to as they can in this."[82]

This school became one of the best known and most highly regarded schools for black youth in the country. Although it was known as the "Tuskegee of the North," the Bordentown School, as it came to be known, offered both vocational training and a classical education, including courses in Latin. Students were given both a solid education and training in a trade. Luminaries in the black community, including both W. E. B. Du Bois and Booker T. Washington, supported the school and lectured there. Albert Einstein lectured there. The residential school was a self-contained community; students grew their own food and maintained the campus with the skills they learned. Eventually, the school housed 400–500 students each year. One scholar has referred to it as the "capital of Negro New Jersey" in the early decades of the twentieth century.[83]

Although the school later became coeducational, the original idea was a response to a strong perception that black girls in New Jersey needed education that focused on their specific needs. Why did Governor Abbett support an ambitious project that focused on black girls? What arguments did the ministers who led the group that met with the governor use? Rev. Rice's report listed some of the points those who endorsed the project were making. One argument was that "the colored people have had less training and chances for training in the United States." Yet, the bulk of the arguments focused on critiques of black mothers as women who were not adequate to train their daughters. First, black girls were not getting the "home training" they needed because "the mother before them has not had such training." Second, even when black girls were able to attend public schools, a "large amount of instruction given" to them was "lost, from the fact that it is not preceded or supplemented in the home or family training." And how was the need for special training for girls evident? Rev. Rice articulated the source of concern within the black community of New Jersey: "All who have studied these people in their homes, on the streets, on excursions or in public conveyances will agree that a school such as is here anticipated is needed."[84] His use of the term "these people" clarifies that for the ministers and others who called on the governor, this was a class issue. Working-class black girls were not being trained how to act like ladies, and their behavior when they were in public was a source of embarrassment and chagrin for some community leaders.

Several months later, Mossell wrote a column that outlined what kind of girls' behavior the black community was concerned about. When conductors on streetcars asked young women to move forward in the car to redistribute weight so it would be easier for horses to pull the car, they "[would] not budge a step." The conductor would have to ask them "repeatedly" to move. Young women would "take up all the room possible" by spreading their skirts "while others stand." They would stay seated and wait for "men to rise" to give up their seats for mothers with babies or the elderly. They would take shelter in the covered open-air markets when it rained and refuse to "give an inch" to other women. Mossell wrote, "We often wonder what they can be thinking about. . . . Let us cast a thought toward the sufferers in the daily thoroughfares and common carriages from the thoughtless behavior of ill-bred women."[85] Yet one must read this purported critique of the behavior of black women and girls very carefully. While Mossell may well have been concerned about how young black women behaved on public conveyances and in public markets, it is clear from other context she offered that in her eyes the chief offenders were well-to-do white women, not black girls. She identified the offenders as "women, regardless of race or condition." She described the topics of conversation of these women as who wore what at the opera or the theater. The women she described wore bustles and veils, items that working girls were unlikely to wear on the way to and from work, and were careless about how they held their umbrellas, which mussed up the hair, scratched the faces, and disarranged the veils of other women. Mossell was describing, very quietly and between the lines, what it was like to be a black woman in crowded public spaces populated by thoughtless white women with class privilege. What was ostensibly a critique of how black girls behaved in public was actually a description of how black women, even professional black women, were invisible to the white women with whom they shared their public space.

Thus, while the ministers who supported the Bordentown school expressed concern and anxiety about how young black women behaved in public, Mossell wrote about the *experience* of being a young black woman in public. She wrote about being invisible to privileged white women who jostled up against her and caused damage to her appearance and attire. While the ministers seemed to be saying that young black women were taking up *too much space* and not being ladylike enough, Mossell very carefully and guardedly wrote about what it felt like to be crowded into spaces where white women took more than their share of public space.

Good Homes and a Wider World: A Tension Unresolved

Mossell was not able to travel much in 1886 and 1887, the period of her tenure as editor of "Our Woman's Department." Her daughter Mary was born in 1885, and she was caring for a young child during these two years. Her second daughter, Florence, was born in 1887, so for some part of that year, she was pregnant while she was editing the column. These responsibilities kept her close to home.[86] Her solution as she edited the column from her home on 924 Lombard Street was to bring the world to her door. In August 1886, she asked her readers to send her information on "the Negro Problem": "If any one who may have chanced to read a number of articles on the subject would drop us a card stating the title of the book or magazine containing such, it would . . . be of value. We make these requests believing that there are many who do not write themselves who would be glad to assist in any way possible in making known the good accomplished by our people."[87] Her request signaled to her readers that she valued their work as readers and the collective knowledge that was present in the black community.

Because Philadelphia was a center of labor and race activism, local events sometimes offered a window on a wider world. In December 1886, she reported about two such events. The first had international import. English race activist Catherine Impey spoke at a meeting at the home of Robert Purvis, a longtime activist for black rights. Because she was not a U.S. resident, she could say things that local blacks could not, and she spoke very forthrightly. Her voice thus became a vehicle for Mossell to relate her own views. She reported: "She said that only menial offices were open to [the colored people of this city], opportunity to become skilled laborers and clerks being denied them by the hostility of the trades-unions and that they could not rent houses in any respectable locality however respectable they themselves might be."[88] Attendees, who included Rev.

Charles G. Ames, Rev. Matthew Anderson, Rev. B. T. Tanner, and Fanny Coppin, formed an organization at the meeting for the purpose of publishing a paper that would "present facts to the friends of the colored people" and provide the black community with information about job opportunities.

The second event Mossell reported in December 1886 related to the labor movement. Well into the twentieth century, labor unions in the United States excluded blacks. One of the rare exceptions was the Knights of Labor, a radical union that flourished in the 1880s.[89] The Knights welcomed both blacks and women, and Mossell reported that the Henry George Assembly of the Knights, a Philadelphia local, was welcoming cooks and domestic servants as members. "Many new members were admitted and the assembly is reported as progressing rapidly," she wrote.[90] Both of the events she reported at the end of 1886 pointed toward the future for black workers in Philadelphia, a labor force that included significant numbers of young black women who were looking for new opportunities and a wider range of options.

In January 1886, Mossell encouraged black women to become independent entrepreneurs as owners of restaurants. Although she acknowledged the difficulties of such enterprises ("many restaurants are started by women and fail"), she urged potential proprietors to think in terms of perfecting a few dishes that would particularly appeal to a female clientele, to hire female waiters, and to decorate their establishments in ways that would "make the place more homelike" and enable the customer to "forget that she is eating in a public place." Simple food, served well would meet the needs of women in public life and would prevent "many a severe headache, fit of ill temper, or attack of dyspepsia." Restaurants that focused on the needs of women in this way "would really by the good [they] would do have a right to be classified under the head of benevolent institution[s]."[91] Mossell envisioned an urban economy in which skilled businesswomen could build careers and provide services for other women. In the process, black businesswomen would strengthen the black community, make it easier for other black women to accomplish their goals in public life, and provide employment for young black women.

Mossell did not limit her economic dreams for black women to large cities. She also encouraged black women in smaller towns and cities to find ways to earn incomes through their domestic skills. In response to a letter writer from Wilkes-Barre, Pennsylvania, who wanted to start a store that commissioned home work and asked for advice about what type of articles she should commission, Mossell wrote that "in small towns a number of ladies having an interest in the industrial success of their sex could band together in aid of such work." She suggested that one of the group rent a house with a storefront that could sell "goods of all description, the work of nimble hands" on commission. Noting that such stores existed in Philadelphia, she listed the possibilities: "preserves, cake, bread, fancy work of all kinds, aprons, dolls . . . knitted goods . . . hand made laces, nurses caps and aprons, dusting caps, waiters aprons, gingham and white aprons, sack and skirts of calico," and her list continued. "Any item that cost $2 or less should sell well in a city the size of Wilkes-Barre," Mossell said. While she did not discuss advertising, finding a large-enough market, economies of scale in supplies, health risks associated with producing goods at home, or any of the other issues that urban reformers had begun to talk about in relationship to home work, she did say that "ladies in reduced circumstances" could work together and support themselves, particularly if a charitable institution could be persuaded to bear some of the initial startup costs of setting up a storefront that sold home-produced goods on commission.[92] In the mid-1880s, Mossell was confident that any black woman who was willing to work hard and create economic opportunities for herself had a chance of success.

However, the difficulty almost every woman faced in a capitalist, industrialized United States was something she was deeply ambivalent about. On the one hand, she firmly believed that mothers should be at home so they could guide their children, particularly since so many families were new to urban environments. She believed that children inherited tendencies from their fathers that mothers needed to work to correct: "Though having great confidence in a mother's influence we hold that the inherited tendencies received from the father and the practical example he may set by words and deeds go farther to shape the son's cause than a mother's counsel." Since men's values were tainted by the lax morality of the public world, this meant that mothers who wanted to raise honest, principled children, particularly sons, had a full-time job.[93]

However, the women who devoted themselves to making a good home for their families and raising children with strong values were in a difficult position economically. Many had given up the income they had earned as teachers in order to fulfill these roles, Mossell noted. They had given up economic independence and had become "women who need to be cared for." This was an uncomfortable position for Mossell to contemplate because she deeply admired the woman "who can take care of herself, when circumstances require it." But she came down firmly on the side of the community over the career aspirations of individuals: the need of a community just one generation away from slavery to train children in the values that would lead to steady employment, respect in the community, and an ethic of care for all vulnerable members was simply greater than the personal ambitions of individual women.

Mossell cited several examples of undesirable behavior within the black community in this issue of her column. She spoke of the petty thievery that purportedly was rife within the black community, noting that some attributed this to the history of slavery. "It is known that slaves felt a part ownership in their master's property," she wrote and told the (perhaps apocryphal) story of the slave who cooked and ate his master's turkey, saying that "he belonged to his master and the turkey also, and the turkey was as much the master's inside of him as out." Mossell saw this story in black and white terms and was not inclined to see its radical critique of the ownership of human beings.

Mossell also connects undesirable behaviors in the black community to poor parenting among mothers and fathers. She deplored men's easy acceptance of loose morals as a necessity for success in the world of work:

> Men have to pass through a certain amount of vice to see the world and open their eyes. In fact, to so great an extent is the different methods of thinking and speaking carried that one can generally decide when hearing a man exclaim "oh, that's a woman's way of thinking or doing" that it is on the side of strictness, and when it's a man's idea of the matter it is on the lax side of morals. No true mother gives her daughter a lax rule for her guidance, but men constantly give such to their sons both by word and example.[94]

Mossell acknowledges that mothers were needed in the home. Yet the dependence this choice entailed was a circumstance that "no high-spirited woman" could endure without pain. The best she could do to resolve the tension between women's needs and community needs was to issue a strong manifesto: mothers were "entitled to all the rights and privileges and have all the claim upon the respect and kindness of men that could possibly be claimed or awarded to the most successful and enterprising workers among women in any department of the world's work."[95]

Yet the tension between individual and community needs was never fully resolved for Mossell. She continued to describe the successes of independent women and to provide information about new opportunities for working girls. She described the success of sculptor Edmonia Lewis, who in 1883 had unveiled her sculpture *Adoration of the Magi* at St. Mary's Chapel in Baltimore.[96] She reported that Miss Lucy C. Laney was working with the Presbytery of Savannah, Georgia, on plans to start an industrial school. Miss Alice Baker had begun her work as a missionary in Haiti for the AME church. A church bishop had said that Baker's service surpassed even their fondest hopes. When the first medical school in France opened its doors to women, one of the first to enroll was "a colored girl." Mrs. M. E. Lambert had become editor of the *St. Mathews Lyceum Journal.* Opportunities seemed to be opening for black women and girls, and Mossell wanted to make sure that her readers were aware of them.

Conclusion

As one of the first black women journalists to edit an advice column for black women and girls in the early black press, Gertrude Bustill Mossell had a great responsibility. Her columns provided a space where black girls and women could find information about the everyday concerns they faced at home and in the workplace. Instead of being read aloud, as newspaper articles were in earlier decades, the advice columns of the 1880s were for private reading and spoke directly to individuals. The straightforward and direct language of advice columns drew readers in and sustained their interest, and Mossell nurtured this connection by encouraging her readers to write to her at her home address. Like Nellie, the daughter in the article that opened this chapter who clipped articles for her scrapbook, one can imagine black girls clipping Mossell's columns and placing them carefully into their scrapbooks as they imagined possible futures, perhaps as wives and mothers, perhaps as civic actors, perhaps as doctors or writers. Mossell made sure her columns covered a broad field of possibilities, and each black girl who read them, if she were so inclined, could make her own book of knowledge tailored to her own hopes and dreams, an arsenal of advice and information in a scrapbook. Mossell's advice columns situate her as an important literary activist of the mid-1880s, particularly in her writing for women and girls. She was prolific even before she published her best-known book, *The Work of the Afro-American Woman* (1894), and she continued to write and publish for decades after her two-year editorship of "Our Woman's Department."

Mossell's work in the 1880s focused on the everyday concerns of black girls in the workforce. Black girls, particularly girls on the cusp of womanhood, were a central component of her writing, and her starting assumption was that they were invested in living dignified lives. Her concern for the future quality of life of black girls was an important part of her black feminism. Mossell's column in the *New York Freeman* gave her access to thousands of readers across the nation. The next chapter turns to the work of her colleague and neighbor in Philadelphia, Frances E. W. Harper, who wrote serialized fiction to address these themes.

4. Moving the Boundaries

Black Girlhood and Public Careers in Frances E. W. Harper's Trial and Triumph

TRIAL AND TRIUMPH, A NOVEL Frances E. W. Harper serialized in the *Christian Recorder* in 1888–1889, tells the story of a black girl who comes of age in an urban city in the North in the post–Civil War years. Harper used the novel as a platform for delivering the messages to the black community that were featured in her lectures after the Civil War and into the late nineteenth century. A remarkable feature of the novel is the absence of institutions and organizations that lobbied for the rights of northern and southern blacks in these decades. This novel was written with the goal of promoting change at the preinstitutional level—within the homes of black families.

Harper's decision to publish *Trial and Triumph* in serial form in the popular newspaper the *Christian Recorder* gave a broad and growing African American reading community access to her work. The story was so popular that subscribers wrote in for back issues so they could catch up on installments they had missed.[1] Serialization helped democratize literature by putting new work into the hands and homes of every economic and social class on a regular basis.[2] We can well imagine this serialized story being read aloud to new arrivals to northern cities who had left the South, like Grandmother Harcourt and her husband, for better opportunities.

The *Christian Recorder* was a logical choice for Harper. The African Methodist Episcopal church, which published the journal, was her religious home at the time and was one of the leading venues where black writers could publish fictional anecdotes and serialized novels. In addition, as Eric Gardner argues, the *Recorder* may be viewed as a "public meeting place" that increased "multiple literacies" within the black community by teaching such subjects as "genre and geography, politics and poetic form, religion and rhetoric." It served as a site for discussing “real-world concerns and struggles and embody[ing] the black community’s debates on gender roles, household structures, a massive war [and] questions of freedom and faith.” Subscribers to the paper had access to information about diverse issues and to many African American voices that were otherwise absent from the dominant print culture. The *Recorder* functioned as a congregation of sorts for readers who were working to build community after the war. The average subscriber to the *Christian Recorder* was a married black man in his forties living in the Northeast with significant ties to the church and his family.[3]

The *Recorder*’s status as a family paper made it an attractive site for black writers seeking to publish fiction with black girl figures whose actions reinforced the concepts of racial reconciliation and duty to family values. Stories about girlhood helped advance the church’s mission by presenting images of well-functioning families with well-run households. Importantly, during the war, other stories about black childhood functioned as “textual interactions” between black soldiers, their families, and the church. These “soldier-subscribers,” as Eric Gardner calls them, would have read the *Recorder*’s girlhood stories and imagined their households functioning efficiently in their absence.

Serial publications introduced a literary form that helped black women gain access to the public sphere. Weekly installments meant that readers came to every issue primed and eager to engage with the material. As black readership grew, the black press became a viable option for novelists seeking to serialize their fiction in the nineteenth century. The growth of literary societies and increased access to printing technologies led to the development of a substantial reading community in the North.[4] In the late 1880s, the message of hope and a brighter future in *Trial and Triumph* would have been greatly encouraging to this population. And in laying out the social landscape of the black community in a northern urban center, it would have provided them with valuable information they needed as they planned their futures. As Michelle Campbell Toohey notes, Harper’s serialized novels “addressed the complex social and political concerns of the postwar black community with the intimacy required for building community from the inside.”[5]

This chapter analyzes the novel through the lens of two questions. First, what material from her own life did Harper weave into her story? Second, what kind of preparation for the future did Harper present for northern black girls in the 1880s?

Drawing upon Autobiography

In *Trial and Triumph*, a black girl named Annette Harcourt is orphaned at an early age after being born under the shadow of scandal. She is raised by her maternal grandmother, who does not understand her granddaughter very well but is fiercely devoted to the goal of raising a moral person who will not repeat the mistakes of her mother. That goal includes giving Annette as much education as she can. Grandmother Harcourt refuses to put Annette into domestic work when she reaches young adolescence and gives her freedom to read instead of doing housework. The young Annette has a passionate and impulsive personality that is a great trial to the grandmother, who does not know how to help Annette govern her impulsiveness.

Mrs. Lasette, a kind family friend and a former teacher who knew Annette's mother well, takes the girl under her wing and shows her broader horizons. Mrs. Lasette supports and encourages the grandmother when other family members argue that Annette should leave school and go to work. She is the one Annette turns to when she faces racism in a newly integrated school and when her heart is broken as a young woman. It is through this neighbor that Annette hears many debates about issues of concern to the northern black community.

By the time Annette graduates from school as valedictorian of her class, she has learned to combine her passionate interior self and her intellect. She delivers an effective and deeply moving speech to a mixed-race audience about the history of her race from their time in Africa to the present time in the novel. After her marriage plans fall through, she goes south to teach the children of freedpeople and becomes a valuable and much-loved member of a southern community.

Frances Smith Foster feels that *Trial and Triumph* may be the most autobiographical of Harper's novels.[6] It is true that there are numerous parallels between Annette's life story and Harper's own, and there is evidence in the novel that she drew on life experiences in other ways. But caution is warranted here. Like Maria W. Stewart, Harriet Wilson, and Harriet Jacobs, Frances Harper drew on her life experiences as raw material that she used to create new forms of fiction. In the case of *Trial and Triumph*, Harper wrote a novel that spoke to the black community, specifically the working-class black community and especially young black women, on multiple levels. The novel showed these audiences a way ahead. It also showed parents and community members how to interact with and raise young black girls who had rich interior lives and passionate emotions. Harper's message about such black girls was that they could become valuable resources to the community if they were carefully and properly nurtured. Thus, an exploration of the parallels between Harper's life experiences and characters and incidents in the novel offers us a way to look at how Harper the novelist used and shaped such material to suit her purpose as Harper the race advocate at a particular moment in the history of her people.

I begin with a look at origin stories. In the novel, the fact that Annette was born is almost glossed over. The focus is on the shame of her mother's unwed pregnancy:

> Lucy, her youngest child, the pet and pride of the household returned home with a great sorrow tugging at her heart and a shadow on her misguided life. It was the old story of woman's weakness and folly and man's perfidy and desertion. . . . Sorrow had wasted her strength and laid the foundation of disease and an early death. Religion brought balm to the wounded spirit, but no renewed vigor to the wasted frame and in a short time she fell victim to consumption, leaving Annette to the care of her mother.[7]

The last words of the quote, "leaving Annette to the care of her mother" is the announcement of the child's birth. All of the focus is on the wrongdoing and sorrow of her mother. We learn that Annette is a "wronged and disinherited child" and that she "had entered life sadly handicapped . . . [as] the deserted child of a selfish and unprincipled man and a young mother whose giddiness and lack of self-control had caused her to trail the robes of her womanhood in the dust."[8] The story of Lucy, Annette's mother, serves as a cautionary tale of how *not* to raise daughters. While her hardworking mother provided for her physical needs, she failed to ensure that Lucy had proper supervision and guidance when she came of age. She allowed Lucy to be in situations without a male family chaperone and did not give her the spiritual ballast she needed to see through the façade of a charming but unworthy man. Annette's grandmother says, "It seemed to me as if my poor girl just worshiped him. I did not feel that he was all right, and I tried to warn my dear child of danger, but what could an old woman like me do against him with his handsome looks and oily tongue."[9] Because of this "antenatal history," as Harper refers to it, Annette is regarded as a wronged child (her wealthy father abandons her) and as a girl who is in danger of inheriting her father's lack of self-control and her mother's poor judgment.[10]

Harper's early childhood bears some similarities to Annette's. We know that she was born in Baltimore in 1825 and that her mother died when she was three years old. Her father is absent from any biographical detail about this part of her life. We know that both parents were freeborn, but as her friend William Still observed, the family was still "subjected of course to the oppressive influence which bond and free alike endured under slave laws."[11] However, the father is never named and is barely mentioned. He was clearly gone before Harper's mother died. William Still, very subtly, suggests that the relationship with the aunt who took her in may not have been a happy one. He wrote that "she fell into the hands of an aunt" and that during her girlhood Harper "had many trials to endure which she would fain forget."[12] Hallie Quinn Brown wrote that "her childhood days were desolate."[13] The feeling that she was an outsider was compounded by the status of her race in a slave-owning republic. She later said, "Not that we have not a right to breathe the air as freely as anybody else in Baltimore, but we are treated worse than aliens among a people whose language we speak, whose religion we profess and whose blood flows and mingles in our veins. Homeless in the land of our birth and worse off than strangers in the home of our nativity."[14]

The one family asset of an orphaned free black girl living in a slave state was an uncle, William Watkins, who operated a school for black children. William had high standards and offered a strong curriculum that included the Bible, classical literature, music, and philosophy in addition to reading, writing, and arithmetic.[15] While practicing his trade as a shoemaker, he had taught himself languages and medicine, and sometime in the 1820s he opened the Watkins Academy for Negro Youth. He trained his students in elocution, preparing them to be leaders of their race. He taught his students to regard their voices as instruments and was "so signally precise that every example in etymology syntax and prosody had to be given as correctly as a sound upon a keyboard."[16] He was also a local leader in the African Methodist Episcopal church and was a frequent contributor to abolitionist newspapers.[17] From her uncle, Harper inherited training in public speaking, a devotion to the abolitionist cause, and a lifelong commitment to the Christian faith. However, his methods in the classroom were harsh. A former student who later graduated from Princeton and became a highly respected minister recalled that Watkins used a strap to make "profound orthoepical, orthographical, geographical and mathematical impressions" and that he was "strict from the first letter in the alphabet down to the last paragraph in the highest reader."[18] No matter how young the student was, they would learn or face the strap. Thus, both at home and at school, it is likely that young Frances Watkins contended with a complex mixture of gratitude for being cared for and educated and resentment because of harsh treatment. The fact that she did not attempt to reunite with either the aunt who raised her or the uncle who educated her after she was put out to work may speak volumes about her feelings about these relatives.

Harper spent the early years of her womanhood as a teacher and an abolitionist lecturer. She also contributed financial resources to the Underground Railroad. She was a strong supporter of John Brown and sent money to his widow after he was executed. She published several volumes of poetry before the Civil War and published poetry in the abolitionist press.[19] Thus, while Frances and Annette shared the experiences of the early loss of parents and being raised by extended family members, Frances Watkins was of an earlier generation than the character she created and her formative years were shaped by slavery and the goal of eradicating it.

Another difference is that while the black girl character she created was protected from domestic work and completed her education even though her grandmother was poor, Harper herself was put out to work at age thirteen. We do not know the circumstances or why this family decision was made. She was responsible for sewing and caring for the children of a Baltimore bookseller in her new situation, likely in the home of the Armstrong half of the prominent bookselling and publishing firm of Armstrong and Berry.[20] But she did not abandon her studies.[21] By that time, she knew that she wanted to be a poet, and within a year her literary efforts had impressed the wife in whose household she worked, who encouraged her. We learn from her friend Still that "through the kindness of her employer, her greed for books was satisfied so far as was possible from occasional half-hours of leisure." She spent her free time reading and studying, "rarely trifling away time as most girls are wont to do in similar circumstances."[22] Armstrong and Berry published classics such as William Whiston's translation of *The Works of Flavius Josephus* and sold advice literature such as Margaret Coxe's *The Young Lady's Companion*, texts such as *Elements of Rhetoric and Literary Criticism* by J. R. Boyd ("designed for common schools and academies"),[23] and fiction by women such as *Sowing and Reaping: Or, What Will Become of It* and *Sorrowing, Yet Rejoicing, or a Narrative of Recent Successive Bereavements in a Minister's Family* by Mary Howitt, who was advertised as the author of another book, *Strive and Thrive*.[24] Young Frances had access to the most recent publications in genres that enabled her to continue her education and learn what women were writing. This influence doubtless encouraged her to continue her own efforts, and probably within two years of being put out to work (Still says "scarcely had she reached her majority," likely meaning age sixteen),[25] she was publishing poems in the black press. Around 1845, likely while she was still doing domestic work in the home of the Armstrongs, she published her first volume of poetry, *Forest Leaves*.[26]

It is clear that Harper drew on her own experiences when she described key moments in her character Annette Harcourt's life. Harper tells us that Annette's valedictorian address, titled "The Mission of the Negro," was "a remarkable production for a girl of her age." At one point, "it seemed as if the sorrow of centuries was sobbing in her voice," but then "her voice grew musical" when she began to speak of the "mission of the Negro," which she characterized as "grandly constructive." The work of the black community, Annette boldly told her mixed-race audience, was to "build over the ruins of the dead past, the most valuable thing that a man or woman could possess on earth, and that is good character," to "lift up the banner of the Christian religion from the mire and dust into which slavery and pride of caste had trailed it." As she spoke, "it seemed as if she had fused her whole soul into the subject." The impact on the white members of audience was undeniable; her speech was the "sensation of the hour," and "men grew thoughtful and attentive, women tender and sympathetic as they heard this member of a once despised people, recount the trials and triumphs of her race, and the hopes that gathered around their future."[27]

Annette's public speaking triumph is the result of careful nurturing by numerous members of the community that raises her. Her grandmother has worked with her over many years to help her learn to govern her passionate nature, her friend and surrogate mother Mrs. Lasette has helped her broaden her understanding of her race and its tasks, teachers and former teachers who now do manual labor have cultivated her interest in literature and public speaking. Most important, in this triumphant moment, Annette has harnessed her emotions, her interior life, and her intellect in the service of a speech that moves her entire audience. She has overcome the obstacles that racist white teachers attempted to create and she has learned to speak in a way that opens people's hearts. Clarence Luzerne, a friend of Mr. Thomas whom he has invited to hear the speech of the black girl whose intellect he has nurtured so carefully over the years, finds himself unexpectedly impressed. He tells Mr. Thomas that Annette has great potential to do good for her race because "her heart has supplied her intellect." He confirms something that Mr. Thomas and Mrs. Lasette have recognized in Annette: "it is the inner life which develops the outer life."[28]

The press described the impact of Harper's public speaking in similar ways in the 1850s, when she worked to persuade white northerners to take up the abolitionist cause, and the 1870s, when she spoke to black and mixed audiences about how to move forward after the war. When she lectured in Philadelphia in 1856, the *Provincial Freeman* wrote that "the lady like ease and modesty of her deportment and the poetic beauty and pathos of her speaking alike delight and surprise her hearers." A year later, when she spoke to a white audience in Norristown, Pennsylvania, a white newspaper reported that she "melt[ed] her audience into sympathy and tears for the poor slave."[29] She often spoke extemporaneously, without notes and responding to cues from her location and her audience. A clipping from a paper that Harper characterized as "one of the leading advocates of rebeldom" reported that it was clear that her speech was not "cut and dried . . . for she was as fluent and as felicitous in her allusions to circumstances immediately around her as she was when she rose to a more exalted pitch of laudation of the 'Union,' or of execration of the old slavery system. Her voice was remarkable—as sweet as any woman's voice we ever heard, and so clear and distinct as to pass every syllable to the most distant ear in the house." On that occasion, her "quaint humor" frequently brought her entire audience of 500 to laughter. Harper knew what it felt like to hold an audience in the palm of her hand and move them with her words, and she used that experience as she described a key moment in the life of her character Annette Harcourt.

The Setting of the Novel

Trial and Triumph is remarkable for its almost exclusive focus on domestic settings and private interactions. The black church is mentioned in the novel, but only for the purpose of planting the idea that churches should hire all-black workforces when they needed construction work done. The public school system in the city of "A.P." is mentioned, but it serves as a platform for Annette's trajectory—from the object of a teacher's attempt to degrade her (she assigns a white boy to sit next to her as a punishment) to the triumphant public speaker who moves white men and women to seriously consider racial issues from the perspective of a black person. When Annette goes south as a young teacher, she does so through a private arrangement, not through an organization. Black women's groups, which were beginning to flourish at the time the novel was written, are virtually absent; we see only Mrs. Lasette's informal salons in her home and the "mothers' meetings" Mrs. Lasette holds in Grandmother Harcourt's neighborhood to "try to teach mothers, who in the dark days of slavery had no bolts nor bars strong enough to keep out the invader from scattering their children like leaves in wintry weather, how to build up light and happy homes under the new dispensation of freedom."[30] However, these are "meetings," not clubs or organizations, and they are held in homes among neighbors and friends. They are proto-organizations. Even Harper's beloved temperance organizations are not mentioned. Each message that Harper wants to convey through the novel is imparted in private debates or one-one-one conversations. Harper clearly wants her readers to understand that individual actions and words have a significant impact on the welfare of the black race.

However, a careful reading of the text reveals some clues about what city Harper was writing about, the city she calls only "A.P." most of the time, although she did slip one time and refer to it only as "P."[31] We are told that Grandmother Harcourt was a free black woman in the South at one time but had become "restive under the privations and indignities which were heaped upon free persons of color" and that she and her husband had sold their property at a loss and moved their family north so their six children could have an education.[32] This migration likely took place before the onset of the Civil War. Throughout the nineteenth century, Philadelphia was the city with the largest population of free blacks, and it was the first major city in a free state a southern black family migrating from the South would reach. Philadelphia was a likely destination for free blacks leaving the South before the war.

We also learn that Mr. Thomas, a friend of the Harcourt family, loses his job as a teacher when the public schools in the city integrate: "He had spent several years in the acquisition of knowledge and was proving himself an acceptable and conscientious teacher, when the change came which deprived him of his school, by blending his pupils in the different ward schools of the city."[33] Although public opinion in "A.P." has changed enough to "admit the colored children into the different schools," it was not ready to contemplate having black teachers for white children, and the black teachers of the city find the door to their occupation suddenly closed to them. This detail makes it likely that the fictional city of "A.P."

is Philadelphia. In 1881, the state of Pennsylvania passed a law that mandated integrated schools throughout the state after a black father challenged the segregated system that emerged when the state passed a law in 1854 establishing public common schools.[34] Although this law was largely ignored because it had no enforcement provision, it is the only law that called for integration in the period 1865 to 1889 that I have been able to locate for a northern state. Also, we know that in Philadelphia, decisions about public schools were made at the ward level in the nineteenth century, and Harper carefully states that school integration took place "in the different ward schools of the city."[35]

The fact that the schooling of black children in the North in the decades after the Civil War was an issue that could quickly become volatile makes it unlikely that the novel was set in another northern city. Far from welcoming black students, most school districts practiced a de facto form of segregation that violated the ethos of the common school movement. The careful balance between betrayal of the core national principle that every child should have a basic education and the practice of excluding black children relied on the silence of black parents. When those parents decided to challenge a school district, community peace quickly broke down.

Another clue that Philadelphia is the city Harper drew upon for this novel comes from the geography she describes. Grandmother Harcourt lives in a courtyard neighborhood that hovers on the edge of worse neighborhoods in the city. According to Evelyn Bodek Rosen, Philadelphia did not have the overcrowding and filth of other northern cities such as Boston and Philadelphia in the nineteenth century, because the city's architecture developed horizontally, not vertically. However, this was not the case in "certain decaying precincts of Southwark and Moyamensing and in single alleys and courtyards," where slumlike conditions prevailed.[36] These nineteenth-century communities were the locations of the city's Third, Fourth, and Thirtieth Wards. The most likely location for the Tennis Court enclave that Harper describes is the Fourth Ward, which by 1890 was home to 2,573 blacks and was just blocks from Harper's Second Ward home on 1006 Bainbridge Street, which she had bought in 1871.[37]

In 1905, a survey of housing in Philadelphia by Emily Dinwiddie noted that "the type of common court in Philadelphia has been characterized as a horizontal tenement," adding that the description was accurate. Shared outdoor toilet facilities, shared water supply fixtures, shared use of courts and passageways meant that no one felt responsible for cleanliness and maintenance. Dinwiddie noted that while a tiny fraction of tenement houses in Philadelphia had janitors, in the many courts she visited in the city, there was no caretaker. Houses were crowded together with little or no space between them. She reported, "In many of the courts there is only surface drainage, slops are thrown out into a gutter, and if the alley is not properly paved and graded, as is often the case, the foul water remains in stagnant pools before the houses."[38] Harper describes some of these conditions in the Tennis Court enclave: she tells us that there is only one point of entry, which meant that there was no through street and thus no city services; that the walls of the houses are so thin that people can hear neighbors talking through them; and that the court is so narrow that women sitting on their front steps can converse with each other across the court comfortably.

Another clue that makes Philadelphia the likely setting of the novel is the fact that Mrs. Lasette, the wealthy matron who becomes Annette's confidante and surrogate mother, lives in the Nineteenth Ward, where there "are not a half dozen colored children." The federal census confirms this: in 1890, Philadelphia's Nineteenth Ward housed 55,249 whites and only 275 blacks. Mrs. Lasette tells Rev. Lomax that her husband bought land there in the early days of their marriage, when land was cheap and they were poor, even though it meant that they lived "more than a mile" from the city's business district. This geography is right for Philadelphia, although Harper may have truncated the distance to serve the plot. In the late nineteenth century, the southern edge of the Nineteenth Ward was just over twelve miles from Market Street. Annette frequently visits Mrs. Lasette, and the cost of public transportation for a trip that long would have been prohibitive for a young girl from the Tennis Court neighborhood.

What does identifying Philadelphia as the likely setting of the novel tell us? It enables us to analyze Harper's message more clearly because we can ground it in the social reality that she knew. The members of the social circle she mentions in the novel have diverse economic backgrounds, from the poverty of Grandmother Harcourt to the wealth of the Lasettes and Clarence Luzerne. In fact, a large proportion of the characters in the novel are economically secure, even the professionals who had to struggle to establish themselves. We learn that Annette's uncle had to teach school in the first years after he earned his medical degree because "it takes a young doctor some time to gain the confidence of an old community" and of course, what Harper does not say, because no white hospital or medical practice would hire a black doctor in the 1870s.[39] But by the time Grandmother Harcourt dies and Annette needs a home within the family, her Uncle Thomas's "beautiful home" is "very different from Grandmother Harcourt's "humble apartments."[40]

Another professional who eventually succeeds is Mr. Thomas, the schoolteacher who loses his job when the schools in his ward integrate. For a while Mr. Thomas is unsure about his future, but even in his difficulty he works to help a young man who has lost his job as a clerk in a store because his employer has learned that his mother is black. Mr. Thomas counsels young Charley Cooper not to attempt to pass as white because that course of action will inevitably separate him from his mother, who has already suffered enough. The clear implication is that Charley is the product of rape that occurred when his mother was in slavery.[41] In fact, Mr. Thomas is very familiar with the racial dynamics that young Charley must contend with. He was also born as the result of a white man's rape of his mother, as we learn later in the novel.[42] Instead, Mr. Thomas asks a white employer who is his friend to hire Charley. Both Charley and Mr. Thomas prosper. Charley succeeds because he avoids alcohol, works hard at his job as a "utility man" who does "almost anything that comes to hand"[43] for his employer, devotes himself to his mother, and eventually marries the wealthy daughter (and only child) of the Lasettes. Mr. Thomas prospers because he had the foresight to learn the trade of carpentry in an industrial school in the South before he began teaching school. He finds a manual labor job unloading boats at the docks, but when his employer realizes that he has carpentry skills he gives him a contract to design and build a warehouse for him. Harper tells us: "Against the odds which were against him . . . he was enabled not only to build up a good business for himself, but also to help others, and to teach them by his own experience not to be too easily discouraged, but to trust pluck more than luck, and learn in whatever capacity they were employed to do their work heartily as unto the Lord and not unto men."[44]

Thus, in the world Harper describes in *Trial and Triumph*, black men can find good and meaningful work if they are willing to work hard, to take work below their level of training, and to establish good networks in both the black and white communities. Several times in the novel women castigate black men who have been unable to find work. One woman criticizes a "great hulk of a man shambling around complaining of hard times, and that he can't get work" whose household relies upon the income of his wife, who takes in laundry. Several times in the novel Harper expresses her disappointment with a young generation of black men who frequent saloons, who "[take] life as a holiday," "young men with cigars in their mouths and the perfume of liquor on their breaths" who look on hard workers such as Charley Cooper as "milksops."[45] Harper's message was that black men who were willing to work diligently at any job, so long as it was honest work, would eventually prosper and be able to support families. Over the course of the novel Mr. Thomas moves from the status of unemployed teacher to become a business owner who employs other blacks and is a "happily married" man. The word "pluck" appears in the novel numerous times. Mr. Thomas resolves that "if pluck and energy were of any avail . . . he would leave no stone unturned in seeking employment."[46] Even though he finds door after door slammed in his face by white employers, he refuses an offer of employment by the wealthy black saloon owner Frank Norris, Annette's father. Instead, he takes a job unloading cargo on the docks, and his patient and persistent delivery of good work eventually catches his employer's eye and leads to a brighter future. Harper tells us that "pluck and perseverance prevailed."[47] Rev. Lomax exclaims that he is "full of hope for the future of our people. . . . We are now passing through a crucial period of our history and what we need is life—more abundant life in every fibre of our souls; life which will manifest itself in moral earnestness, vigor of purpose, strength of character and spiritual progression."[48] Like her contemporary William Alexander, who published *History of the Colored Race in America* in 1887, Harper believed in 1889 that the possibilities for the black race were "endless." Alexander wrote: "Time will erase the memory of their wrongs, and by earnest and intelligent endeavor they will soon reach the position for which God designed them—an intelligent and noble people."[49]

In Philadelphia, there was some evidence to support this assessment of pluck and perseverance in the 1880s. Some schools had been integrated, public transportation was integrated, black men were voting and even had some political influence at the ward level, and a rapidly growing black community was sustaining institutions that previous generations had created, such as the Institute for Colored Youth (founded in 1837). Philadelphia was also the headquarters of the National Equal Rights League, which was founded in 1864. The Pennsylvania branch of the league had successfully fought for the 1881 law integrating schools. Some black professionals were beginning to break down barriers in the city, including Caroline Anderson, who in 1878 graduated from the Philadelphia Women's Medical College, and Nathan Mossell, who graduated from the University of Pennsylvania Medical School in 1882 after much resistance. By 1884, thirty-five black men were on the city's police force. Even though black men and women were being excluded from the new jobs that an industrializing North was creating, there was reason to believe that this was a temporary setback and that once black people had proved themselves, those doors would open too. As Dickson T. Bruce has noted, "racial barriers were not seen as impregnable" in the 1880s.[50]

Despite her optimism, Harper did not sugarcoat the present. She spoke the truth about what she saw: black families crowded in "tenements and alleys" because white landlords would not rent better properties to them, lack of access to land, discrimination by white employers and white laborers who refused to work with blacks, the struggle of biracial people to adapt to life in the North, debates about whether school integration was desirable, the difficulties of raising children when saloons were located in black neighborhoods, black girls who became prostitutes, and black boys who became drunkards. But in each case, Harper believed, black people had the power to make right decisions that would open doors to them. In this novel, the central problem is not white racism but what black people choose to do when they confront it. Mrs. Lasette discusses her husband's friends who were not willing to buy land in the Nineteenth District when he did shortly after the war. Decades later, instead of owning comfortable homes they are "crowded in tenement houses or renting in narrow alleys and little streets." Black men who encounter discrimination in the job market can solve their problem either by creating networks that include white employers or by starting their own businesses. Mothers who keep their children away from saloons will fend off disastrous futures. As Annette's story illustrates, when doors are closed in the North, young women can take their skills into the South, where they will be valued.

Governing Interiority

In 1895, journalist and writer Victoria Earle Matthews spoke to the First Congress of Colored Women of the United States, the precursor to the National Association of Colored Women, which was founded the following year. Her topic was "The Value of Race Literature." Matthews dismissed the notion that what was called "American literature" reflected the experience of all Americans and looked forward to a time when literature written by African Americans would "rightly interpret our unappreciated contribution to Christianity and make it into universal literature." She said, "Our history and individuality as a people, not only provides material for masterly treatment; but would seem to make a Race Literature a necessity as an outlet for the unnaturally suppressed inner lives which our people have been compelled to lead." Yet she insisted that such a new literature should do more than record the great accomplishments of members of the black race. In fact, the essential components of such accomplishments lay in how people conducted themselves in their day-to-day interactions with others. Quoting Harriet Beecher Stowe, Matthews said: "What can any individual do? . . . There is one thing every individual can do. They can see to it that they feel right—an atmosphere of sympathetic influence encircles every human being; and the man or woman who feels strongly, healthily and justly on the great interests of humanity, is a constant benefactor to the human race."[51] Thus, each person's interior life had the potential to be a source of great influence, and in the artist's hands, depictions of that inner life could become expressions of universal human experience that would enter the canon of great literature.

Interiority is one of the themes of *Trial and Triumph*. The central trial young Annette Harcourt faces is not oppression by whites but her struggle to master her passionate temperament. Her triumph is the fact that she learns to govern that passion and to harness her interiority as a source of power that she can use to benefit her race. At the beginning of the novel she is a young and wild child whose ungovernable behavior causes her grandmother to despair. Annette is unkind and disrespectful to adults in her neighborhood and does impulsive, vengeful acts, such as pouring oil on the steps of a neighbor woman she dislikes. When Grandmother Harcourt confronts her and asks her why she did such a thing, Annette, who is not actually sorry, struggles to find an answer. At first she says that she "did it for the devil" because "the preacher said the devil makes people do bad things." Grandmother Harcourt rejects this explanation, pointing out that the preacher had said that the devil *tempts* people to do bad things, but people can choose not to do them. Annette then admits that she did it "just for fun" because the neighbor is always telling on her and trying to get the grandmother to beat her. She is unable to understand the value of a community of women who watch over all the neighborhood children. All she can see is that a neighbor is trying to curb her freedom, and she retaliates in the only ways she knows how.

Grandmother Harcourt is tempted to use corporal punishment on this occasion, but she is painfully aware that Annette is not a happy child. She cries out in her sleep and "never seems light-hearted and happy."[52] To Grandmother Harcourt, it seems as if the child is carrying some of the grief her daughter Lucy experienced as a shamed, degraded, and abandoned unwed mother. Annette has inherited the sorrowful consequence of her mother's moral misstep, and Grandmother Harcourt does not know how to heal that wound. She does not know how to help her granddaughter learn to manage and control her feelings. When a neighbor cautions her that "Annette needs wise guidance, a firm hand and a loving heart to deal with her. To spoil her at home is only to prepare her for misery abroad," Grandmother Harcourt replies "I am afraid that I am not equal to the task."[53] Harper later tells us that while Grandmother Harcourt works hard to provide for Annette's physical needs, "to her a restless child was an enigma she did not know how to solve." She also does not know how to meet Annette's emotional needs. Grandmother Harcourt was "not demonstrative in her affections" and "for the hunger of the heart she had neither sympathy nor comprehension."[54]

Fortunately for Annette, other members of her community see potential in her and step in to help. The most significant female presence in her life outside the family is Mrs. Lasette, the wealthy matron who once was her mother's friend. Mrs. Lasette and her husband have risen from poverty to wealth (although we do not hear what Mr. Lasette's business is), and after bearing one child, a daughter, she chooses to "[pour] a new interest into the welfare of her race."[55] Mrs. Lasette accomplishes this largely through one-one-one personal relationships: "she soon became known as a friend and helper in the community in which she lived." Mrs. Lasette is a particular friend to young people on the cusp of adulthood. Young black women come to her for advice about sex and marriage, and young black men consult her about job prospects. Harper tells us that "to all her heart was responsive."[56] One of the black men she has influenced is Mr. Thomas, who boarded with her for a time while he was training to be a teacher.

Harper was likely drawing on her own childhood experiences when she described Annette's early love for poetry in the context of a family whose members do not understand her talent. In Mrs. Lasette, she found a friend

> who understood her better than her grandmother, and who, looking beneath the perverseness of the child, saw in her rich possibilities, and would often speak encouragingly to her. Annette early developed a love for literature and poetry and would sometimes try to make rhymes and string verses together and really Mrs. Lasette thought that she had talent or even poetic genius and ardently wished that it might be cultivated and rightly directed; but it never entered the minds of her grandmother and aunts that in their humble home was a rarely gifted soul destined to make music which would set young hearts to thrilling with higher hopes and loftier aspirations.[57]

Like Harper, who was encouraged to pursue her desire to become a poet by Mrs. Armstrong, the bookseller's wife, Annette finds encouragement outside her family.

Mrs. Lasette helps Annette process her feelings when she encounters racism at the newly consolidated school from both her classmates and the white teacher. When Annette responds to a racial taunt from Mary Joseph, the daughter of an Irish saloonkeeper, by calling her a "mick," Mrs. Lasette uses moral suasion and the Socratic method to show Annette that she is responsible for governing her feelings and rising above the moral standard of behavior she sees in whites:

> "Who made Miss Joseph?"
>
> "Why, the Lord, of course."
>
> "And who made you?"
>
> "He made me, too."
>
> "Are you sure that you did not make yourself?"
>
> "Why, of course not," said Annette with an accent of wonder in her voice.
>
> "Does God ever make any mistakes?"
>
> "Why, no!"
>
> "Then if any one calls you black, why should you get angry? You say it would not make Miss Joseph angry to say she looked white, or red and rosy."
>
> "I don't know; I know I don't like it and it makes me mad."
>
> "Now, let me explain the reason why it makes you angry to be called black. Suppose I were to burn my hand in that stove, what would I have on my hand?"
>
> "A sore place."
>
> "If it were your hand, what would you do?"
>
> "I would put something on it, wrap it up to keep from getting cold into it and try to get it well as soon as I could."
>
> "Well, that would be a very sensible way of dealing with it. In this country, Annette, color has been made a sore place; it has been associated with slavery, poverty and ignorance. You cannot change your color, but you can try to change

> the association connected with our complexions. Did slavery force a man to be servile and submissive? Learn to hold up your head and respect yourself. Don't notice Mary Joseph's taunts; if she says things to tease you don't you let her see that she has succeeded."

She concludes the lesson by advising Annette not to put herself "on the same level" as Mary Joseph by quarreling with her.[58]

Mr. Thomas uses the same combination of moral suasion and the Socratic method with Charley Cooper when he loses his job because of racism. He tells Charley that it is not the color of his skin that his employer found objectionable but the fact that he was "connected by blood with a once enslaved and despised people on whom society had placed its ban, and to whom slavery and a low social condition had given a heritage of scorn." According to Mr. Thomas, Charley was fired because of the failed manhood of his employer, who lacked the courage to follow his instinct and retain a good worker and instead bowed to pressure from public opinion. Mr. Thomas says that he pities such men, for "there never was slave more cowed under the whip of his master than he is under the lash of public opinion. The Negro was not the only one whom slavery subdued to the pliancy of submission."[59] In both of these examples, Harper imparted her belief that right feelings and right conduct had the power to both elevate the black race to its rightful and natural moral place and, with time and patience, to wear down the whites who were excluding them from opportunities. Harper seemed to be saying that if black people could only understand the logic of racism, they could attack it at its roots and slowly but surely remove the basis for it. It is understandable that in the 1880s, before the virulence of lynchings and Jim Crow slammed doors closed for so many blacks and before it became clear that most whites had no intention of ever expanding job opportunities for black workers, Harper, a lifelong activist who had seen what moral suasion could do in the decades-long campaign to end slavery, still could believe that it would be an effective tool for convincing whites to leave behind prejudice that she firmly believed no longer applied to the postwar context.

As part of her Socratic conversation with Annette, Mrs. Lasette referred to the deep historical roots of her people, connecting the young girl with the figure of Cleopatra:

> Learn to act as if you realized that you were born into this world the child of the Ruler of the universe, that this is his world and that you have as much right in it as she has. I think it was Gilbert Haven, a Bishop of the Methodist Episcopal Church, a man for whose tombstone I do not think America has any marble too white or any laurel too green, who saw on his travels a statue of Cleopatra, which suggested to him this thought, "I am black, but comely, the sun has looked down upon me, but I will make you who despise me feel that I am your superior."[60]

Here, Harper took a bit of poetic license. Gilbert Haven saw William Wetmore Story's statue of Cleopatra at the British Museum in the early 1860s on a trip to Europe. In *The Pilgrim's Wallet*, the book he published in 1864 about his travels, he wrote about the profound impression seeing an African queen in marble had made upon him: "I think [the] artist the bravest American except John Brown. He has made a negress the model of America,—an African prophetess the seer of America."[61] The message Haven heard from the ancient African jeremiad was this:

> I belong to a despised race, but you shall feel that I am your superior. What if my forehead is low, and cheek-bones high, and lips thick, and nostrils not undistended? What if all the characteristics of the negro are stamped upon my countenance? You shall acknowledge that they are no drawback to my power; that they may even be the weapons of my conquest. . . . Your selected representatives and rulers, they shall be my worshippers. . . . Their passion, their infatuation, shall teach all your race the folly and criminality of your pretended natural abhorrence of my blood. It is negro blood; and your Antony, the type of your beauty and culture; your Caesar, the representative of your highest qualities of mind and will,—these shall seek alliance, at any sacrifice, with the African. They shall teach Caucasians of every age and clime that my blood is as good as theirs,—is one with theirs; that it is as great an honor and privilege for you to marry me, as for me to marry you. The time has been when, in my person and in that of these proudest names of your race, this truth was recognized. It will be again. It will be universally.[62]

Haven drew upon an African past to imagine a future in which racial equality would be a universal truth and in which there would be no barriers between blacks and other races. Harper repurposed Haven's radical message of racial equality into a call for pure actions: "Annette, I want you to be so noble, true and pure that if everybody should hate you, that no one could despise you."[63]

Residents of Philadelphia had a chance to see another statue of Cleopatra, one created by a black woman artist, in 1876, at the Philadelphia Centennial Exposition. Edmonia Lewis's *The Death of Cleopatra* depicted the African queen on her throne in a scene popularized by Shakespeare: at the moment when she has chosen to be bitten by a poisonous snake rather than surrender her crown, or as Susanna Gold describes it, "having chosen to suffer death rather than succumb to imprisonment and humiliation at the hands of her Roman conqueror."[64] Gold argues that Lewis's choice of this moment for a work of art that would be displayed in a national setting was deliberate: the statue "responds to the ambivalence of the Centennial culture that celebrated one-hundred years of a nation built on founding principles of unity and liberty, but haunted by centuries of African slavery, the recent Civil War, and the rapidly failing efforts of Reconstruction."[65]

In drawing attention to art that portrayed figures from an African past, Mrs. Lasette introduced Annette (and Harper introduced her readers) to a world in which visual representation of Africans opened minds to broad views of the place of the black race in geopolitical relations and offered ideas through visual means that would have been perceived as inflammatory in print or as oratory in the immediate postwar decades. Harper drew upon popular mass market Egyptian iconography that would have been familiar to readers of the period. Her reference to a well-known statue of Cleopatra as a touchstone for racial pride is similar to Frederick Douglass's description of his mother's appearance as similar to an image of the Egyptian ruler Ramses drawn from a statue in his 1855 autobiography, *My Bondage and My Freedom*. Michael Chaney argues that Douglass's comparison of his mother to an Egyptian statue offers a glimpse of Douglass "in the very act of self-creation."[66] Mrs. Lasette's reference to Cleopatra as an icon of racial pride gives the orphaned Annette an ancestral connection to a distant past that had not yet been torn asunder by slavery and offers her a means of constructing a self who can envision a life beyond the harsh conditions of the Tennis Court neighborhood.

Each chapter in *Trial and Triumph* shows a bit more of Harper's strategy for moving the race forward. Black men should prepare for multiple occupations and be willing to move backward in the hope of eventually moving forward. Black institutions such as churches should hire black workers. Black community members should form their own businesses and then hire other black employees. The community should look for opportunities to integrate with white institutions and should form friendships with white people so they can show them by example and through moral suasion that black people deserve every opportunity that whites do. Mothers should raise children with strong moral values. Children should be given as much education as possible so they will become leaders who are a credit to their race.

These are all external tasks that will take place in the public realm. But an equally important theme in the novel is the task Annette faces of learning to govern her interiority. By the time she is an older adolescent, her interiority has all but taken over her life. When her grandmother must leave their home for long periods to do her work as a sick nurse, Annette is perfectly content to be alone. Neighbors hear her "sing[ing] and recit[ing] at the top of her voice and run[ning] up and down the stairs as if a regiment of soldiers were after her."[67] Her aunt tells Mrs. Lasette that the girls her age make fun or her because "she is very odd and queer and often goes out into the street as if she never saw a looking glass. . . . Why, Annette just makes herself a perfect laughing stock."[68] All Annette cares about is reading and writing poetry. The women in her family, most notably her Aunt Eliza, devalue this talent. When Annette shows her some of her poetry, saying "that is one of my best pieces," Aunt Eliza replies

"You seem to think there must be something very great about you. . . . Can you cook a beefsteak?"[69] Aunt Eliza continues, "I know where you want to get. You want to get among the upper tens, but you haven't got style enough about you for that."[70] Even Annette's grandmother criticizes Annette: "She's got too many airs for a girl in her condition. She talks about writing a book, and she is always trying to make up what she calls poetry. I expect that she will go crazy some of these days. She is all the time talking to herself, and I just think it is a sin for her to be so much taken up with poetry."[71] Surely drawing upon her own experience as a talented but orphaned black girl, through the character of Annette, Harper depicts the frustration of trying to develop a creative talent while family members attempt to pressure her into "practical" domestic labor. In response, Annette is in danger of withdrawing so far into herself that she is unable to relate to her community.

Fortunately for Annette, Mr. Thomas continues to nurture her intellectually even after he is forced to leave the teaching profession. He tells her that when she does well in school, she is not just a good student but that she is "a representative of her branch of the human race" who is on the cusp of winning victories for her entire race. Harper tells us that this sense of racial pride and the possibility that she can contribute to it "increases her determination and rouses up all the latent energies of her nature, and she labors day and night to be a living argument of the capability in her race."[72] Yet Mr. Thomas is troubled, for he knows that when she graduates, Annette will face obstacles: while the white girls in her school will find "unclosed doors, and open avenues," because of her black skin, the doors of factories, workshops, and school rooms will be closed to her.[73] However, he has faith that Annette will find a solution when the time comes and continues to encourage the budding poet he sees. He understands that "poetry was a passion born in her soul" and calls her "our inveterate poet."[74]

Grandmother Harcourt does not live to see Annette reach adulthood. On her deathbed, she extracts a promise from her son Thomas, a doctor, that he will take care of her. So for the last years of her girlhood, Annette lives in the beautiful home of her uncle and an aunt who does not want her and despises her because she has not mastered all the domestic skills. As she enters the household for the first time and her aunt greets her, Annette finds that "there was no warm pressure in the extended hand. No loving light in the cold unsympathizing eyes which seemed to stab her through and through."[75] The aunt barely speaks to her and excludes her from events on her side of the family, saying that Annette is not part of that family. Annette, who is grieving the loss of her grandmother and the loss of her status as a loved child, struggles once more to master her emotions. Mrs. Lasette's daughter, Laura, tells her that Annette's aunt has said that her "tear bags must lay near her eyes and that she will cry if you look at her, and that she is the strangest, oddest creature she ever saw."[76]

When she hears this harmful gossip, Mrs. Lasette responds in two ways. First, she tells Laura the story of Annette's "antenatal history"—that is, the story of her parents—as a cautionary tale for a daughter of marriageable age. She tells Laura of the perils of young women who entered domestic service some two decades earlier. These girls, particularly girls with mothers from the South, were unprepared for the freedom of the social life an urban center offered working-class young people: "Our dear old mothers were generally ignorant of books, but they did try to teach good manners and good behavior; but I do not think they saw the danger around the paths of the inexperienced with the same clearness of vision we now do."[77] Mrs. Harcourt, who had "unbounded confidence" in the children she had moved out of the South so they would have better opportunities, allowed her daughter Lucy to go to social events such as "excursions, moonlight drives and parties of pleasure" unaccompanied by male relatives. When a handsome stranger comes to town Lucy falls for him completely, and soon they are planning to be married. But when Lucy tells him she is with child, he abandons her and Lucy must withdraw from society completely for the length of her pregnancy. She loses all position in her social circle. In addition, her widowed mother must support her and her child, as Lucy dies, likely from consumption, when Annette is still a baby. The absence of safeguards during her courtship years and her lack of preparedness for sexual pressure from a handsome newcomer brought sorrow, shame, and economic hardship to her family. In this narrative, though, Lucy is presented as a victim, as one who was not given the knowledge she needed to navigate her social situation. It is her mother, Grandmother Harcourt, who is ever so gently blamed for her part in Lucy's tragedy. She failed to properly prepare her cherished daughter.

Mrs. Lasette also responds by including Annette on the guest list of the graduation party she hosts for Laura. Harper tells us that it is more than a "mere pleasure party"; it is the equivalent of our modern-day networking events. Harper tells us that at Mrs. Lasette's parties, "rising talent was encouraged, no matter how humble the garb of the possessor."[78] As a model hostess, Mrs. Lasette sees to it that every guest has a suitable conversation partner, and she introduces the wealthy southerner Clarence Luzerne to the "shy and easily embarrassed Annette," who finds herself socially isolated from peers who have tired of her "faults of temper."[79] Mr. Luzerne, already impressed by Annette's powerful valedictorian speech, finds conversing with her to be a rare intellectual pleasure, and soon the two have begun a courtship. Annette has found a potential mate who appreciates her for her talents and her intellect, the same qualities that ostracized her among peers and family members. They read books together and find that they think alike on many issues. Their views of the ideal marriage are the same. They seem perfectly matched to each other. As Annette plans for marriage and domesticity, it seems that her future is secure. She will be a wife and mother who will raise a new generation of worthy community members. Because Mr. Luzerne is wealthy, Annette has an opportunity to replicate the role Mrs. Lasette has modeled for her.

But Harper gives her a test of character. Clarence Luzerne's wife, whom he had long assumed to be dead, suddenly reappears, ill and in dire need of help. Annette proves the depth of her character, the fruit of many conversations with Mrs. Lasette, by instantly moving to help this suffering woman. She does much more than merely go through the motions; she sits by her bedside for days, caring for her tenderly. When the wife regains consciousness and perceives the feelings between Clarence and Annette, she offers to divorce her husband so he will be free to marry his love. Harper raises the stakes by telling her readers that Luzerne feels comfortable with this and would be willing to divorce his wife. Annette's future hangs in the balance, and the decision is entirely up to her. Without hesitating, she tells Mr. Luzerne that "the great end of life is not the attainment of happiness but the performance of duty and the development of character. The great question is not what is pleasant but what is right."[80] She refuses to marry him because marriage is a sacrament that cannot be broken, even though it breaks her heart to make her choice. His wife has a prior claim on him, even though they have been separated for many years. Here, Harper shares her view of the importance of marriage to a readership still recovering from the effects of slavery and the upheavals of the war.

Readers could see from this chapter that Annette has made great progress in learning to govern her interiority. She masters her deepest feelings for the man she loves and makes what Harper presents as the right choice. Her duty is twofold: to respect the bonds of marriage and to ensure that a suffering woman will get the best possible care. Lest there is any doubt that Annette has triumphed over her formerly ungovernable nature, in the next chapter we see just how far she has come. She immediately turns to Mrs. Lasette, not to wallow in her grief, but to ask for help. Her first thought is that she must "have some active work which will engross my mind and use every faculty of my soul."[81] She is ready to integrate her interior life with useful work for her community.

For Mrs. Lasette, this is Annette's true graduation day. She has come through her trial successfully. Mrs. Lasette tells her that she is "glad that you have been so true to conscience and to duty; glad that you have come through your trial like gold tried in the fiercest fire; glad that my interest in you has not been in vain, and that I have been able to see the blessed fruitage of my love and labors."[82] Annette is one of Mrs. Lasette's greatest successes: through careful nurturing of a black girl, she has helped create a young woman who is ready to dedicate herself to her community and use all her talents for the benefit of others.

Service to the Race

As Harper had done almost two decades earlier, Annette takes her talents into the South. Through an arrangement with a friend, Mrs. Lasette finds a school where Annette can do the work she prepared for at the normal school: she will be a teacher. Thus, Grandmother Harcourt's strategy of educating Annette even though she would not be able to teach in the integrated schools of her city is vindicated. When a daughter criticized her for keeping Annette in school so long, she responded that she had promised Mrs. Lasette that she would give Annette a full education and she intended to keep that promise, adding, "Maybe something will turn up that you don't see just now. When a good thing turns up if a person ain't ready for it they can't take hold of it."[83] Annette's success in finding a place for her talents drives home the message that Harper plants in several places in the novel: prepare yourself for the future you want and then work to make that future happen. But the solution for Annette reflects the harsh reality that many doors were closed to professional black women in the North in the 1880s.

In the South, Annette is valued as a welcome addition. Harper makes clear, though, that it is not just her training and skill that wins her friends. She connects with black people in her new setting by opening her heart: she finds "opportunity among the freedmen to be a friend and sister to those whose advantages had been less than hers." Her secret is that she "roused up her soul to bear suffering and to be true to duty" and in doing so she finds joy.[84] Little children love her, the "street gamins" know she is their friend, the elderly women she cares for call her "dear child." She helps young boys make the right choices as they begin their careers; and one mother says that she has been "the making" of her daughter. People of all generations treasure Annette because of the kind and generous help and good counsel she gives their community.

Annette thus replicates the role that Mrs. Lasette played in the northern city of "A.P.," with the key distinction that she does so as a single woman, not the wife of a wealthy man. She is giving of her essence, from the resources she has created by unifying her interior and exterior. All of the knowledge she has of the black race—of their history and accomplishments, of the ability of black women to contribute to their communities—unites with her deeply felt emotional world and with her soul.

Annette's new life in the South mirrors the experience Harper had when she toured the South as a lecturer after the Civil War. Harper was likely grieving also when she first began this endeavor. Her husband, Fenton Harper, had died in 1864, and the life she had known as a married woman and co-manager of a farm had just imploded. The farm had been purchased with her earnings from writing and lecturing, and when her husband died, she lost her investment to her husband's creditors. She wrote that the administrator "swept the very milk-crocks and wash tubs from my hands."[85] The experience made the injustice of property laws very real to her. She was keenly aware that if she had died instead of her husband, no property would have been seized to repay the family's debts.

For the next six years, Harper toured the South at her own expense almost constantly. She gave lectures in any place the freedpeople could offer. One time she arrived to find that the lecture hall was a brush arbor. She wrote to William Still: "Shall I call it an edifice or an improvised meeting-house? Well, it is called a brush arbor. It is a kind of brush house with seats, and a kind of covering made partly, I rather think, of branches of trees, and an humble place for a pulpit."[86] She sometimes lectured twice a day, often working at the limit of her strength and often requesting a friend in the North to withdraw funds and send them directly to a freedperson who needed help. Just as she had done before the war, when she sent every dollar she could spare to support the work of the Underground Railroad, after the war, she contributed cash, the money she paid for housing, and her knowledge to the freedpeople. She did not settle into a home of her own until 1871, when she moved to Philadelphia, and even after that she continued to make lecture tours among the freedpeople of the South for most of a decade.

What she saw in the latter 1860s and 1870s was a deeply unsettled and violent society. In several letters, she reported that a freedperson had been murdered just before or just after she visited a community. In 1867, she wrote about a young black woman who was so elated when the Union troops reached her town that she said that she "was going to marry a Yankee and set up housekeeping." She was arrested for incendiary speech "and then brutally hung."[87] Later that year she wrote that she was about to travel to a town where a freedman had been shot because he had "[given] offence by some words spoken at a public meeting."[88] Another time she learned of a young man who was murdered after he had married a white woman: "there was . . . no investigation by jury," she wrote. She never changed her plans when she heard of such events.[89]

She spoke to black audiences, to black and white audiences, and, in some cases, to groups that consisted of black women only so she could speak more freely about private matters. She wrote from Greenville, Georgia, as she was preparing to speak to a group of women: "I am going to talk with them about their daughters, and about things connected with the welfare of the race. Now is the time for our women to begin to try to lift up their heads and plant the roots of progress under the hearthstone."[90] She spoke on rural plantations and in cities and towns, in the rudest of structures and in court houses and legislative halls.[91] She never had difficulty finding an audience, and she never charged a fee. For her income, she relied on what people were able to give in a freewill offering. One time her only payment was a vase of roses on the table she stood behind.[92] All of this she did on her own, "influenced in her labor of love, wholly by the noble impulses of her own heart, working her way along unsustained by any Society."[93]

Harper carried a message of hope and progress. She sometimes used her own life story as an example of what was possible. The editor of a southern newspaper reported in 1871 that in her lectures, "she . . . draws a graphic picture of her own marvellous advancement from utter obscurity to the platform of a public lecturer, honored by her own race and applauded by their oppressors. While we regret, as she says, that her experience . . . is exceptional, it is easy to anticipate the harvest of such a sowing."[94] She told freedpeople that they had "muscle and brain power" that they needed to use. "Get land, every one that can, and as fast as you can," she advised. "A landless people must be dependent upon the landed people. A few acres to till for food and a roof, however humble, over your head, are the castle of your independence, and when you have it you are fortified to act and vote independently whenever your interests are at stake."[95] Frances Harper still believed in the core values of the republic, after all of the ways those values had been perverted in her lifetime, and she used her resources to educate freedpeople about the virtues of independence and the importance of the vote.

Harper also saw good reason for hope. She wrote to Still of numerous examples of freedpeople who had acquired enough land to run a prosperous farm, often through the labor and management of a woman. She wrote an article for the *Englishwoman's Review of Social and Industrial Questions* in 1878 entitled "The Coloured Women of America" that listed the many ways that freedwomen in the South were the means of sustenance and progress for their families. She quoted from a letter from a southern woman, who told Harper that "there are many women around me who would serve as models of executiveness anywhere." These women were managing farms, buying land and homes, raising vegetables, selling cakes, knitting hose, and producing sugar with a crew of hired men. They were using every skill and resource they had to provide security for their families and education for their children.[96] And they were succeeding.

"Oh, if some more of our young women would only consecrate their lives to the work of upbuilding the race!" she cried out to William Still. "Oh, if I could only see our young men and women aiming to build up a future for themselves which would grandly contrast with the past—with its pain, ignorance and low social condition."[97] Frances Harper believed that the young women of the North had the knowledge and capacity to help their southern counterparts craft new lives in freedom, through the sharing of knowledge about issues that ranged from literacy and other types of formal education to information about the North, cultural mores of the free black community, and, of course, Christianity. But Harper issued one crucial caveat: all of this was possible only "if one takes with her a manner that unlocks other hearts."[98]

In the character of Annette, Harper created the kind of young black woman who was needed in the South. She could not be a person who was focused too intensely on her creativity and saw work in the South as a stopgap or as a stepping-stone to bigger things. She could not be a person who was withdrawn and too focused on her interior life. She could not be a person like some of the girls in *Trial and Triumph* who obsessed about pretty clothes and the size of the homes they wanted. The northern black woman who went South to work needed to be fully integrated within herself and very clear that all of her resources were to be used for the benefit of others. And she needed to do her work with an open heart and a welcoming spirit. Only after Annette had been through her trials, many of which were the same ones Harper had endured, could she be the special kind of person who could work effectively in the South. And only when a black girl had been carefully nurtured and encouraged and believed in could she know how to give those same gifts to others.

Harper sent Annette into her life's work as a single young black woman. She knew that freedom from obligation to a husband or a family gave a northern black woman in the South essential room to maneuver, and she knew that it was important for her readers to see the example of an independent young woman who found useful work to benefit her race. Such a woman would need the freedom to make quick decisions and work long hours. She would need the ability to travel if a need arose in a nearby town. And in giving Annette a position through a private network, she freed her from obligation to the board or management of a northern, likely male-dominated, organization. Annette was beholden only to the community where she was working, just as Harper had been beholden only to her own bank balance as she traveled through the South.

Yet Harper also understood that it was important for black men and women to work together. *Trial and Triumph* is the story of a community of black men and women who are working together to move forward. Mr. Thomas and Mrs. Lasette often consult with each other about how to overcome particular difficulties. Grandmother Harcourt relies on her son to provide for Annette in the last years of her childhood. Mrs. Lasette holds gatherings that bring men and women together for the purpose of discussing important issues. At the end of the novel, Clarence Luzerne and Annette reunite as older and more experienced friends. Mr. Luzerne's wife has died and he is free to marry. Yet Harper leaves the end of their story somewhat ambiguous: "He had come not to separate her from her cherished life work, but to help her in uplifting and helping those among whom her lot was cast as a holy benediction, and so after years of trial and pain, their souls had met at last, strengthened by duty, purified by that faith which works by love, and fitted for life's highest and holiest truths."[99] Harper refers to Annette as the love of his *spirit*, not the love of his heart. Will they marry? Or will devotion to uplifting the race come first for two dear friends who understand each other perfectly? Harper leaves the ending to her readers to imagine.

Conclusion

Trial and Triumph is, in essence, an epistolary letter from Harper to her people. She even draws the parallel at one point, through the words of Mr. Thomas, who wishes that pleasure-loving, beer-drinking young black men will "strive to be more like those of whom it was said, 'I write unto you, young men, because you are strong.'"[100] This is a quote from I John 2:24, a New Testament epistle from the Apostle John to an unnamed first-century church. As did John's letter, the novel gives advice to an embattled community about surviving and doing well. Harper names the difficulties the northern community is struggling with and gives practical advice about how to overcome them. She offers hope and encouragement. She records the many connections between the formerly divided northern and southern parts of her "congregation" and encourages her readers to strengthen these ties.

In 1892, Frances Harper spoke to the Brooklyn Literary Society on the topic of "Enlightened Motherhood." Using the same phrase that Annette used in her valedictorian speech, Harper told her audience that the work of mothers was "grandly constructive." She spoke of the home as the place where children "should be trained for useful citizenship" and warned that if the education of daughters was neglected, they would not be able to properly raise strong men and virtuous women. In Harper's vision of racial progress, women were at the center of the grand construction project the black community was engaged in. They set the moral tone in their homes by training their children to aspire to something better than the "arrogance, aggressiveness, and indomitable power" that prevailed in a nation that had all but abandoned the republican values of her youth.[101] The need for classic republican values is a theme of *Trial and Triumph*. Harper has described a community of virtuous citizens who do their best every day to improve the welfare of their society. Those who are not familiar with those values (such as, perhaps, Grandmother Harcourt) come to grief and those who reject them in favor of self-interest (Frank Miller, idle young men, selfish aunts) are excoriated. The novel also conveys the viewpoint of a former abolitionist. Every act that is done should be a moral act that will benefit the race, she tells her readers. Even conversations are measured by this standard. Harper has no patience with idle gossip or frivolous chatter. The great abolitionist orator valued words and sought to show her readers how much good they could do.

Trial and Triumph offers a template that shows how to nurture young black girls, particularly those who have suffered losses and have unusual natures and do not seem to fit in with the rest of the community. Harper wrote from her own experience of loss, of harsh treatment from relatives, of feeling compelled to explore her identity as a poet when others felt she should be working to support herself, of finding useful work in service to her people. One suspects that she also wrote from her own experience about the struggle a young black girl experiences as she learns to integrate a deep interior life with an unusual intellect in the service of meaningful work. Certainly the possibility the novel creates of independent work for single young black women drew upon her experiences before and after the war, first as an unmarried abolitionist lecturer in the North and later as a widowed emissary to the freedpeople of the South. Writing from her own life, Harper offered a conduct manual that was wrapped in an entertaining story that reached her community and opened their hearts.

The ending of the novel contains a program for young black women activists that could be seen as a lens of hope. As the conversations and dilemmas in *Trial and Triumph* indicate, educated young black women such as Annette were unable to thrive in the postbellum North due to racism, lack of opportunities, and structural inequalities. Thus, Harper encouraged black female activists such as Annette to leave the North and establish a "beautiful" home in the South. Annette creates "a beautiful place of fragrance and flowers" in her new home.[102] Harper creates a domestic sphere for Annette where she surrounds herself with community members and becomes "the beloved friend of old and young."[103] It is in this domestic and activist space that Mr. Luzerne arrives. When his wife dies, Mr. Luzerne finds "Annette's location and start(s) Southward with a fresh hope springing up in his heart."[104] The passion that Luzerne feels is matched by Annette's desire, as Harper lets us know: when she hears Mr. Luzerne's unmistakable footstep, it "[sends] the blood bounding in swift currents back to her heart and [leaves] her cheek very pale."[105] Through these expressions of shared passion, Harper constructs an equation of sexual desire for young black women activists in the nineteenth century that must rest on certain predetermined standards. To enter into a sexual union, a young black woman must occupy a space of opportunity where she might gain economic security, create and maintain a beautiful home, and engage in purposeful, activist work in the community. Only after Annette achieves these ideals does Mr. Luzerne seek her out to "claim the love of his spirit."[106] This recipe for single black women activists and single black men suggests that taking the necessary steps to acquire emotional and physical spaces of integrity, activism, and purposefulness is necessary to ensure that each person has gained a level of independence and personal happiness before entering into a partnership or marriage. In the 1880s, suggesting that a young black woman establish her own professional sphere and networks before marriage was forward-thinking. Only after Annette and Mr. Luzerne have evolved, matured, and overcome "years of trial and pain" could their souls "[meet] at last."[107] The reverse migration from the North to the South that Annette makes suggests that for black women and girls, an alternative trajectory might be the necessary course for successful and productive futures.

By the last decades of the nineteenth century, the spaces black girls needed to be successful had evolved. In the antebellum era, black girls made creative use of cramped garrets and attics. In the immediate postbellum decades, the literal and figurative spaces of the newspaper advice column offered them information about what resources they needed and how to acquire them. By the 1880s, Harper was envisioning that young black women needed the physical space of an entire home as the base for their movement into society. *Trial and Triumph* ends on a note of hopefulness. A young, black woman has established her own home and her own life without the aid of a man. She is surrounded by community members and friends. She has found purpose in her life before she enters a relationship or marriage. Frances Harper has written a picture of renewed hope for black women and girls at the end of the 1880s.

In the last lines of the novel, Harper steps outside her role as omniscient narrator and speaks directly to her readers. She writes, "under the guise of fiction, I have essayed to weave a story which I hope will subserve a deeper purpose than the mere amusement of the hour, that it will quicken and invigorate human hearts and not fail to impart a lesson of usefulness and value."[108] The intriguing phrase "under the guise of fiction" hints at the many points of autobiography in the novel. Yet in Harper's hands, the autobiographical becomes much more than that. It becomes a map for the future in a moment in black history when it was possible to peer down the road and see reason for hope. By moving her autobiography into the 1880s, Harper emphasized her theme of progress. The young girls of that decade, Harper felt, had a better social context in which to plan for their futures than she herself had had. They no longer had to contend with indentured servitude. Slavery was part of the past. Despite many obstacles, she believed there was reason to prepare for a better future. The task now was to continue building up the race by helping each other and by being prepared for every door that opened. In the social world *Trial and Triumph* presented, a black girl is the iconic representative of this strategy.

5. Black Girlhood in Early-Twentieth-Century Black Conduct Books

IN "OF THE MEANING OF PROGRESS," the fourth essay in W. E. B. Du Bois's *The Souls of Black Folk* (1903), a black girl's desire for education and her untimely death serve to define the barriers to social and economic improvement for African Americans at the turn of the twentieth century. As a new teacher, Du Bois travels south, "beyond railways, beyond stage lines, to a land of 'varmints' and rattlesnakes," until he reaches a poor black community in need of a teacher.[1] Du Bois meets Josie, a black girl with a "longing to know" and with dreams "to be a student in the great school in Nashville."[2] This yearning "hovered like a star above this child-woman amid her work and worry, and she studied doggedly."[3] Capable, selfless, and noble, Josie "had about her a certain finesse, the shadow of an unconscious moral heroism that would willingly give all of life to make life broader, deeper, and fuller for her and hers."[4] Josie "seemed to be the centre of the family: always busy at service, or at home, or berry picking; a little nervous and inclined to scold, like her mother, yet faithful, too, like her father."[5] Despite Josie's fortitude and devotion to duty, Du Bois grows weary of "this little world," views his life in the community as "dull and humdrum," and leaves the South and the school Josie cherishes.[6] After her teacher departs, Josie becomes "thin and silent," yet she "worked the more." Dashed dreams dim Josie's once-bright future, but she "shiver[s] and work[s] on, with the vision of schooldays all fled, [and] with a face wan and tired." Josie travels to Nashville to find work but returns to find her brother jailed and her sister pregnant. She continues to work, but when "one summer's day some one married another," Josie's heart finally breaks, and she "crept to her mother like a hurt child, and slept—and sleeps."[7] Du Bois's ability to "wander," "muse," and "journey" contrasts sharply with the horizons of Josie's life, which are shaped by an underdeveloped education and limited opportunities, her disenchantment when she realizes that her hard work is not enough to improve her own life and the life of her community, and personal and family disappointments, all of which contribute to her premature death. The story Du Bois tells illustrates how Josie's obligation to uphold principles of progress and shoulder the responsibility for her entire family and for her community becomes a burden that is too heavy and ultimately leads to her demise. Josie's story reveals the toll racial advancement at the turn of the century could take on committed individuals, especially when societal structures of poverty and racism restrict this progress.

African American educator and activist Fannie Barrier Williams highlighted what could happen when black girls in literature served merely to illustrate the problems associated with race advancement at the turn of the twentieth century. In her 1905 essay "The Colored Girl," Williams criticized how black girls were often presented as symbols of the problems of the race: "The term 'colored girl' is almost a term of reproach in the social life of America. . . . She is not known and hence not believed in; she belongs to a race that is best designated by the term 'problem,' and she lives beneath the shadow of that problem which envelopes and obscures her."[8] Williams claimed that what black girls truly wanted was "to be respected and believed in. This is more important than position and opportunities."[9] For Williams, the focus should be on the interior desires and aspirations of black girls instead of seeing them as figureheads who were assigned responsibility for carrying the weight of the entire race. Williams condemned black intellectual thought that limited black girls' choices. Black girls "need encouragement to do whatever her hands find to do, and to be protected and honored for it. If the colored girl of character and intelligence must cook, who shall say that she is not deserving of the honors of the best social life as the girl who plays the piano or manipulates a typewriter," she wrote.[10] Whether black girls cooked or "manipulate[d] a typewriter," Williams insisted that men should "place a higher premium on character than we do upon the quality of her occupation. . . . Let her be loved, admired, encouraged, and above all things, heroically protected against scorn and contempt of men, black as well as white."[11] Today's national neglect of black girls is connected to a long-standing and ongoing conversation among black intellectual activists about how representations of black girls served simply to support bourgeois values that linked their comportment, careers, and conduct to class hierarchies. Williams and other black women inserted their voices into this debate by focusing on black girls.

In this chapter, I argue that black activists at the turn of the twentieth century insisted that certain behaviors of black girls were essential components of racial uplift. Literature published at the beginning of the twentieth century sought to manage black girls in the public sphere by correcting behavioral traits, relying on religious beliefs, and promoting education as paths to good citizenship. These restrictions were outlined in conduct manuals and behavioral guides that targeted black girls. Instead of recommending that black girls acquire an education that would prepare them for uplift work or that they pursue their own career paths, conduct books instructed them to acquire an education that would prepare them to care for others. They taught black girls to defer to black male leadership and that they were to follow rules that would prepare them for their future roles as wives and mothers. They inhibited their natures and restricted their ability to exercise free will. These instructions constituted another form of violence toward young black women.

Conduct was an important topic among African American activists at the turn of the century. The language, iconography, and coded messages of decorum in black conduct books taught black girls traditional rules of domesticity as part of an attempt to control representations of African Americans in the public sphere. Conduct books written by African Americans promoted an image of a black community that was cultured, malleable, law abiding, and religious. These texts were produced as black populations were migrating from southern states to northern and western cities during the Great Migration of the early twentieth century. This movement—both the physical movement of people and the movement of southern culture into the North—changed the geography of both interracial and intraracial relations. Within the black community, middle-class northerners became very anxious about representations of the race, and their writings reflect a collision of classes, manners, dialects, and lifestyles. Conduct books offered specific behavioral protocols that reflected the concerns of these black elites.

These conduct books were written mainly to protect African Americans against the systemic, racialized violence in the form of lynching and rape. Historian Rayford Logan calls the post-Reconstruction era (1877–1917) the nadir in U.S. race relations.[12] During this period, conservative white Democratic federal and state governments passed Jim Crow laws that created a system of legal racial segregation in public and private facilities in the South. Restrictions on voter registration and voting methods, such as poll taxes and literacy and residency requirements disenfranchised most blacks and many poor whites. White violence against black men and women in the forms of rape and lynchings intensified racial tension. The mass publication of white supremacist literature, such as Thomas Dixon's illustrated novel *The Leopard's Spots: A Romance of the White Man's Burden 1865–1900* (1902) and its sequel, *The Clansman: An Historical Romance of the Ku Klux Klan* (1905) contributed to harmful racist ideologies by presenting the false idea that black criminality was rampant.

In response to the violence of the period, conduct books encouraged a view that proper conduct, harmonious courtship, and marital relationships could provide blacks access to the social and political circles from which they were largely excluded.[13] To promote these ideals, black writers published manuals that encouraged readers to adopt the genteel characteristics they felt were representative of the cultured, well-mannered "New Negro."[14] The construct of the "New Negro" was generated during the period 1895 to 1925 to counter the image in the popular imagination of the black person as base, uneducated, immoral, and undisciplined—in other words, devoid of all characteristics that separated the "lower" forms of human life from the supposedly more advanced forms.[15] To promote this new image of black humanity, black intellectuals wrote prescriptive manuals that featured exemplary characters who modeled moral integrity and behavioral codes that whites would recognize as the embodiment of bourgeois manners.[16]

One popular instructional manual, *Floyd's Flowers*, offers a good example of the language, iconography, and coded messages of decorum that surrounded black girls at the turn of the twentieth century. *Floyd's Flowers* was written by educator and activist Silas X. Floyd and illustrated by artist and educator John Henry Adams. First published in 1905, Floyd's conduct guide went through other editions, including a new edition in 1925 that was retitled *Charming Stories for Young and Old*.[17] Floyd graduated from Atlanta University in 1891 and was a public school principal in Georgia for five years. By 1902, he had received honorary degrees from Morris Brown College and Atlanta University. His work can be found in several periodicals of the early twentieth century, including *Sunday School Times*, the *New York Independent*, and *Lippincott's Magazine*. *Floyd's Flowers* was widely read at the beginning of the twentieth century. Its compilation of 100 short stories provided black parents with advice about how to raise their children as morally correct citizens and productive members of society.[18] Using girls and boys as protagonists, Floyd prepared readers to face prejudice at an early age and taught protocols of racial etiquette and lessons on moral refinement. Scholars consider *Floyd's Flowers* a "historical rarity" and an early black textbook that taught young black readers "conventional morality and the self-help philosophy." While Floyd taught black children "a glimpse into their rich historical heritage," he deemphasized slavery and "preferred instead to stress the responsibilities of freedom."[19]

Reading Floyd's text correctly means one must consider text and image together to draw out the full meaning. Although the simple line drawings in the book may seem pedestrian, their messages of racial awareness, economic inequality, and a collective sense of well-being were intended to resonate deeply with readers. Henry Louis Gates Jr. and Gene Andrew Jarrett argue that African Americans tried to control the cultural politics of racial representation through artistic forms that were "more accessible and emotive than literary art."[20] In the book's preface, Floyd explains the power of images to elicit emotional responses: "There is something in a picture, even though the subjects be foreign to us, which readily takes hold of our innermost feelings and becomes companionable to the extent that we find ourselves loving that something whatever it is: a man, or a humble dog, or an old homestead, or what not."[21] With their ability to stimulate the imagination, images combine with the written text to shape people's beliefs. Frances Smith Foster argues that collaboration in New Negro texts was a necessary part of representing racial identity.[22] Such teamwork among writers and artists had occurred earlier in the African American literary tradition (for example, in the sketches in Mrs. Amelia A. E. Johnson's *Clarence and Corinne: Or, God's Way* [1890]) and continued into the twentieth century, taking shape in texts related to new black institutions (the Niagara Movement, the National Association of Colored Women) and in the creation of black literary magazines (*Crisis*, *The Brownies' Book*) and black newspapers (*Opportunity*, *New York Age*).

In later editions of the book, photographs replaced sketches. The human subjects in these photographs presented alternatives to the caricatured images of blacks that regularly appeared in the mainstream press and thus accomplished the cultural work that Floyd's text could not achieve on its own. In her work on African American children's literature of the Harlem Renaissance, Katharine Capshaw Smith argues that the image of the black child at the turn of the century embodied the racial tensions of the period.[23] Analyzing this little-known literature adds to the conversation about the canonical texts of this period that we read for messages about racial performance. We no longer have to lean as heavily on novels such as Wallace Thurman's *The Blacker the Berry* (1929), Jessie Fauset's *Plum Bun: Or, a Novel without a Moral* (1929), Nella Larsen's *Quicksand* (1928) and *Passing* (1929), and Claude McKay's *Banana Bottom* (1938) because we can look at other works by African Americans that link black girls to cultural ideals of behavior. The information in *Floyd's Flowers* supplements the knowledge we gain from these texts and helps us see a fuller picture of the African American experience at the turn of the century.

The Discourse of Conduct Books

Floyd's Flowers belongs to a group of texts by black intellectuals who adapted the rhetoric of older conduct books to target a population of black readers. These included W. E. B. Du Bois's *Morals and Manners* (1904) and Booker T. Washington's *Working with Your Hands* (1904). In *Morals and Manners* Du Bois addressed the "Negro problem": "There is without a doubt a deep-seated feeling in the minds of many that the Negro problem is primarily a matter of morals and manners and that the real basis of color prejudice in America is the fact that the Negroes as a race are thotless [*sic*] in manners and altogether quite hopeless in sexual morals, in regard for property rights and reverence for truth."[24] In his essay "Industrial Education for the Negro" (1903), Washington stated that African Americans must "learn the secrets of civilization—to learn that there are a few simple, cardinal principles upon which a race must start its upward course." Adoption of these "secrets of civilization" would cultivate productive citizens.[25] Washington fashioned an image of the well-mannered, business-minded man who transcended plantation stereotypes. This new subject would be urban, industrialized, and well-mannered. He would have knowledge of the world but would remain committed to the black race and to the transformation of America through black culture.

Racial progress based on conduct and outer appearance signified the black elite's awareness that their own destiny was inseparable from that of the masses.[26] As African Americans left the South during the Great Migration, black intellectuals encouraged poor and working-class populations to learn certain behavioral codes in order to gain a sense of personal worth and dignity in a racist society. Floyd thus suggested that black girls who publicly exhibited lower-class behavior negatively affected how the dominant culture perceived blacks and that this had serious consequences for the entire race. These texts emphasized the role of the black elite as instructors of the black reading public.[27] Floyd adapted lessons from these texts to teach his readers how to manage the body through a conservative agenda that promoted propriety, morality, and decorum. Many black conduct books emphasize that effective parenting would give children a life of happiness and encourage their capacities and possibilities. One example is *The Brownies' Book* (1920–1921), edited by W. E. B. Du Bois and Jessie Fauset, which consisted of stories and advice that promoted racial pride and unity among black children.

In *Golden Thoughts on Chastity and Procreation* (1903), African American coauthors Professor and Mrs. John W. Gibson advised young black girls to avoid political debates, speak politely, and apologize readily. They told them to shield themselves from unwanted advances and not tell personal jokes. The Gibsons maintained that because black girls were responsible for the moral, mental, and physical states of coming generations, their training needed to produce superior individuals. Professor and Mrs. Gibson maintained that the guidelines they presented in their book should be practiced in every American home. They argued that "it is important to study the illustrations as well as the content, because combined, they tell their own story; they tell the coming of a new aristocracy, a people powerful in strength, morals, culture, wealth and refinement." The pictures in their book told a story "of the steady growth, development and advancement of the colored American in the teeth of all kinds of obstacles, hindrances and forcible laws."[28] The Gibsons believed that heredity determined a black child's capacities and possibilities even before conception and argued that effective parenting and nurturing could potentially overcome bad hereditary traits and make it possible for the next generation to have happy lives. Their chapter on girlhood emphasized how important it was for girls to have training in both domestic skills and knowledge of art and literature. Like Josie in Du Bois's "Of the Meaning of Progress," the black girls in the Gibsons' text shoulder the responsibility of racial representation for their families and for the race at large.

In *Don't! A Book for Girls* (1891), African American author Robert Charles O'Hara Benjamin instructed black girls to avoid "idleness, flirting, dancing, vindictiveness, backbiting, gossip, and slangy speech."[29] This text is an early example of advice for black girls that paid particular attention to the changes in behavior that should follow puberty, including how to sit, talk, and walk. These directives suggested that some of the problems of the black race were attributable to deficiencies in the morality, decisions, and behavior of black girls. Benjamin wrote *Don't!* because he believed that black women and girls had not received the same "philanthropic largesse" as men after emancipation and were therefore in need of direction and instruction.[30] He advised black women to remain single rather than marry a man whose lack of morals would only create a dysfunctional household.[31] Instead of focusing on the desires and hopes of black girls, Benjamin focused on what he deemed to be more pressing objectives, such as teaching girls which actions were appropriate for their gender, silencing their voices, and discounting their opinions. The very title of the book demands reticence and restriction and excludes free choice.

Floyd's Flowers is part of a body of work that addresses girls' emotional, physical, and sexual health. In 1897, Dr. Mary Wood-Allen wrote *What a Young Girl Ought to Know*, a sex and health-education manual that discussed sex, nutrition, sleep, breathing, health, exercise, menstruation, and creative power.[32] In her role as national superintendent of the Purity Department of the Women's Christian Temperance Union, Dr. Wood-Allen, a white woman, argued that the knowledge her book offered provided a means of protection for girls and women: "Life will be safer for the girl who understands her own nature and reverences her womanhood, who realizes her responsibility toward the race and conducts herself in accordance with that realization."[33] Girls who violated laws of health were hurting not only themselves but also future generations: "Girls of today are the mothers of the future. . . . The physical strength or weakness of each individual girl affects the average health of the nation."[34] Wood-Allen's message implied that immorality was a source of degeneracy. In the chapter, "The Period of Puberty: Passing from Childhood to Womanhood," Wood-Allen urged mothers to teach young daughters about sexual health and morals. Avoiding these subjects, she claimed, would hurt both the child and humanity at large: "Many parents neglect to give their children the information and advice needed at the period of adolescence because, not possessing full knowledge as to the phenomena of such a time and not realizing the dangers of silence, they feel diffident and embarrassed about referring to this subject."[35] Wood-Allen argued that "a mother might feel a natural pang at the thought of disturbing the vestal purity of her girlish imagination," but enjoined mothers to be decisive and strong instead of remaining silent when teaching their daughters.[36]

Turn-of-the-century manuals such as *Morals and Manners*, *Working with Your Hands*, *The Brownies' Book*, *Golden Thoughts on Chastity and Procreation*, *Don't! A Book for Girls*, and *What a Young Girl Ought to Know* were intended to extend the work of advice columns to give black parents and their daughters information that was important for the growth and well-being of young, black girls. Although these books put information on behavioral practices into the hands of black readers, they advocated rigid rules that limited the lives and restricted the feelings of black girls. Silas Floyd drew from these conduct guides and repackaged their messages in a book on racial etiquette. He presented himself as an authoritative voice. The frontispiece of the manual reinforced his upper-class status and his credibility as a teacher of such etiquette by pairing his photograph and one of artist John Henry Adams with stenciled images of their white equivalents: Floyd's image was placed next to an image of a white male scholar surrounded by books, and Adams's photograph was juxtaposed with an image of a white painter (see figure 5.1).

"Dutiful" Girls in *Floyd's Flowers*

In "Thanksgiving at Piney Grove," Floyd provided an example of how black girls could contribute to racial progress through proper education. The story focuses on Grace Wilkins, the daughter of farmer Solomon Wilkins and his wife Amanda. The Wilkinses, like so many black families in the South at the turn of the century, were poor farmers, in this case in Georgia's Black Belt. Amanda must work alongside her husband for the family to survive economically. Floyd does not say so in so many words, but the impression is left that Grace has been shortchanged because she has not had the benefit of a mother who was a full-time homemaker. A sketch of Grace before she attends industrial school emphasizes her unruly hair and vacant facial expression (see figure 5.2). Readers are informed that Grace does not pay much attention to her appearance; her grooming regime consists of giving her face a "lick and a promise" in the morning. She does not own a toothbrush, and she does not pay much attention to her hair. When Grace turns fourteen, "an uneducated colored preacher" advised the Wilkinses to send Grace to "one of the normal and industrial institutes for the training of black boys and girls of the South." This institute is a thinly veiled reference to Tuskegee Institute. Grace later tells her parents about "the great school and . . . the great man at the head of it."[37] They reluctantly agree and send her to the industrial school for a term of eight months. When Grace returns home to spend the summer with her parents, they immediately notice

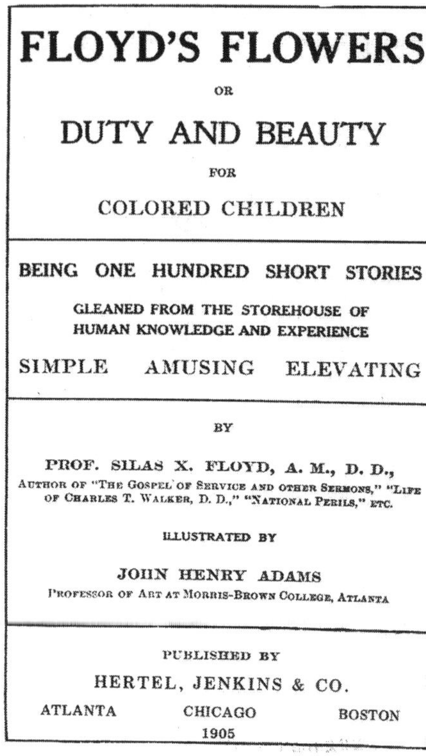

FLOYD'S FLOWERS
OR
DUTY AND BEAUTY
FOR
COLORED CHILDREN

BEING ONE HUNDRED SHORT STORIES
GLEANED FROM THE STOREHOUSE OF
HUMAN KNOWLEDGE AND EXPERIENCE
SIMPLE AMUSING ELEVATING

BY
PROF. SILAS X. FLOYD, A. M., D. D.,
AUTHOR OF "THE GOSPEL OF SERVICE AND OTHER SERMONS," "LIFE OF CHARLES T. WALKER, D. D.," "NATIONAL PERILS," ETC.

ILLUSTRATED BY
JOHN HENRY ADAMS
PROFESSOR OF ART AT MORRIS-BROWN COLLEGE, ATLANTA

PUBLISHED BY
HERTEL, JENKINS & CO.
ATLANTA CHICAGO BOSTON
1905

FIGURE 5. 1. Frontispiece and title page of Floyd, *Floyd's Flowers*.

FIGURE 5. 2. Grace before going to school. Floyd, *Floyd's Flowers*.

a new hygiene routine that Floyd describes in detail. She "dressed differently and talked differently." She brushes her teeth twice a day with a toothbrush, an item that is new to the household.[38] She is careful to "keep her hair well combed every day." She even moves differently. Her mother, speaking in confidence to her husband shortly after Grace's return, says "Dat gal's sho got a new walk on her!"[39] Grace's parents repeatedly note that her newly acquired rituals for hair care, dress, and hygiene are habits she "had never had before." Thus, Grace's behavior is not something she has learned from her parents.

Grace's new practices make "a deep impression upon Solomon and his wife," and they decide to "work hard and stint themselves in order that they might keep her there until she finished the normal course." Grace's parents will sacrifice so she can have a normal school education that will prepare her for a career as a teacher.[40] The narrative emphasized Grace's physical transformation from an unruly girl into a "Grace-ful" woman. Her toothbrush, combed hair, and washed face become markers of cultivation. Her education at the industrial school transforms her into a civilized young woman. Grace's transformation in this story critiques the negative influence that race, inheritance, and environment could have on the physical and psychological development of the black race if no intervention was made.[41] Floyd teaches readers that new behaviors are neither innate nor inherited; they can be learned, and anyone can learn them.[42]

Through Grace's story, Floyd contrasted his interpretation of the "Old Negro" (Grace's parents) with the "New Negro" in the form of the cultured and educated young woman Grace becomes. This contrast conveys a gap in class and between the generations that his lessons were intended to reduce; Floyd's story suggested that Grace's transformation would also reform her parents. Grace's parents "join[ed] in heartily in the movement" and helped Grace build her own school when she returned to Piney Grove as a teacher.[43] Like many black intellectuals, Floyd was "deeply invested in the enterprise of building black national identity through literary constructions of childhood, suggesting that the child who reads the texts has a duty to reform backward parents."[44] Floyd's story argued implicitly that when one (young female) individual changed from an old way of life to a new one, that change would have a ripple effect that would elevate the race. The transformation of one black girl benefited not just herself and her parents but her entire community and beyond; readers learn that "the Piney Grove Academy [Grace's school] soon became the model school for the surrounding counties."

The image of Grace at graduation embodies what Floyd presented as successful, self-governing womanhood (see figure 5.3). Adams's illustration depicts a neat and well-groomed Grace in a full skirt and crisp blouse. Her expression is carefully neutral. According to Katharine Capshaw Smith, Grace's lack of pronounced facial expression, a characteristic that she maintains from childhood

FIGURE 5.3. Grace's graduation. Floyd, *Floyd's Flowers*.

to adulthood in Adams's drawings, suggests that "restraint and self-control become primary political tools. Floyd is deeply concerned with adopting a mask to hide emotional displays."[45] Grace's dispassionate face during her girlhood and at graduation suggests her life has little room for play, pleasure, or enjoyment.

Floyd presented the new Grace as the embodiment of the ideal female New Negro. After Grace opens her Piney Grove Academy for the black children of her community, she holds a Thanksgiving Day ceremony in which she tells the audience about Frederick Douglass, Booker T. Washington, and Paul Laurence Dunbar. At the end of the ceremony, the town's pastor announces that his son intends to marry Grace, whom he views as "one of the best women in the world."[46] He invites the townspeople to attend the ceremony, which he performs that same day. Floyd positions Grace as the politically aware intellectual center of her community *and* as a woman who can fulfill the domestic role of a wife.

Grace's story begins with change and ends with marriage. This trajectory suggests that marriage, rather than her achievements, is Grace's ultimate reward for her education and cultivation. Although Grace portrays all the attributes of a woman qualified to educate and mobilize her race as head of her own school, she will teach texts written by men, maintain a gendered role as wife, and fulfill marital obligations. The image of Grace at graduation looks staged and constrained. Her form appears lifeless, inhibited, and demure. She has graduated into a physical presentation that conveys that she has learned to control herself, her movements, and her manner. She knows not to look directly at the artist. She has learned the physical social mores that were assigned to her gender. This representation intimates that her future, too, will amount to a life of prescriptions. In his 1907 essay, "Rough Sketches: A Study of the Features of the New Negro Woman," artist John Henry Adams described the model black woman as "an admirer of Fine Art, a performer on the violin and the piano, a sweet singer, a writer mostly given to essays, a lover of good books, and a home making girl."[47] Adams's sketch presented a version of Grace as a young woman who had made a transformation from an uncultured girl to the ideal woman his article described. Young women who made the transition to become members of the new black aristocracy were expected to be educated and cultivated and to be efficient homemakers.

In "Industrial Education for the Negro" (1903), Booker T. Washington joined Floyd in emphasizing black girls' domestic education and hygiene over formal education:

> I have gone through the South, and into the homes of the people of my race, and have found women who could converse intelligently on abstruse subjects, and yet could not tell how to improve the condition of the poorly cooked and still more poorly served bread and meat which they and their families were eating three times a day. It is discouraging to find a girl who can tell you the geographical location of any country on the globe and who does not know where to place the dishes upon a common dinner table. It is discouraging to find a woman who knows much about theoretical chemistry, and who cannot properly wash and iron a shirt. . . . Our knowledge must be harnessed to the things of real life.[48]

Washington further highlighted the relationship between girls' domestic education and self-governance and leadership in *Working with the Hands* (1904), his sequel to *Up from Slavery* (1901). In this manual, Washington wrote about what kind of education girls should have. The book included photographs of girls sewing and doing other industrial activities that they had learned at Tuskegee Institute. Claiming that "the hands, the head, and the heart" must work together, Washington outlined his solution for educating black girls in the South:

> These girls, now more than fifty in number, are taught simple lessons, receive short practical talks on behavior at home, on the streets and elsewhere. We also have a small library for them, and each one is allowed to draw the books she wants, to keep two weeks or longer. We also have picture books on the table for the younger children and pictures for the walls of the room. A friend gives two hours of her time on Saturday to these children, and it delights one's heart to see the improvement in them in all directions, especially in their quiet and becoming conduct on the streets.[49]

Washington advocates both training in domestic skills and basic education. However, despite his mention of classes and reading, Washington seemed more focused on girls' improved conduct in public than on their intellectual development.

Floyd emphasized black girls' domestic roles and their contribution to the collective well-being of the black race in other stories. "Mary and Her Dolls," for instance, illustrates how Mary's love for her black dolls and her budding awareness of inequality could be channeled into a lesson about her future role. The story opens with a description of how dolls and other toys are an important part of black children's upbringing:

> Was there ever a time when little boys and girls, especially little girls, did not love dolls and did not have something of that nature to play with? It is not only amusing, it is inspiring to see the little children making merry with their dolls and their toy animals and their little express wagons and their wooden guns and their toy steam engines and their whistles and their balloons . . . and a hundred and one other things.[50]

While Floyd mentions a number of playthings for children, dolls are the focal point of the story. Mary's father, Dr. Smithson, asks Mary to give one of her five dolls to a less fortunate girl (see figure 5.4). Since her father is clearly a member of the black middle class, Mary's refinement and awareness can be attributed to his influence. However, instead of parting with one of her precious dolls, Mary decides to use her own money, with which she had intended to purchase "a little iron bank," to buy a doll for the less fortunate girl.[51]

Mary's independent spirit in managing her own money represents a modern outlook that conveys a mature, if not maternal, way of thinking: "She was glad that her papa had understood how she loved her dolls and glad to find that none of her beloved children was missing."[52] The story of Mary and her dolls illustrates how independent spirits were channeled toward the domestic, dutiful role that was expected of women. Like Grace's mother, whose role is peripheral,

FIGURE 5.4. Mary and her dolls. Floyd, *Floyd's Flowers*.

Mary's mother is never given any attention in the story. In Adams's illustration, Mary seems to replace her mother. She appears older than her suggested age and maintains the posture of a mother as she gazes at her dolls with a look of deep concern. Floyd's stories work alongside, and sometimes seem to be attempting to replace, the tutelage a biological mother might give her children. Mary found a way to keep her collection of dolls and still do what was expected of her. Although Floyd's messages to black girls were prescriptive, girls who knew how to read his stories carefully could draw the lesson that it was possible to fulfill cultural expectations without sacrificing everything that was important to them. Mary offers a counterpart to Du Bois's Josie, whose self-sacrifice was her destruction.

Textual images of black girls playing with dolls appear throughout *Floyd's Flowers* and suggest that the acquisition of black dolls fostered racial pride and increased black consciousness. Michelle Mitchell documents how the National Baptist Convention recognized the need to make "colored dolls" more accessible to black consumers and to promote the idea that dolls helped shape black children's self-esteem. In 1908, the convention launched several such initiatives.

Baptist women organized Negro Dolls Clubs in 1914 and hosted "doll bazaars" at Christmas, and black Baptists formed the National Negro Doll Company. Mitchell's recounting of the history of black dolls explores how "race dolls were powerful toys," as black reformers "considered the placement of certain kinds of material culture within domestic spaces to be a symbol of collective progress."[53] However, although Floyd discusses "the power in dolls," he specifically emphasizes the dolls' connection to "domestic life, skills, and the acquisition of maternal feeling."[54] Thus, Mary's dutifulness was designed to inspire young readers. Her plain dress and demeanor are as unpretentious and straightforward as she is herself. Her determination to keep and care for her dolls as she would her own children reinforces ideals of domesticity. Mary's perfect fulfillment of the gendered role of caring for her dolls in preparation for motherhood conveys Floyd's message about the need to prepare girls to become women who could maintain the safety and cohesiveness of their families.[55]

"True Little Ladies": Floyd's Beautiful Girls

In *Floyd's Flowers*, black girls were not just dutiful community members who learned about the domestic sphere; they also defined female beauty. The ideals of beauty Floyd presented involved both aspects of conduct, such as manner and mood, and aspects of outward presentation, such as dress. They encompassed all aspects of respectability and informed black girls on how to conform to social codes of behavior through their appearance and their interactions with others. According to Floyd, black girls functioned as expressions of beauty and were responsible for representing the race when they appeared in public places.

In "Directions for Little Ladies," Floyd offered specific instructions about behavior that dictated how a black girl should act at home, in public spaces, and in everyday life. "A true little lady" will always say, "'I thank you' whenever someone assists her"; she is "never loud and boisterous on the streets, in public places, or at home"; she is clean and well-dressed because "every true little lady hates dirt"; "she will not tattle or seek to gossip; she loves Sunday school and church; she loves her mother and will help her mother in any way; finally, a true little lady will be a Christian." These guidelines leave little space for girls to develop their imaginations or participate in unguarded or playful activity. The rhetoric reveals how training black girls' bodies involved modifying their thoughts.[56] The instructions directed black girls toward a conventional and formulaic way of thinking and behaving. Even directions about how to behave outwardly are circumscribed: the "little lady" will "love . . . Sunday school and . . . church" and "be a Christian." The ideals Floyd presented were intended to have the effect of replacing youthful behavior, natural curiosity, and high spirits.

THE "DON'T-CARE" GIRL.

FIGURE 5.5. The 1922 Don't-Care Girl. Floyd, *Floyd's Flowers.*

In stories that focus on the indecorous behavior of black girls, such as in "The Loud Girl" and "The Don't-Care Girl," Floyd warns that behaviors such as yelling and not attending to personal appearance diminish "beautiful traits." Floyd writes that the "don't-care girl" (see figure 5.5) and the "loud girl" (see figure 5.6) are "two things of which we have seen enough of in this world" and that children who exhibit such behavior are "things; they are hardly worth the dignity of being called human beings."[57] The "loud girl" is "always an object of pity and she is a sorry object for her own contemplation." The "don't-care girl" is "the worst girl in all this world" because she "doesn't care what people think or say about her conduct; the girl goes to every 'hop,' to every party," and she "stays out late at night with the boys."[58]

Floyd warned black girls that indecorous behavior broke a series of laws—conventional, parental, and divine. Floyd told them that taking delight in unruly

FIGURE 5.6. The loud girl. Floyd, *Floyd's Flowers.*

behavior was shortsighted: "It is a foolish thing to take delight in trying to shock people by your boisterous ad unladylike and unbecoming conduct. Every really wise and nice girl does care a good deal for the good opinion of others, and particularly for the good opinion of persons older than she is. She recognizes the fact that the laws of conventionality and of good society are based upon what is right and what is proper, and that no girl can with propriety set them at naught."[59] Even worse was the impact irreverence had on parents: "Some girls go so far as to say they "don't-care" what their own fathers and mothers think. The wild girl who says this is setting at defiance not only the human parental law, but also the law of god, which plainly commands children to obey their parents."[60]

Floyd further suggested that by behaving like ladies, black girls could eliminate the tarnished reputation of black women, whom whites had stereotyped as impure, immodest, and overly sexual. Floyd wrote, "Every day such flippant girls are treading on dangerous ground, and someday, unless a merciful God prevents it, she will come to open disgrace and die and go to torment."[61] Black females of all ages were very vulnerable to rape and sexual abuse at the hands of white men, and sexual violence was a subtext that every black person would have been aware of from a very young age. One element of Floyd's concern may have been that brash behavior would put girls at risk. His stories emphasized how "Loud Girls" and "Don't-Care Girls" would be perceived as not caring about the value and safety of their own bodies; this type of behavior may have made them more vulnerable to assault. Girls who read these two stories carefully might have concluded that ignoring social rules was a tacit message that they would be willing participants in any violence inflicted on their bodies.

An illustration in "The Loud Girl" depicts two black girls exhibiting what Floyd defined as immodest behavior. Their gestures—one clenches her hands into fists, while the other raises her hands in the air as if ready to clap—suggest aggression. Widespread legs, open gaping mouths, boyish hats, and rumpled clothes depart from the feminine ideal of the period. In these stories, the stakes for the black community increase when black girls engage in rowdy behavior and wear unfeminine dress in public places. "The Loud Girl" describes three black girls who ride in a streetcar and make a ruckus while eating chocolates, talking and laughing loudly, and throwing candy at one another. Passengers who enter the streetcar stumble over the girls' outstretched legs. The behavior and dress of the three girls suggest a highly charged, unruly performance that contributes to the girls' diminished moral character:

> They all wore boys' hats. One wore a vivid red jacket with brass buttons, and another had on a brass belt. A third one had on a most conspicuous plaid skirt. This third one had a box of bonbons, and when the three were seated she opened the box and offered it to her companions, saying as she did so, in a voice loud enough and shrill enough to be heard in every part of the car: "it's my treat; have some, chums!"[62]

Floyd critiqued the black girls' inability or unwillingness to observe how their behavior in public could affect others' perceptions of them. The occurrence of this behavior on a streetcar, a public space in an urban setting, suggests that the girls would attract the kind of attention that would lead to assumptions about their sexual mores. Their disregard for the public space of the streetcar and for propriety adds to a sense of sexual degeneracy that Floyd tacitly condemned. He read the brass on their clothing as fake gold, a vulgarity and showiness that should not be displayed in public. When read against the grain, however, this story conveys alternative messages. The girls' brass buttons and brass belt serve several functions. Brass is a protective, defensive shield that anticipates danger and guards the girls against unwanted solicitation or threats of violence, suggesting that the girls, although rambunctious, have a resiliency that is durable and flexible like the metal they wear. The girls demonstrate boldness, ammunition that reinforces an aggressive, *offensive* stance against danger.

Floyd's streetcar scene echoes a similar scene in Pauline Hopkins's novel, *Contending Forces: A Romance Illustrative of Negro Life North and South* (1901). In a chapter in which black people from the community gather in a parlor to discuss "questions of the day and their effects upon the colored people," Mrs. Davis relates an incident when she chastised a group of black girls who were acting unruly on a streetcar:

> Some o' them was a-standin' up in thet car, an' every once in a while I noticed thet a passenger'd squirm as ef suthin' had hit him. Finally I got so mad I jes' couldn't see along with sech antics from them critters a-disgracin' theirselves and the whole o' the res' o' the colored population, an' I jes' elbowed myself into thet crowd o' young jades—what's thet (as Will murmured something under his breath), was they gals? Yas, they was; young *jades*, every one o' them! Now what do yer think they was a-doin? . . . *They was a-trampin' onto the feet of every white man an' woman in thet car to show the white folks how free they was!* I jes' took my ambriller an' knocked it into two or three o' them thet I knowed, an' tol' em' I'd tell ther mothers.[63]

Although Mrs. Davis is a respectable member of the black community, Hopkins gives her dialect speech to signal respect for someone from a lower class who has a sense of manners and decorum. Her concern is not only that the black girls act so badly that their behavior affects "the whole o' the res' o' the colored population"; she is also dismayed because they demonstrate bravado and "show white folks how free they was." Mrs. Davis's choice of the word *free* is sarcastic and suggests a disjuncture between freedom and bad behavior. Mrs. Davis disapproves of the fact that black girls are expressing their unrestricted movements and actions in the form of poor decorum. This streetcar scene expresses different understanding of freedom between a younger generation and an older generation. The older generation might abide by severe restrictions on bodily behavior that black people imposed on themselves in an attempt to avoid violence. This code necessitated strict standards of behavior lest the community be judged and condemned by the behavior of one or a few. However, these loud girls have not known slavery and thus have a different understanding of freedom. In one sense, the bad behaviors black girls exhibit in these turn-of-the-century sources are evidence of progress. These girls are having normal adolescent experiences of testing limits and trying out unsanctioned behaviors, and they are participating in these actions outside the home.

The standards of behavior Floyd presented in his writings were, in part, an attempt to protect girls from the rampant dangers of the Jim Crow era. However, some African American women in this period felt it was necessary to speak loudly and act in unexpected ways in order to advance racial progress. Activist Ida B. Wells wrote inflammatory articles and spoke publicly and openly about violence toward African Americans. Her actions demonstrated an unwillingness to stay silent even though she was constantly in danger. However, while she spoke clearly and directly against injustice, she did not behave in a way that would have distracted from her message. The irony of the message of "The Loud Girl" is that the attributes that Floyd assigns to the "loud girl" reveal the kind of black girl who could channel her passion and become a woman who is self-assured and confident. Such a young woman would need the capacity to speak boldly and "shoot her head way up in the air" when she addressed others. The characteristics of the "loud girl"—who is loud, bold, and defiant—are those of someone who is strong-willed, independent, and outspoken. Some of the most prominent African American women writers created protagonists who were the embodiment of Floyd's "loud girl." One example is Frado in *Our Nig* (1859), who acts "loud" when she refuses beatings from Mrs. Bellmont and blame for things she did not do. Her "loudness" is a form of self-protection despite the punishment she often receives for asserting herself. Yet the politics of respectability, as Evelyn Higginbotham suggests, attached shame to such behaviors because of fear that they would fuel derogatory racial stereotypes and that they would make black women even more vulnerable to rape by white men.[64] Black women were exhibiting the types of behaviors that would send messages to the public that they were present and their lives mattered. This kind of message necessitated using their bodies in ways that ignored Floyd's directions. Activist women such as Ida B. Wells had mastered loudness; they knew how to use their voices intentionally and effectively.

The black boy characters in *Floyd's Flowers* conveyed expectations for boys. While Floyd said that unruly black girls were "the worst girl[s] in all this world,"[65] he encouraged unruly boys to behave better because they were "made for better things."[66] In "The Rowdy Boy," "A Plucky Boy," "Directions for Little Gentlemen," and "The Bad Boy—How to Help Him," Floyd described unacceptable behavior for young black men. He asserted that it was easy to identify a "rowdy boy" anywhere in society because "there are certain marks or appearances which he carries about with him and which are never absent," such as smoking, poor dress, lateness, and criminal behavior.[67] "The Rowdy Boy" gave boys the encouraging message that they were "made for better things."[68] It suggests that modifying bad behavior would remove an obstacle to a bright future. The implication was that unlike girls, whom Floyd expected to remain in the home, boys would leave their homes and make an impact on the world.

Floyd portrayed model black girls as "modest and quiet."[69] He advised them not to speak much. His model black girl was good-natured, delicate, and gentle. The body of the girl in Figure 5.7 is calm and self-contained rather than out of control, with arms and legs that flail. Her stature is tall and upright. In her hand she holds a closed fan, which suggests modesty and propriety and mimics her body, which appears closed, drawn in, and turned away from any confrontational stance. Her neatly coiffed hair and long full skirt are properly maintained—she does not need to wear a cap, and her clothes are wrinkle-free and neat. The black girl's hair is partially pinned up, a style that Shawn Michelle Smith argues is "a sign of modesty" among middle-class women at the turn of the twentieth century.[70] The black girl in the image exhibits true womanhood, guided by a quiet demeanor and crisp outward appearance. The sketch illustrates that Floyd's proper model of black girlhood focuses less on the improvement of intellect than on the development of moral character and outward appearance.

The good-natured black girls in *Floyd's Flowers* appear to be lighter in skin tone, in contrast to the "loud girl," whose skin is noticeably darker. The illustrations in Floyd's text thus seem to suggest that character is contingent on skin tone. The hair is also an indicator of character. The model black girl's hair is long and carefully coifed, in contrast to the short, coarse, and curly hair of the "loud girls." Stereotypical racial characteristics thus make claims about character: darker-skinned black girls are loud, while lighter-skinned black girls are "modest and quiet." This differentiation based on skin color suggests that Floyd aligned his text with the white supremacist discourse that equated dignity with white or lighter-hued skin. His text encouraged an idea of uplift that centered class differences on color and superficial exterior characteristics such as dress and hair, regardless of an individual's merit or intellect. This mindset points to an intraracial division along class and color lines that created further divisions among African Americans and decreased a sense of community.

In "Keeping School," the combination of text and images teaches young black readers the importance of education at an early age. In the story, Tootsie, a black girl who is unable to read, learns to read by looking at the pictures in a Christmas book and connecting the pictures with the words in the text. Floyd states that "every boy and girl in America ought to go to school" because school is one of "the best institutions" and is "connected with the life of our nation."[71] Tootsie, who is too young to attend school, studies despite her young age by incorporating reading into her everyday play. She prepares herself by creating her own school at home through play and imagination: "There was no schoolhouse, and no teachers; nothing only just little Tootsie; not even her dolls; just simply Tootsie sitting all alone on the couch near the window."[72] Tootsie imagines a large school that has sixty pupils. She looks through Christmas books, attempting to connect words with images. Tootsie eventually teaches herself to read by asking family members to help her with unfamiliar words:

> [She] would ask mama and grandma, or whoever happened to be nearest, what the words of the picture-story were. She would then say the words of the story over to herself, and look at the picture. Next day she would read over the words

FIGURE 5.7. Modest and quiet. Floyd, *Floyd's Flowers.*

> of the same story as far as she could remember them, and when she came to a word that she did not know, up she would jump and go ask someone what it was.[73]

Floyd's text thus teaches young readers like Tootsie how to weave educational pursuits such as reading into their recreational activities and to keep school foremost in their minds even when at play: "Maybe one reason why Tootsie learned so fast was because her school is just like play to her and not like work. Of course, it is easier to play than it is to work. But could you think of any better thing to play than to play keeping school? Why not try it?"[74] In language that is

FIGURE 5.8. Keeping school. Floyd, *Floyd's Flowers*.

simplified to accommodate his youngest readers, Floyd conveyed the idea that children's play should be purposeful (see figure 5.8).

Floyd demonstrated how Tootsie was connected to and protected by her black family. The reference to Tootsie's "mama" and "grandma" emphasizes generational literacy and recognizes Tootsie's lineage in a black family and in a household that is supportive of her educational pursuits. That Tootsie was able to ask not only her mama and grandma for help but also "whoever is nearest" suggests that she, like Annette in *Trial and Triumph*, is a part of a community of tutors invested in her learning.

Black Girls in the 1922 Edition of *Floyd's Flowers*

Later editions of Floyd's text addressed the continuing unease generated by increasing numbers of black migrants in urban settings. In the 1922 edition of *Floyd's Flowers*, Adams's sketches were replaced by photographs. The composition of the photographs were identical to the composition of the images in the sketches, but because they were photographs of living people, they intensified Floyd's messages about behavior, decorum, and appearance. The photographs were more realistic, more true to life, more aligned with the modern era and its technologies. They served to draw a wider range of readers into the text by offering qualities of drama and seriousness as well as farce and silliness. In her work on photographic images of the New Negro, Deborah Willis notes that African American artists used photography to refute and critique stereotypes and caricatures. She argues that photographs "transformed the visual representation of black America, both in the public realm of popular culture and within the intimacy of the family album."[75] Perhaps photographs combated popular racist images more powerfully because photographs resonated with black people as treasured items that were preserved in black family albums. They offered a sharper portrayal of real life that had the capacity to capture a sentiment. Photographs that visually realized the dreams and desires of the black community and captured a spirit of transformation contrasted sharply with mass-produced images in the mainstream publishing world that reinforced widely held stereotypes that sought to diminish the humanity of African Americans.[76] Maurice O. Wallace and Shawn Michelle Smith note that "African American intellectuals, authors, orators, and activists understood, responded to, and utilized photography to create new spaces for self and community in the nineteenth and early twentieth centuries. . . . [T]hey put photographs to striking use in their varied quests for social and political justice, plumbing and expanding the political power of the photograph."[77]

Extensive photographic records of African Americans at the beginning of the twentieth century represented them in dignified attire and poses to reinforce a model of uplift that promoted aspects of refinement such as cleanliness, leisure, and literacy. These portraits captured a stylized elegance that sought to portray ideals of race advancement. In the 1922 publication of "Thanksgiving at Piney Grove," for example, the photographic images of Grace's transformation enabled readers to observe that although she was from the "black belt of Georgia" and her parents spoke in dialect, Grace could change her lifestyle and mannerisms through education and could become a dignified woman. The photographs offered readers representations of an actual woman with whom they might relate. Floyd felt it was important for readers to clearly observe the meaning of her change. Grace's "before" image is a headshot that reveals only her lopsided grin and unruly hair, thus exaggerating the sense of absurdity associated with her unawareness of hygienic practices (see figure 5.9). Her "after" image, in contrast, reveals a full-body portrait of Grace after she graduates (see figure 5.10). She stands posed and stiff in a long skirt and blouse. Her hair is styled and her expression hints at a slight smile. Turned to her side and away from the camera, she holds onto a chair in an awkward stance. The image of Grace in a full dress and coiffed hair, yet holding onto a chair for support, suggests that she is refined and dependent, educated and submissive.

As Grace's transformation indicates, Floyd's text aimed to change the public image of African Americans by reinforcing the need for a return to domestic

FIGURE 5.9. Grace before going to school. 1922 edition.

ideals. His text and Adams's images became a parental presence that replaced the black mother as the nurturing figure. Instead of the black mother, black male figures—Floyd, Adams, the minister in Grace's story, and Dr. Smithson (Mary's father)—become authoritative figures who guide black girls into a domesticated role. In contrast, the black mother appears as a backward and undeveloped figure; in Grace's story, she speaks in dialect and represents the "Old Negro," and she is altogether absent in the stories of Mary and Tootsie. Floyd's text thus conveys the notion that the middle-class black male will assume the role of uplift for the black race while black women and girls support him by maintaining the domestic sphere. He presents black girl figures who might have enjoyed imagination and play in their youth, as Tootsie does with her Christmas books and as Mary does with her dolls, but whose youth and imaginations are channeled into domestic roles and standards of behavior that require them to be modest, matronly, and quiet.

GRACE'S GRADUATION.

FIGURE 5.10. Grace's graduation. 1922 Edition.

Conclusion

Even as his cultural narrative showed how codes of behavior reflected racial achievement and advancement for African Americans, Floyd reveals the rigid representations of femininity that black activists of the era relied on to resolve social and political crises of racial representation during the New Negro era. By the turn of the century, it had become clear that the optimism Frances E. W. Harper and Gertrude Bustill Mossell had expressed in the 1880s was no longer accurate. Both writers had advised black girls to carefully monitor their outward appearance and behavior so they could take advantage of new opportunities. They believed that acting correctly would open doors for all blacks, and for black girls in particular. Harper also acknowledged the existence of the rich interior world of black girls and encouraged them to develop and harness their interiority as a tool for moving forward. She believed that whites could be reasoned with and convinced of the merits of the social justice claims of blacks, particularly regarding work. However, the rapid increase of industrialization had not brought new job opportunities to black workers, young black men and women did not have equal access to education, many blacks with college degrees found it difficult to get work in their chosen profession, the civil and political rights of black citizens were contracting instead of expanding, and there was very little of the interracial dialogue that Harper had modeled in *Trial and Triumph*.

After the flourishing of new work by African American women writers in the post–Civil War decades, few works of fiction by African American women were published during the decades surrounding the turn of the twentieth century. Instead, black women published nonfiction and plays that reflected the tumultuous, violent period. Ida B. Wells published her 100-page pamphlet the *Red Record* in 1895. The previous year, in 1894, 197 black persons had been put to death by mobs who gave the victims no opportunity to make a lawful defense. Wells-Barnett noted that southern white men did not consider that blacks "had any right which a white man was bound to respect."[78] The social context of racial violence shaped the literary productions of black women writers at the turn of the twentieth century.

African American women playwrights wrote and staged antilynching plays in the early decades of the twentieth century that revealed how black households thrived and survived even with the loss of husbands, sons, and fathers. Koritha Mitchell explores how these antilynching plays "helped their communities to live, even while lynching remained a reality that would not magically disappear."[79] The plays "served as mechanisms through which African Americans survived the height of mob violence—and its photographic representation—still believing in their right to citizenship."[80] These plays include Alice Weld Grimké's

Rachel (1914) and Alice Dunbar-Nelson's *Mine Eyes Have Seen*, published in 1918.[81] Mary P. Burrill, another African American woman playwright, "was one of the earliest playwrights to dramatize African Americans taking up arms against whites for the injustices of lynching."[82] Her first play, *Aftermath*, was published in the *Liberator* in April 1919.[83] Georgia Douglass Johnson, described as "the most prolific" black woman playwright, wrote *A Sunday Morning in the South* (1925), *Blue Blood* (1926), *Safe* (1929), and *Blue-Eyed Black Boy* (c. 1930). Myrtle Smith Livingston wrote *For Unborn Children* (1926), and there were plays by black men, such as G. D. Lipscomb's *Frances* (1925) and Joseph Mitchell's *Son-Boy* (1928).[84] African American women playwrights "refused to feature physical violence; their scripts spotlight instead the black home and the impact that the mob's outdoor activities have on the family. Indeed, the dramas most commonly depict exactly what mainstream discourse denied existed: loving black homes."[85]

These literary productions are the lens through which we must understand books such as *Floyd's Flowers*. Within the context of a dangerously violent period for African Americans, Floyd was attempting to teach black children behaviors and strategies that would increase their chances of survival. It may be the case that the racial hatred expressed in Jim Crow laws, lynching, and other forms of violence against blacks shocked black communities back into the focus on exteriority and conduct that we see in Floyd's writings. While Harper urged young black women to go deeper than outward physical appearance and focus on developing the internal resources of intellect and interiority in the 1880s, Floyd returned early-twentieth-century readers to the concept that intellect and morality must manifest visibly on the black body. He presented homilies for children that emphasized that dressing well and behaving correctly were essential behaviors for black children. E. Azalia Hackly continued this emphasis on propriety of outward appearance in her 1916 conduct manual *The Colored Girl Beautiful*: "The body is like a camera, it tells the truth; it is the outward sign of inward grace, or vice-versa."[86]

Perhaps the best way to assess how the changes in social context affected literature about black girls at the turn of the twentieth century is to analyze Gertrude Bustill Mossell's ten-page short story *Little Dansie's One Day at Sabbath School,* which she published as a chapbook in 1902.[87] Little Dansie, "our little heroine," as Mossell the narrator calls her, is the child of a worker on a "great cotton plantation" near Atlanta.[88] The story is not clearly anchored in time; the events could have happened anytime from the 1870s to 1902. We learn that Dansie's parents "tried to give her the advantages they had not enjoyed in their youth," although their poverty limits what they can offer.[89] Dansie has little education; she is worried that the other children will laugh at her ignorance when she attends her church's Sabbath school for the first time. Her parents have little money to spend on their cherished child; her "poor clothes" are another thing she worries about as she prepares to enter the Sabbath school.[90] Providing transportation to this church, which is far from their home, appears to be the one advantage they can offer.

The school Dansie attends is a Sunday school, and the lessons taught there are centered on teachings from the Bible. The Sunday that Dansie attends, a visiting minister, a "gentleman from a distance," comes to the classroom to speak to the children. His "kind voice" charms Dansie, especially because "the words he had chosen were so simple that she had understood them all." He chooses two texts from the Bible: "Greater love hath no man than this, that a man lay down his life for his friends," and "Peradventure for a good man some would even dare to die."[91]

After the lesson, the visiting minister takes Dansie's hand and accompanies her home, where he visits with her father. Dansie overhears the two men talking and learns that the minister, Mr. Ellsworth, "her new friend," is going deaf: "Although his voice still charmed the listener he was himself fast becoming powerless to hear the sweet music of loved voices around him."[92]

In the next scene of the story, the Sabbath school pupils are boarding a train for an annual "woods meeting," a revival meeting. We learn that "teachers and pupils, parents and friends, were on hand," but there are so many children that it is difficult to supervise them as they board the train. Older children are responsible to watch over the younger ones such as Dansie, "but so eager were the little ones that this proved quite a task."[93] Dansie is almost beside herself with excitement about the trip, but she focuses her attention on Mr. Ellsworth, the new friend who has won her heart. She sees him cross the tracks to talk to someone on the platform and then turn around and walk toward the train to board it. Because of his hearing loss, he does not hear a train bearing down on him from further down the tracks. We learn that "Dansie sees it first of all." She rushes from her seat on the train and takes his hand, pulling him off the track. Too late her adult friend sees the danger and "leaps aside, dragging Dansie with him."[94] But her dress gets caught on the wheel of the train and Dansie is gravely injured.

She is taken to the Children's Hospital Dispensary, where Mr. Ellsworth and "the faithful doctor" sit by her side all night. They know she will not survive, but Mr. Ellsworth hopes that she will regain consciousness so he can offer some word of comfort to her. She awakens long enough to repeat one of the verses from the lesson he taught the Sabbath school class: "Peradventure for a good man some would even dare to die."[95] These are her last words; within a day she is gone. Mr. Ellsworth speaks at her funeral, which is described in great detail. He speaks to the congregation of "how truly [Little Dansie] had learned the lesson of self-sacrifice; how she had learned the lesson of giving all for others, even her own beautiful life."[96]

Mossell intended this story to be a presentation of the ideal of Christian love. The moral of the story is that Dansie's selfless example of love for others leads "the un-Christian" ones who attend her funeral "to come forward and test the love of this Friend, who had laid down His life for them." As the narrator, Mossell tells us that "the response was overwhelming, and such a revival as was begun then and there was never heard of before in that community."[97] Dansie's death served to revitalize the Christian community on the plantation. Her example of self-sacrifice strengthened the black church in her corner of rural Georgia.

But underneath Mossell's intended message of Christian love and the revitalization of a Christian community are many other messages that were shaped by the harrowing experiences blacks had endured in the North and in the South since the 1890s. To whites, for example, trains were a symbol of the triumph of industrialization and progress. But to southern blacks at the turn of the twentieth century, a train was a painful reminder of segregation, and in this story, it is a threat that bears down inexorably on a male leader of the black community. In addition, emancipation has not brought much material improvement to Dansie's parents; they contend with grinding poverty and cannot afford to buy many things for their child, despite their desire to give her better chances in life than they had as children.

We see black institutions—the Sabbath school, the children's hospital—but they do not seem to be effective vehicles for caring for children. The Sabbath school cannot provide adequate adult supervision when the children go on the annual excursion; if enough adults had been present, Dansie would never have been able to get off the train so impulsively. And the doctor at the children's hospital is powerless to heal Dansie; all he can do is sit in vigil by her bed and wait for her death.

We see male leaders, but they seem to be flawed. The minister who cannot hear perhaps symbolizes male leaders who are not listening to the concerns of women and children. All he can do as a communicator is deliver his message; he cannot hear the responses of others. He is kind and well-meaning, but he does not adequately compensate for his handicap, and this is the reason Dansie encounters danger.

The absent mother is curious. We know she exists, but we know nothing about her. Dansie reads almost like a motherless child, a child who is desperately hungry for the love of an adult. She attaches herself to Mr. Ellsworth almost immediately, and her love for him guides all of her subsequent actions in the story. Most of all, Dansie plays adult roles. Instead of relaxing and enjoying her first train ride, she is hypervigilant and entirely focused on Mr. Ellsworth. She knows of his hearing loss because of an adult conversation she has overheard, so she has knowledge the other children do not have, and she feels responsible to act on that knowledge. When Mr. Ellsworth is in danger, she is the first to see the train approaching. Why didn't other adults at the train station look out for the visiting clergyman? Why did the responsibility fall on the shoulders of a little girl?

The overall picture presented in this story is of a community whose adults are not focused enough on the safety of children. Of course tragedies such as the one that befell Dansie can happen in the blink of an eye even when loving adults are properly vigilant. But this is a story about "our little heroine," and the reader is encouraged to see the events through her eyes and from her perspective. From that standpoint, the story is telling young black girls that they should be willing to sacrifice everything to protect the leaders of their community, the men in their lives. In the context of the lynchings that were taking place throughout the South and even in the North, this concern for the safety and well-being of black men is very understandable. But turning that concern into a type of socialization that forestalls even the future of black girls is disconcerting and difficult to read. It is painful to think of young black girls absorbing a message of self-sacrifice so complete that even death is possible. Unlike the black girls Harriet Wilson, Harriet Jacobs, Maria Stewart, Frances E. W. Harper, and even Mossell herself in the 1880s wrote about, Little Dansie has no opportunity to plan for a better future. She has no opportunity to even think of a future. Her life is cut off, ostensibly for the good of her community. She is the martyr who provides the spark that becomes a powerful religious revival.

It is interesting to read this story backward in time, through the lens of "Theresa—A Haytien Tale," the anonymously written story published in *Freedom's Journal* in 1828 that I discussed in Chapter 1. Both stories feature girl heroines. Both girls take action to benefit their people. Both girls overhear adult conversation and make decisions to act based on that knowledge. Both are praised for their contributions to community welfare. But in a curious way, there is more hope in the 1828 story than there is in the story written seventy-four years later. Theresa has a strong mother who is willing to take on nontraditional roles to protect her daughters. Dansie has two parents, but they are unable to adequately clothe her, she has little education, and her parents cannot protect her when she enters the public world of excursions and trains.

Granted, Theresa, who is older than Dansie, knows what to do with the information she obtains through overhearing adult conversation. She knows that the right thing to do is to take that information to the adult who will know what to do with it. Dansie, in contrast, feels responsible to keep the information she learns to herself, and this partially contributes to her death. If more people had known of Mr. Ellsworth's hearing loss, they might have been more solicitous of his welfare at the train station. Theresa is not interested in self-sacrifice. She is interested in independent action that will move her people forward toward greater freedom. Dansie is almost obsessed with self-sacrifice. Once she hears from the man who charmed her and won her little heart that this is the ideal, she is virtually programmed to follow that script, and her dying words remind the men by her bedside that she has fulfilled her purpose. One has to wonder why Dansie is so vulnerable to such passionate love for a near-stranger. It does not seem like her parents have the time to spend with her to feed her need for love, like the children in *Floyd's Flowers,* whose parents read to them and talk with them about each step of their development. Dansie's parents are present mostly through their absence. Likely the fact that they work on a large plantation is the explanation for that. Clearly they love their daughter and want the best for her. But the post–Civil War agricultural system of the South seems to be taking every resource they have.

Despite the positive message Mossell intended to convey of Christian love and self-sacrifice, the story she wrote—for children—was one of poverty, hardship, early death, flawed adults, and an unsafe public world. In 1902, Mossell's outlook was much more pessimistic than it had been twenty years earlier, when she counseled young women about how to plan and strategize for a happy life. The decades of Jim Crow laws, barriers to employment, discrimination in education, KKK violence, the use of terror to prevent black men from voting or holding public office, rigid control of access to land in the South, and the murders of thousands of black men had taken their toll. It was not that the future looked less bright in 1902 than it had in 1828 or 1880, it was that it was difficult for Mossell to even see a future for young black girls at the turn of the century. In a sad and curious way, there is more hope for a future in the 1828 story of Theresa than there was in the 1902 story of Little Dansie. But in 1902, it was clear that although slavery had ended, oppression had not. There was no longer one clear goal for everyone to focus on, and the future looked very uncertain. It is worth noting that this story was written before the Niagara movement, before the birth of the NAACP, before the Harlem Renaissance. This is a story from the depths of the nadir of race relations in the United States.

But the future that was to come had more promise than Mossell could envision in 1902. The women writers of the Harlem Renaissance were being nurtured and schooled or were beginning their careers as self-supporting professional women in that year. Zora Neale Hurston, who was eleven, was growing up in all-black Eatonville, Florida, where her father was mayor and then the minister of the town's largest church. Angelina Weld Grimké had just completed her education at an integrated normal school and was in her first year of teaching English in Washington, D.C. Nella Larsen, who was also eleven, was attending public school in Chicago and was navigating the black and white worlds that she explored so deeply in her novels. In 1902, Alice Dunbar-Nelson found the resources to leave her husband Paul and begin a new career as a teacher in Wilmington,

Delaware. These and other black women writers delved deep into the world of black female interiority in their writing and contributed significantly to the canon of literature by black women. Although their work went in directions that Frances E. W. Harper, Maria Stewart, and Gertrude Bustill Mossell could not have foreseen and likely would not have approved of, they fulfilled their vision of a world in which black girls could grow up to become women with important things to say.

Epilogue

The Changing Same? Next-Generation Black Girlhood

IN 1966, AMIRI BARAKA, writing as LeRoi Jones, introduced the concept of the *changing same* in the context of his exploration of rhythm and blues and jazz. He argued that while both of these musical forms came from the same African American root, jazz was stuck in a pattern of the changing same. In contrast, rhythm and blues was a more honest expression of lived experience and the desire for freedom. The "new music" began by being free of "the straitjacket of American expression sans blackness."[1] Almost two decades later, Deborah McDowell appropriated the concept of the changing same in her examination of the development of black feminist literature from the 1890s to the 1990s.[2] Both authors argued that powerful forces in U.S. culture have stifled or ignored the development of African American creative expression. As I conclude this study, I find myself thinking about this concept of the changing same. When considering the state of black girlhood in U. S. society, where should the emphasis be—on the potential for change or on an acceptance of the hard reality of the same? In particular, are the obstacles for black girls so deeply rooted in this culture that there is little room for forward movement?

Black Girlhood in the Nineteenth Century creates a language for talking about black girlhood. The images and tropes some nineteenth-century black writers created to describe black girls have had a long staying power. Today, black girls are often misrepresented in the media, often in bewildering ways that attack them. This book offers a theoretical landscape for identifying and naming such attacks and for seeing beyond them to look at what black girls are actually doing, thinking, and dreaming.

Nineteenth-century writers, both male and female, understood that black girls had power. The male newspaper editors of the antebellum period offered static, two-dimensional girls who were obedient and adopted Christian values, or who were (or would be) very sorry that they had not. These were the ideal black girls in the minds of black male activists who would (they hoped) become "ideal" women who were concerned largely with running households and raising children. The ministers of the late nineteenth century were more overt in their attempts to control black girls and offered examples of "bad" or troublesome girls as cautionary tales of who not to become. In their attempts to control and rigidly program black girls, these men were tacitly admitting that girls had the power to upset their plans and hopes about black women.

Black women writers saw the power of black girls as a positive resource for survival and the future of the race. They wrote about black girls who fought against oppression and abuse, girls who moved across urban landscapes, girls who had inner desires that should be nurtured and cultivated, girls who attended college, girls who had the capacity to follow innovative career paths in an industrial city. They advised girls to have a deep sense of self-respect. They wanted them to succeed at what they chose to do.

This group of black writers introduced tropes of black girlhood: the dutiful, obedient Christian girl; the youthful girl; the "prematurely knowing" girl; the self-respecting working girl; the educated girl; the girl who uplifts the race; the "Don't-Care" girl; the "Loud Girl." Whether they saw a fullness of potential or a threat to the elevation of the race, nineteenth-century black writers assigned black girls the tremendous responsibility of representing the race in everything they did and said. How they dressed, how they groomed themselves, how they moved, what they said and how they said it: all were scrutinized carefully by black leaders and authority figures. Black writers projected idealized images of black girls to reading audiences, and they expected girls to shoulder the responsibility of presenting the race in a positive light from a very young age.

Toni Cade Bambara, author of the short story collection *Gorilla, My Love* (1972), marked the absence of focused literary attention on black girls in the 1970s: "The initiation or rites of passage of the young girl is not one of the darlings of American literature. The coming of age for the young boy is certainly much more the classic case. I wonder if it all means that we don't put a value on our process of womanhood."[3] In the appendix to *The Bluest Eye* (1970), Toni Morrison wrote that she selected a poor black girl as the novel's protagonist because she wanted to "dramatize the devastation that even casual racial contempt" can bring to vulnerable young black females.[4] For Morrison, a black girl was the figure best suited to articulate a society's incendiary practices of racial hatred toward its most marginalized members—poor black people.[5] She wrote *The Bluest Eye* (1970) to give voice to those on the periphery: "Little black girls who were props, background, those people were never center stage and those people were me."[6]

A decades-long absence of critical attention to black girls in U.S. fiction has had serious consequences for how they are interpreted and understood. This book offers a literary genealogy of black girls and a language for talking about black girls. Because of the absence of such a lexicon, the boundaries about what is proper and what is not vis-à-vis black girls do not exist. Commentators today often do not regard the age of a young black girl as a marker of innocence. Black girls are not viewed as children and young people who need protection and care. Instead, they are the unwilling recipients of actual physical attacks, and attacks in the press, on social media, and in other modes of public commentary.

The most prominent example of such attacks is the way the media has commented about Sasha and Malia Obama. In one sense, the Obama daughters are a refreshing example of young black women who are nurtured and protected. Their mother, the First Lady, keeps them out of the public eye to a large extent. They are carefully raised and educated and are surrounded by people who love them. For many black observers, they were a heartening addition to the visual landscape of the nation. Cheryl Wall recounts that at President Barack Obama's first inaugural address, "one of the joyous moments . . . was the sight of Malia and Sasha Obama. . . . For the first time in history, if only for a day, the most adored children in the world were two little black girls."[7]

Yet their youthful innocence has been violated in shocking ways in social and other media. When Malia Obama appeared in public wearing a T-shirt with a peace sign and dark sunglasses, a commenter on the Free Republic Web site said that she looked like a "typical street whore." When President Obama signaled his approval of the FDA's decision to lower the age limit on the Plan B birth control pill, Andrea Tantaros asked, "So I'm just wondering, at age 15, is the Obama daughter, Malia, going to go on birth control? Are they gonna put her on birth control?"[8]

When the Obama daughters good-naturedly participate in public events, they are sometimes criticized. At the 2014 press conference to pardon the turkeys chosen for the president's Thanksgiving dinner, Malia and Sasha were present, as is traditional. They stood behind their father as he made jokes and made a valiant attempt to present turkeys as the national bird in a scholarly context. The girls tried hard to comport themselves properly. Like most teenage girls, they tried several postures. They searched for the right body language to play the role of dutiful presidential daughters. They smiled in the right places. But in one moment, Malia folded her arms across her body, cocked her right hip a little bit, and looked away from her father. Sasha gazed off into space. The girls broke their roles as First Daughters and were typical teenagers for just a moment. It was this moment Elizabeth Lauten, communications director for a Republican member of Congress, chose to comment about on Twitter: "Dear

Sasha and Malia, I get you're both in those awful teen years, but you're a part of the First Family, try showing a little class. At least respect the part you play."[9] Lauten scrutinized every movement, every body posture of the two girls and pounced on them as "Don't-Care Girls" for the brief time when they behaved in ways she deemed inappropriate. Over a century after Silas Floyd introduced the "Don't-Care Girl" in *Floyd's Flowers,* black girls are still scrutinized so closely that they do not have the freedom to be actual people.

Even when black girls accomplish incredible feats, they come under vicious attacks in the media. A memorable example is the stir that resulted from the relationship between Olympic gold medalist Gabrielle "Gabby" Douglas and her host and surrogate (white) mother, Missy Parton. In August 2012, Gabrielle Douglas made history when she became the first African American female to win the Olympic All-Around title in gymnastics at age sixteen. Long aware that her daughter had a talent for tumbling, Natalie Hawkins, Gabrielle's mother, enrolled her daughter in gymnastics to provide a "safe place" for her to play when she was six years old.[10] Gabrielle honed her skills in her hometown of Virginia Beach. She soon caught the attention of renowned gymnastic coach Liang Chow, who offered to develop Gabrielle's skills at his gymnastic camp located 1,200 miles away in West Des Moines, Iowa. To defray costs, Gabrielle lived with a white family in Iowa that consisted of Missy and Travis Parton and their two young daughters.[11] The Partons became Gabrielle's surrogate family for two years. They made every effort to make Gabrielle feel at home, "giving her free rein of the house, buying her a pool pass, taking her to weddings, and eventually teaching her how to drive."[12] Missy Parton's decision to accept Gabrielle into her household was a benevolent, charitable act, but the offer was predicated on another, more personal reason. In an interview, Missy Parton explained that she recently lost her mother and hoped that Gabrielle's presence in the Partons' household would fill a void: "God never took something away without filling the hole, without replacing it with something," she said. "And for us he just happened to replace it with a 16-year-old black girl."[13]

The offhand comment that Gabrielle would fill a "hole" in the Partons' household reminds us of a common trope of early African American literary history in which enslaved black girls fill voids in white households and become slaves/surrogate daughters to surrogate white mothers. Gabrielle assuaged Missy Parton's loss by enabling her to play a benevolent role as the surrogate white mother who clothes, feeds, and cares for a black child. However, Gabrielle did not feel entirely at home in Iowa. She "remembers thinking when she arrived that she must be the only black person in the state."[14]

Despite the hardships of being separated from her mother and her community, Gabrielle succeeded in reaching her goal as an athlete. At first, news coverage hailed Gabrielle's journey from poverty to gold medal Olympian as a "quintessentially American tale." However, she was attacked in social media forums during the 2012 Olympics when she appeared at a competition with an "improper" ponytail. The press blamed Gabrielle's absent black mother for her "unruly hair" and assumed that her surrogate white mother was too culturally disconnected to provide proper care for a black girl.[15] Suddenly Gabrielle was an inadequately mothered girl who, like Grace in *Floyd's Flowers*, did not know how to groom herself properly. Even as she competed successfully toward an Olympic Gold Medal, how she looked was more important to some people than what she accomplished. In her moment of triumph, she was criticized as a black girl who was not representing the race properly.

Gabrielle responded vigorously to the criticism, which she was unaware of until she won her second gold medal. "I don't know where this is coming from. What's wrong with my hair?" she said. "I just made history and people are focused on my hair?" Then she rejected the focus on her appearance. "Nothing is going to change. . . . I'm going to wear my hair like this during beam and bar finals. You might as well just stop talking about it."[16] Like Linda Brent in *Incidents in the Life of a Slave Girl* and Frado in *Our Nig*, Gabrielle Douglas rejected criticism that distracted from her ultimate goal of personal fulfillment and freedom of expression. She is the resilient girl who refuses to be hindered.

Louisiana-born Quvenzhané Wallis was just five years old when she auditioned for *Beasts of the Southern Wild* (2012). Wallis made history as the youngest-ever nominee for Best Actress in a Leading Role for her performance as "Hushpuppy," the bold, spirited six-year-old in a film about a black girl from the New Orleans bayou who tries to survive her life of abject poverty with her father.[17] In the film, Hushpuppy grows up without the protection of her mother, who dies when she is young. Hushpuppy receives tough yet nurturing love from her father, who teaches her at a youthful age how to care for herself. At the age of six, Hushpuppy is forced to become "prematurely knowing" when her father falls ill and she must take care of herself and try to heal her father. When the father eventually dies, members of the black community become her surrogate parents. Hushpuppy's life unfolds in a pattern that follows the trajectories of Harriet Wilson's Frado, Maria W. Stewart's Letitia, and Harriet Jacobs's Linda Brent: orphaned at six, strengthened through physical endurance and self-determination, and forced to become prematurely aware when faced with adversity. In this filmic version, the transition from youthful to prematurely knowing is marked by an acute sense of dangerous surroundings and knowledge of the skills that are necessary for survival.[18] Wallis's portrayal of the girl who survives was a tour de force.

Yet she came under attack during the 2013 Oscars when she expressed her joy by holding her arms in a defiant champion's pose, similar to Superman. While the pose was intended to capture her spunk, the *Onion*, a popular media outlet, “illogically sexualized and demonized”[19] her by labeling her “a little cunt” in a tweet.[20] The *Daily Beast* commented that “Best Actress Oscar nominee Quvenzhané Wallis has been called a lot of things, most of them complimentary. Among them: ‘a small force of nature,’ ‘special,’ and ‘extraordinary.’ Now, thanks to The Onion’s Twitter feed, she can add another word she probably shouldn’t hear for another 15 years.”[21] For a moment, her triumphant portrayal of the prematurely knowing girl in the film was overshadowed by the fact that she was forced at the age of nine to become a prematurely knowing girl in real life. The remark, which was an extremely poor attempt to satirize the kinds of commentary that often accompany the Oscars, provoked widespread outrage, and the CEO of the *Onion* issued a somewhat gracious apology that was more about the image of his publication than it was about the harm the insult might have done to a young black girl.[22]

The inability to see Wallis as youthful vividly illustrates the failure of U.S. culture to protect the innocence of black girls, as novelist A. J. Verdelle pointed out:

> I remain convinced that white Americans—not all, but many—cannot see black children for who and how they are. The public is unaccustomed to seeing black girls who do not fit the mold. . . . They do not see this young child—bolstered by serendipity and her own talent and her devoted parents and an amazing film—living a dream, dressing up, attending the Oscars at age nine, nominated in a huge category, at age nine, having seen herself on a forty[-foot] screen, at age nine, having been a cover girl, at age nine, sitting in the most high company, at age nine, smiling with her baby teeth.[23]

Verdelle’s repetition of “at age nine” forces readers to acknowledge that Wallis is indeed a child who deserves protection. The *Onion* writer viewed Quvenzhané as too vocal, too precocious, and, in a deeply misguided attempt at satire, an appropriate target for sexualized violence. Outspoken, confident, focused, and talented black girls disrupt stereotypical assumptions in white America about race. Wallis was chosen to play the lead in the film *Annie* (2014), and it is to be hoped that she will continue to portray roles that break boundaries and present images of black girls as visible and powerful figures. Yet despite this achievement, social media exploded with racist responses to the casting of a black girl in a lead role traditionally given to white girls. Social media responded similarly with racist tweets about the casting of “Rue,” a black girl played by Amandla Stenberg in the widely popular film, *The Hunger Games*. While Rue is described as having brown skin in the book series that is written by Suzanne Collins, people on social media could not imagine a black girl in this role.

The Futurity of Achievements

In February 2015, the African American Policy Institute released a study on the treatment of black girls in schools entitled *Black Girls Matter: Pushed Out, Overpoliced, and Underprotected.* Some of the major findings were that black girls in major cities are ten times more likely to be disciplined than both white boys and white girls, that schools fail to intervene in situations where black girls are sexually harassed, and that black girls get less attention at school than black boys because the girls are perceived to be "more socially mature and self-reliant."[24] In an article about the report, Khadijah Costley White wrote about her memories of schooling, of being disciplined for minor infractions, for not moving right, for not speaking right. Most devastating was her memory of having her teacher give her a bad grade on a report she had poured herself into and was proud of. The teacher thought the words were not her own, that she could not have produced work of that high quality. White wrote that in that moment, "I was overwhelmed by the thought of having to be a black girl for the rest of my life."[25]

White's need to prove her authorship is similar to the examination that Phillis Wheatley underwent to prove that she had actually written her 1773 collection, *Poems on Various Subjects Religious and Moral.* As the first known person of African descent to publish a book of poetry in the New World, Wheatley arguably inaugurated the African American literary tradition. Despite her achievements, Wheatley had to counter efforts by white "father figures," including her master, John Wheatley, and the eighteen men who examined her intellectual capabilities in an attempt to diminish her influence and reject her authorship. Wheatley had to pass an examination that New England's literary elite administered that, according to Henry Louis Gates Jr. was an "[audition] for the humanity of the entire African people."[26] Wheatley passed the examination, and her authorship of the poems was clarified, but the eighteen men still denigrated her as an "uncultivated barbarian from Africa."[27]

In the twenty-first century, black girls represent a future filled with achievements. More than ever before black girls are role models who are successful in many arenas. In sports, film, and literature, black girls are breaking through boundaries and gaining platforms for their talents. Because of their success, there are now consequences for those who attack black girls in the media. Elizabeth Lauten had to quit her job. Andrea Tantaros was widely attacked. Some girls, like Gabrielle Douglas, defend themselves. The public achievements and resilience of black girls help us envision a future generation of black women whose girlhoods will impact their lives in adulthood.

Scholars and activists are producing initiatives that recognize the genius that resides in black girls. Ruth Nicole Brown offers a contemporary activist understanding of black girlhood that draws upon her work with black girls in her organization SOLHOT (Saving Our Lives, Hearing Our Truth!). Of her organization, Brown states, "SOLHOT is not about etiquette training, managing girls' behavior, punishing who they are, telling them who they should be, or keeping them busy."[28] Salimishah Tillet's organization A Long Way from Home supports black girls and young black women who have survived sexual assault. Tanya Torp's organization Be Bold offers educational resources, social services, and moral support to black girls in Lexington, Kentucky.

Black Girlhood in the Nineteenth Century offers a literary genealogy of the cultural attitudes toward black girls the African American Policy Institute studied. It helps explain how we arrived at this point in the United States when black girls are not valued and their accomplishments are undermined. But the attitudes we see today are only part of the genealogy I describe. Some elements of the heritage of black girls' identities have been overlooked for far too long. Strength, determination, an ability to strategize in creative ways, and a capacity to succeed against all odds are also part of the literary heritage of black girls. My hope is that recovering this long-lost heritage will in some way contribute to solutions for black girls of today and tomorrow.

Notes

Introduction

1. Mrs. N. F. Mossell, "Only a Girl," *New York Freeman*, February 13, 1886.

2. bell hooks, Foreword, in hooks, *Bone Black*, xii.

3. Scholars have written memoirs, such as bell hooks's *Bone Black: Memories of Girlhood* (1996) and June Jordan's *Soldier: A Poet's Childhood* (2001). Some have written studies of black girls' lived experiences in early-twentieth-century Chicago and New Orleans, for example, Marcia Chatelain's *Southside Girls: Growing Up in the Great Migration* (2015) and LaKisha Michelle Simmons's *Crescent City Girls: The Lives of Young Black Women in Segregated New Orleans* (2015). Other scholars have engaged the fields of hip-hop pedagogy and ethnography; these include Krya Gaunt's *Games Black Girls Play: Learning the Ropes from Double-Dutch to Hip-Hop* (2008), Ruth Nicole Brown's *Hear Our Truths: The Creative Potential of Black Girlhood* (2013), and *Black Girlhood Celebration: Toward a Hip-Hop Feminist Pedagogy* (2009). Aliyyah I. Abdur-Rahman's *Against the Closet: Black Political Longing and the Erotics of Race* (2013) includes a chapter titled "Recovering the Little Black Girl," which explores the rape and incest of black girls in a twenty-first-century framework.

4. Ernest, *Chaotic Justice*, 6–7.

5. Stewart, "Lecture Delivered at the Franklin Hall," 30.

6. Ibid., 30.

7. Ibid., 32.

8. Delany, "Condition, Elevation, Emigration and Destiny," 274, Delany's italics.

9. Ibid., 273, Delany's italics.

10. Ibid.

11. Harley, "Anna J. Cooper," 88.

12. Crummell, "Black Woman of the South," 106–107.

13. Ibid., 103.

14. Ibid., 105–106.

15. Cooper, "Womanhood," 60–61, Cooper's italics.

16. As Hazel Carby notes, black women writers "reconstructed the sexual ideologies of the nineteenth century to produce an alternative discourse of black womanhood"; Carby, *Reconstructing Womanhood*, 6. See also duCille, *Coupling Convention*; Tate, *Domestic Allegories of Political Desire*; Peterson, *"Doers of the Word"*; Foster, *'Til Death or Distance Do Us Part*; Gardner, *Unexpected Places*; Foreman, *Activist Sentiments*; and Williams, *Dividing Lines*.

17. duCille, *Coupling Convention*, 53, 62.

18. Washington, Introduction.

19. Foreman, "Reading Aright," 332.

20. Jeynes, *American Educational History*, 82.

21. McHenry, *Forgotten Readers*, 3.

22. Ibid., 56.

23. Winch, *Elite of Our People*, 111, 114.

24. Sánchez-Eppler, *Dependent States*, xxv.

25. Jacobs, *Incidents in the Life of a Slave Girl*, 27.

26. The black girl as "not-yet" draws from Spiller's explanation of the captives of the Middle Passage, who were removed from the indigenous land and culture and who are "not-yet 'American' in their movement across the Atlantic. Instead, they were suspended on a body of water and "were also nowhere at all." See Spillers, "Mama's Baby, Papa's Maybe," 455.

27. McDowell, *"Changing Same,"* 37.

28. Wheatley, *Poems on Various Subjects*, xi.

29. "Missing," *Freedom's Journal*, August 15, 1828.

30. "The Little Black Girl," *Liberator*, February 15, 1834.

31. Jacobs, *Incidents in the Life of a Slave Girl*, 27.

32. Ibid., 26.

33. Keckley, "Girlhood and Its Sorrows," in Keckley, *Behind the Scenes*, 374.

34. Ibid.

35. Stewart, *Productions*, 3–4.

36. Larsen, *Quicksand and Passing*, 23.

37. Gwendolyn Brooks, *Maud Martha*, reprinted in Brooks, *Blacks* (Chicago: Third World Press, 2001), 144.

38. Ibid., 163.

39. Ibid., 164.

40. Morrison, *Sula*, 174.

41. Bancroft, *Slave Trading in the Old South*, 83.

42. Jackson, "Talking Book and the Talking Book Historian," 252.

43. Cohen and Stein, Introduction, 3.

44. Frances Smith Foster highlights "the roles of language, religion, and organization in defining and developing an African American press"; Foster, "Narrative of the Interesting Origins," 715. See also Newman, Rael, and Lapsansky, *Pamphlets of Protest*; Levine, "Circulating the Nation," 17–36.

45. Gardner, *Unexpected Places*, 17.

46. King, *African American Childhoods*, 41. Dorothy Sterling's archival study of the lives of enslaved black women and girls on southern plantations contributed foundational work on nineteenth-century black girlhoods to the historical record; see Sterling, *We Are Your Sisters*.

47. Smith, *Children's Literature of the Harlem Renaissance*; Capshaw, *Civil Rights Childhood*.

48. Catherine Driscoll offers a useful historical context for conduct manuals in *Girls*. Carolyn Steedman discusses the changing attitudes toward children and childhood in the fields of the social sciences, law, literature, and medicine in *Strange Dislocations*. Anne Scott MacLeod provides a framework in which to read children's literature in *American Childhood*. See also Dawson, "Miniaturizing of Girlhood"; Roethler, "Reading in Color," 95–105; Sander, *Records of Girlhood*; Graff, *Conflicting Paths*; and Mintz, *Huck's Raft*.

49. Bernstein, *Racial Innocence*, 6.

50. Duane, *Suffering Childhood in Early America*, 3.

51. Williams, "The Colored Girl," 63–65.

Chapter 1. Black Girlhood in the Early Black Press

1. Harris, *In the Shadow of Slavery*, 98. Susan Ryan contends that "U.S. conceptions of citizenship were predicated on a racially recognized 'fitness of self-government,' one that identified the supposedly natural dependence of African Americans as just cause for their exclusion." Ryan, *Grammar of Good Intentions*, 7.

2. Xiomara Santamarina discusses the impact of the lack of employment opportunities in the antebellum North on black men and women: "In a capitalizing and racialized class hierarchy, black men were increasingly excluded from skilled trades and almost entirely excluded from the ranks of a growing professional class. African American men's low wages made it difficult for them to support their families and this made the labor of black women, the group lower than African American men in the economic hierarchy, absolutely necessary." Santamarina, *Belabored Professions*, 15.

3. Ibid., 98, 120. For additional works on black masculinities in the nineteenth and early twentieth centuries, see Vincent Woodard, *Delectable Negro: Human Consumption and Homoeroticism within U.S. Culture* (New York: New York University Press, 2014); Marlon Ross, *Manning the Race: Reforming Black Men in the Jim Crow Era* (New York: New York University Press, 2004); Dwight McBride, *Impossible Witnesses: Truth, Abolitionism and Slave Testimony* (New York: New York University Press, 2001); Reid-Pharr, *Conjugal Union*; and Phillip Brian Harper, *Are We Not Men?: Masculine Anxiety and the Problem of African American Anxiety* (New York: Oxford University Press, 1998).

4. Seventy-one percent of free blacks lived in these three states in 1820; 72.5 percent in 1830; 68.9 percent in 1840; and 64.2 percent in 1850. The lower percentages in 1840 and 1850 are accounted for by the movement of free blacks into the new western states, particularly Indiana and Ohio. Calculated from J. D. B. DeBow, *Seventh Census of the United States: 1850* (Washington, D.C.: Robert Armstrong, Public Printer, 1853), 8, 22, 37, 53, 68, 80, 113, 142, 187, 719, 781, 853, 898, 925, 949.

5. For New York, see Harris, *In the Shadow of Slavery*, 117–118; for New Jersey and Pennsylvania, see Jones, *American Work*, 268.

6. Young, *Antebellum Black Activists*, 36.

7. Ibid., 68–77.

8. Harris, *In the Shadow of Slavery*, 74–75.

9. Moss, *Schooling Citizens*, 60–61.

10. Ibid., 81.

11. In Boston, only 8.5 percent of black men worked in domestic service in 1850; in Baltimore, only 4.4 percent. Moss, *Schooling Citizens*, 180.

12. See Kerber, *Women of the Republic*; and Lewis, "Republican Wife," 689–721.

13. Ball, *To Live an Antislavery Life*, 98.

14. Ibid., 103.

15. Young, *Antebellum Black Activists*, 37; "William Watkins."

16. Moss, *Schooling Citizens*, 102.

17. Calculated from DeBow, *Seventh Census*, 8, 10, 22, 24, 37, 39, 53, 56, 68, 70, 80, 82, 113, 118, 142, 145, 187, 192.

18. Ibid.

19. For information about the emergence of black print culture in the antebellum period, see Vogel, *Black Press*; Dann, *Black Press, 1827–1890*; Bacon, *Freedom's Journal*; and McHenry, *Forgotten Readers*.

20. McHenry, *Forgotten Readers*, 90.

21. Olaudah Equiano, *Interesting Narrative of the Life of Olaudah Equiano: Or Gustavus Vassa, the African, Written by Himself*, edited by Vincent Carretta (1789; repr., Penguin Group: New York, 1995), 51.

22. Ibid., 52.

23. Carby, *Reconstructing Womanhood*, 35.

24. David Walker, *David Walker's Appeal to the Coloured Citizens of the World, but in Particular, and Very Expressly, to Those of The United States of America*, edited by Sean Wilentz (New York: Hill and Wang, 1995), 25.

25. "Formation of Character," *Freedom's Journal*, February 21, 1829.

26. Ball, *To Live an Antislavery Life*, 13.

27. See Kerber, *Women of the Republic*; and Lewis, "Republican Wife."

28. For more information on free black communities in the antebellum North and the creation of civic institutions, see Wilder, "Black Life in Freedom," 215–239.

29. The basic concerns for free African Americans during the antebellum period were voting rights, education, places of worship, and jobs for skilled and unskilled workers. The readership of *Freedom's Journal* consisted primarily of African American men and women in the North who were perpetually plagued by economic, social, and political inequality. See Bacon, *Freedom's Journal*; McHenry, *Forgotten Readers*; and Pride and Wilson, *History of the Black Press*, 4.

30. Pride and Wilson, *History of the Black Press*, 9.

31. Hutton, *Early Black Press in America*, 14–15. See also Dann, *Black Press, 1827–1890*, 4–5.

32. Levine, "Circulating the Nation," 18, 22.

33. Ibid., 23.

34. Anderson, *Imagined Communities*, 35–36.

35. Bacon, *Freedom's Journal*, 51–52.

36. There is some evidence that slaves in the South gained access to *Freedom's Journal*. Jacqueline Bacon notes that in an 1831 letter to William Lloyd Garrison's *Liberator*, correspondent "V" revealed that he looked out his window and "saw a mulatto with a newspaper in his hand, surrounded by a score of colored men, who were listening, open mouthed, to a very inflammatory article the yellow man was reading. Sometimes the reader dwelt emphatically on particular passages, and I could see his auditors stamp and clench their hands. I afterwards learned the paper was published in New-York, and addressed to the blacks." "V," "Walker's Appeal. No. 2," *Liberator*, May 14, 1831, quoted in Bacon, *Freedom's Journal*, 54.

37. Hutton, *Early Black Press in America*, 15. See also Bacon, *Freedom's Journal*, 99–120; and Rael, *Black Identity and Black Protest*, 1–11.

38. Bacon, *Freedom's Journal*, 117. See also Hutton, *Early Black Press in America*, 15.

39. Ryan, *Grammar of Good Intentions*, 7.

40. A short article published on August 31, 1827, described the brutal kidnapping of two black girls: "Two coloured girls aged 9 & 7 years, were kidnapped about 17 months since at Charleston, SC. by a free woman, said to be their aunt and confined between the joists and floor of the house. They were both naked, and their skins had assumed whitish appearance from the dampness and moisture of the place of confinement. The discovery of their concealment was made in an anonymous letter to a magistrate." Charleston was a major port for the buying and shipping of slaves, and the girls were most likely stolen to be sold on the slave market. This article about violence toward these black girls was followed by another on the cost of fruit. Located above the article about the kidnapping was another short segment that described an increase in manufacturing in Worcester, Massachusetts: "In Worcester county, Mass. there are now in operation eleven factories for the manufacturing of woolen cloth alone, which turn out yearly 672,950 yards of broad satinet, 21,300 yards of kerseymore, and 103, 200 yards of broad cloth; the value of which is estimated at $845,882."

The juxtaposition of articles on the disappearance of two black girls, the buying and selling of peaches, and the manufacturing of cloth was intended to draw reactions from readers and remind them of the connections between slave labor in the South and the goods and commodities for sale in the North.

41. Saxe Weimer, "Punishment of a Slave," *Freedom's Journal*, September 12, 1828, reprinted from the *Commercial Advertiser*.

42. Ibid.

43. "Anecdote," *Freedom's Journal*, February 28, 1829, reprinted from the *Boston Evening Bulletin*.

44. McHenry, *Forgotten Readers*, 92.

45. Dann, *Black Press, 1827–1890*, 33.

46. Sanborn, "Plagiarist's Craft," 909.

47. Ibid.

48. Foster, "Narrative of the Interesting Origins," 727–728.

49. While Meredith McGill argues that "reprinting . . . played a critical role in supporting the fledgling black press," her seminal study gives little attention to the im-

plications of reprinting for black readers. McGill states that "for both rhetorical and practical reasons," her book on the intersection of antebellum literature and the system of reprinting between 1834 and 1853 focuses primarily on "the careers and writing of canonical writers." McGill, *American Literature*, 41.

50. Scruggs, "Photographs to Answer Our Purposes," 203–230. See also McGill, "Frances Ellen Watkins Harper."

51. Scruggs, "Photographs to Answer Our Purposes," 230.

52. Jackson, "Another Long Bridge," 193.

53. Brooks, "The Unfortunates," 48.

54. Scruggs, "Photographs to Answer Our Purposes," 230.

55. Gardner, "Children's Literature in the AME *Christian Recorder*," 7.

56. "Missing," *Freedom's Journal*, August 15, 1828.

57. Noble, "Ecstasies of Sentimental Wounding," 295.

58. The scarred bodies of black girls recur throughout African American literature, functioning as repeated, visual reminders of the pain suffered by their lack of protection and subsequent victimization. The black girl's wounds eventually turn into scars. The sight/site of her scar represents visually the physical reality of past pain. The black girl's bodily scar manifests in the reader self-reflexivity. From Frado's beaten and scarred body in *Our Nig* (1859), the marks left from "hundreds of tiny red insects, fine as a needle's point, that pierced through [Linda Brent's] skin" as she hid in the cramped garret for seven years in *Incidents in the Life of a Slave Girl* (97).

59. One article stated that "a medical correspondent of the Portland Patriots, thinks it would be advantageous for females to pass their twenty-fourth or twenty-fifth year before they subject themselves to the cares and fatigues of a married life; as the constitution of few women can be regarded as firmly established until after their twentieth year. Every female who does not have an offer to her taste previous to that age will applaud his advice; but such as may meet with husbands to their mind will judge of their own fitness, and laugh at the Doctor." "Early Marriage," *Freedom's Journal*, November 23, 1827, reprinted from the *Boston Patriot*. The *Boston Patriot*, a semiweekly, was published from 1770 to 1816.

Another article described marriage customs in several countries, emphasizing the duties and practices of young brides: "The Americans marry young; the occasion which the young men have for a wife to assist them in their labours conduces to early marriages and great purity of manners; but the wife who dies is readily replaced by another. She is a necessary friend, and the very soul of the family: she is an indispensable resource for domestic affairs—an assiduous companion, and renders home pleasant in whose parts of the country where neighbours are scarce, and where the children soon quit their paternal abode." "Marriage, Customs, &C, of Various Nations," *Freedom's Journal*, October 5, 1827.

60. Foster, *'Til Death or Distance Do Us Part*, xv.

61. Foster, *Love and Marriage in Early African America*, xviii.

62. As Foster argues, "African Americans considered themselves competent to define and to discipline, to regularize and record for themselves the most intimate aspects of their lives." Ibid., xxii.

63. "An unmarried woman, negligent of her person, has no occasion to look out for a husband—few gentlemen will select ladies for wives, who are not attentive to their graces." "An Unmarried Woman," *Freedom's Journal*, June 20, 1828. See also "The Old Maid's Diary," *Freedom's Journal*, November 2, 1827, 109. These articles are reprinted in Foster, *Love and Marriage in Early African America*, 113 and 109, respectively.

64. "E," "Lines Written on Hearing a Beautiful Young Lady Express a Determination to Live an Old Maid," *Freedom's Journal*, January 25, 1828; Foster, *Love and Marriage in Early African America*, 87.

65. For examples of articles that discuss single black women in the nineteenth century, see the chapter titled "Whether to Marry—and Who?" in Foster, *Love and Marriage in African America*, 83–130.

66. "A Sketch of Comfort," *Freedom's Journal*, June 22, 1827.

67. Ibid.

68. Untitled article, *Freedom's Journal*, May 1, 1827.

69. "Dick Dashall," "Girls 'Have at Ye All,'" *Freedom's Journal*, October 10, 1828.

70. Ibid.

71. Foster, "How Do You Solve a Problem?" 635.

72. "West Indies," *Freedom's Journal*, September 14, 1827.

73. S., "Theresa—A Haytien Tale," *Freedom's Journal*, January 18, 1828, 1.

74. Ibid.

75. Ibid., 2.

76. Foster, "How Do You Solve a Problem?" 634.

77. Bacon, *Freedom's Journal*, 135.

78. DeRosa, *Domestic Abolitionism and Juvenile Literature*, 121.

79. Foster, *Love and Marriage in Early African America*, xix. Foster refers to an article by Sarah Douglas about a black mother having tea with her four daughters: "A Dialogue between a Mother and Her Children on the Precious Stones," *Repository of Religion and Literature and Science and Art* 2, no 4 (October 1859): 156–159. From 1858 to 1863, the *Repository*, which was based in Indianapolis, was administered by black men and designed for black readers. In 1861, its chief editor was John Mifflin Brown. Foster, *Love and Marriage in Early African America*, xvii–xix.

80. "Children," *Freedom's Journal*, July 13, 1827, reprinted from *Dwight's Theology*. Timothy Dwight (1752–1817) was an American academic and educator, a prominent Congregationalist minister, a theologian, an author, and the eighth president of Yale University. He also opened an academy for children in Fairfield, Connecticut.

81. "Honesty," *Freedom's Journal*, May 4, 1827, reprinted from the *New York Chronicle*. Other parenting pieces included a short fictional piece by Washington Irving titled "Ellen; A Sketch from 'Scenes and Thoughts'" (printed on October 5, 1827). The story is about two parents who have lost all of their children in infancy except their daughter Ellen. The story expresses the suffering of the girl figure, but more important is the representation of a two-parent household. The "Summary" section of November 23, 1827, detailed the deaths of two girls in two separate summaries. "Manslaughter," *Freedom's Journal*, November 23, 1827, reported that a jury had returned a guilty verdict to Mrs. M. Carton and Edward Maher " for the murder of the daughter of the former, aged 14

years." "Cotton," *Freedom's Journal*, November 23, 1827, summarized the tragic death of "a little girl, daughter of Mr. L. B. Smith of Saratoga, N.Y., about three years old, [who] was recently burned to death, in consequence of her clothes, *which were of cotton*, taking fire. Woolen stuff should be the dress of children in the winter season." The article indicts the parents for not protecting their daughter (italics in the original).

82. "Both Wrong," *Freedom's Journal*, October 19, 1827.

83. "Evening School," *Freedom's Journal*, October 19, 1827. This is an advertisement for a school created by B. F. Hughes. Another advertisement printed alongside "Evening School" sought interested learners for "The African Mutual Instruction Society for the Instruction of Coloured Adults of Both Sexes" which had reopened its school "on Monday Evening, October 1st, at their former school-room, under the Mariner's Church, in Roosevelt street."

84. For more about the African Free Schools and the campaign of black elites to wrest control of the schools away from the Manumission Society, see Rury, "New York African Free School, 1827–1836," 187–197.

85. Calculated at "Purchasing Power of Money in the United States from 1774 to the Present," http://www.measuringworth.com/ppowerus/ (accessed February 24, 2015).

86. Townsend, *Faith in Their Own Color*, 88. Other black-run schools in New York in this period were also short-lived. The Canal Street High School, operated by Boston Crummell, Thomas Downing, Peter Williams, and others, was in operation from 1831 to 1833. A high school operated by the Phoenix Society lasted from 1836 to 1838. The New York Select Academy, which used the same location of St. Philip's basement as the B. F. Hughes School had and was run by Alexander Crummell and Thomas Sidney, opened in 1839 but lasted less than a year. Townsend attributes the short tenure of these black-run schools to "lack of funds and students" but points out that these multiple attempts show "how important it was for African Americans to take charge of their educational visions"; ibid., 89, 88.

87. Thomas Clapp Cornell, *Adam and Anne Mott: Their Ancestors and Descendants* (Poughkeepsie, N.Y.: A. V. Haight, 1890), 164–165.

88. Mott, Preface. Abigail Mott Moore published this abridgement of Equiano's memoir under her maiden name. While educators praised the ticket system as an incentive to learn, some students found it oppressive. Tickets were taken away as fines for such offenses as blotting a copybook or being late to school. One male student noted that when pupils were "detained at home" for an hour or sometimes for a day or two, they weren't always able to procure a note from parents explaining the absence, "and we, being sometimes disbelieved by the master, are accordingly punished, and thereby discouraged." Quote from "A Dialogue: Spoken between J. M. S. and W. H. at a Public Examination, Written for the Occasion," in Andrews, *History of the New-York African Free Schools*, 138.

89. Rury, "New York African Free School, 1827–1836."

90. Andrews, *History of the New-York African Free Schools*, 54–55, quote on 55.

91. Ibid., 114–115.

92. Ibid., 117.

93. Andrews noted one such case: a seventeen-year-old graduate of his school ap-

prenticed with a blacksmith but was unable to find an employer who would hire him in New York. A friend who owned a factory in Philadelphia agreed to hire him, but his workforce refused to "pursue their business in the company of poor Isaac" because he was black. Andrews noted approvingly Isaac's solution: he "resolved to leave the country and go to the Colony of Liberia." Thus, the free black community lost an educated young man with multiple work skills. Ibid., 118–119.

94. Mott, Preface.

95. Ibid.

96. The Plymouth Committee, "Remarks on the Slave Trade," *American Mercury*, May 1789, 429–430. A transcript is available at "Remarks on the Slave Trade," Sea of Liberty, https://seaofliberty.org/explore/remarks-slave-trade/295 (accessed October 10, 2015).

97. Mott, "Remarks on the Slave Trade."

98. A. M., editorial insertion in Equiano, *Life and Adventures of Olaudah Equiano.*

99. "Remarks on the Slave Trade," in ibid., 25.

100. Rohrbach, *Truth Stranger than Fiction*, 3.

101. The name "Magawisca" is derived from the persona of a young black girl in Maria Sedgwick's novel *Hope Leslie: Or, Early Times in Massachusetts* (1827). In Sedgwick's story, Magawisca is the daughter of a Pequot chieftain of noble birth. She resists the notion that women are to be reserved and weak by "withstand[ing] unwarranted insults and racist slurs with dignity." For example, Douglass used the name "Magawisca" for her story "The Abuse of Liberty," which the *Liberator* published in 1831. Sarah Louise Forten contributed over a dozen poems and essays to several different newspapers between 1831 and 1837. Forten was one of the daughters of Philadelphia sailmaker and community leader James Forten Sr. Forten also wrote a poem, "A Mother's Love," which was published in the *Liberator* on July 28, 1832. Forten also used the pseudonym *Zillah.* Armstrong, *Fragile Freedom*, 105–106; McHenry, *Forgotten Readers*, 64.

102. "Another Slave Case," *Liberator*, October 22, 1863; "The Colored Mother of New England to Her Infant," *Liberator*, July 6, 1833, reprinted from *Weekly Recorder*; "Kidnapping in Boston," *Liberator*, October 29, 1836; W. N., "Riot at Brookfield," *Liberator*, August 23, 1839.

103. "The Little Black Girl," *Liberator*, February 15, 1834.

104. Ibid., italics in original.

105. Pride and Wilson, *History of the Black Press*, 30.

106. Ibid.

107. Fagan, "Americans as They Really Are," 99.

108. Martin Dann argues that the *Colored American* enacted the concept of "imagined communities" by reaching members over a wide geographical area. Dann, *Black Press*, 47–48.

109. Fagan, "Americans as They Really Are," 100; "Title of This Journal," *Colored American*, March 4, 1837. Original spelling and emphasis.

110. Dann, *Black Press*, 48.

111. The newspaper reached readers abroad as far away as Jamaica, where subscribers offered to raise money for the paper. Pride and Wilson, *History of the Black Press*, 31, 34.

112. Ibid., 34.

113. Ibid., 31.

114. "Education of Young Men," *Colored American*, March 4, 1837.

115. C. B. R., "Female Education," *Colored American*, March 18, 1837, 2.

116. Ball, *To Live an Antislavery Life*, 89.

117. Ibid, 94.

118. "I Wish I Were a Kitten," *Colored American*, May 22, 1841, reprinted from the *Sunday-School Visitor*. We do not know much about the *Sunday-School Visitor*.

119. "Order and Neatness," *Colored American*, October 30, 1841.

120. "Maternal Efforts," *Colored American*, July 14, 1838. This article was reprinted and titled "The Father" three years later; Mrs. L. H. Sigourney, "The Father," *Colored American*, October 16, 1841.

121. Fagan, "Americans as They Really Are," 99. Pride and Wilson note that the *Colored American* emphasized that it "was not a private possession, but that it belonged to the reader." Editorials repeated this point throughout the life of the newspaper. Pride and Wilson, *History of the Black Press*, 35.

122. "The Little Hunch Back Girl," *Colored American*, October 7, 1837.

123. "The Shabby School Girl," *Colored American*, October 27, 1838, reprinted from the *Christian Intelligencer*. See also "Truth, The Brightest Gem," *Colored American*, May 16, 1840, reprinted from *Mother's Magazine*.

124. "Very Appropriate," *Colored American*, October 27, 1838.

125. "Riot at Brookfield," *Colored American*, September 7, 1839.

126. "A Beautiful Illustration," *Colored American*, June 16, 1838.

127. "A Heart-Moving Picture," *Colored American*, September 24, 1838. Reprinted from the *Journal of the American Temperance Union*.

128. Ibid.

129. "The End of the Drunkard," *Colored American*, July 27, 1839. See also "'Anna Ross'—A Story for Children," *Colored American*, November 14, 1840, reprinted from the *Christian Intelligencer*.

130. "The Deserted Children," *Colored American*, September 14, 1839. See also "A Victim and His Child," *Colored American*, April 11, 1840, reprinted from the *St. Louis Bulletin*. The article describes a police report about a drunken man who is arrested. "Just as they were about removing the miserable wretch to prison, a little girl about eight years old, barefooted and extremely ragged, came into the room sobbing and crying most bitterly. No sooner did she see her father than she ran to him, knelt down by his side, and motioning the officer away, cried—'Don't take away papa while he sleeps! By and by he will wake up once more and kiss me.'" Once the father sobers, he explains that he was not always a "miserable wretch" but that he "contracted bad habits, which got so strong and old upon my nervous temperament as to make a beast of me. My business was neglected, and my wife died, I do believe of a broken heart. Since that time I have wandered around the world without end or aim, except to procure whisky! I have yet a daughter—at least I had yesterday—a beautiful, tender creature, who still loves me, despite my unworthiness." At this moment a "benevolent sailor" enters the room, "leading the girl by the hand." He has bought her "new and comfortable clothes," rendering her "very pretty and interesting." The sailor pays a fine and father and daughter are

reunited. The editors end this story with a personal message for readers to emulate the actions of the girl: "Now, my youthful readers, was not this an affectionate, good little girl? . . . And will you not try to be like her, although, we presume and hope, you have not a drunken father as this little girl had?" The girl provides the sentimental appeal of the story and functions as an example for others to follow.

131. "A Young Recruit to the Cold Water Army," *Colored American*, April 4, 1840, reprinted from *Cold Water Army*.

132. The five articles are "Multiple News Items," *Colored American*, Saturday, March 21, 1840; "Mothers, after All," *Colored American*, Saturday, March 21, 1840; "Politeness," *Colored American*, Saturday, April 5, 1837, reprinted from the *Youth's Companion*; "The London Scholars," *Colored American*, February 23, 1839, reprinted from the *Sunday School Anecdotes*; and "The Bishop and his Births," *Colored American*, March 28, 1840.

133. The *Colored American* printed advertisements from the *Youth's Cabinet*, a white publication, and reprinted several articles from this publication in the "Children's Department." One advertisement for the *Youth's Cabinet* states: "This interesting and instructive little paper, will be sent round with the Colored American, the present week. It is suited to the capacity of the youth of our country, and is designed, more particularly, for their moral and mental training—yet it always contains Moral and Literary articles, suited to the taste and intelligence of the best informed readers." "Youth's Cabinet," *Colored American*, November 4, 1837, 3.

134. Hutton, *Early Black Press*, 133.

135. Ibid.

136. "Multiple News Items," *Colored American*, March 21, 1840.

137. Ibid.

138. "The Blood Hounds," *Colored American*, March 21, 1840.

139. "The Enlargement of Our Paper," *Colored American*, September 16, 1837.

140. McGill, "Frances Ellen Watkins Harper," 55.

141. "The Political Creed of Thomas Jefferson," *Colored American*, March 21, 1840, reprinted from Richard Hildreth, *Despotism in America: Or, an Inquiry into the Nature and Results of the Slave-Holding System in the United States* (Boston: Whipple and Damrell, 1840), 18.

142. "The London Scholars," offers young readers an equally pious lesson about humility. *Colored American*, February 23, 1839, reprinted from *Sunday School Anecdotes*.

143. "Politeness," *Colored American*, April 5, 1837, reprinted from *Youth's Companion*, which was published in Boston. It ran for 100 years until August 1929 when it merged with *American Boy* and the name changed.

144. "The Bishop and His Births," *Colored American*, March 28, 1840.

145. "Explanation," *Colored American*, March 21, 1840. One reader expressed dismay at the *Colored American*'s suspension: "I must confess I am mortified at the thought, to know that we have but one paper, and it had to be suspended three long months, because the editor could not get the means to meet its expenses." J. B. Vashon, "Good—Very Good," *Colored American*, April 4, 1840.

146. Gardner, "Early African American Print Culture," 76.

147. See "Little Harriet," *Colored American*, June 19, 1841, reprinted from the *Weekly*

Messenger; and "The Favorite Flower," *Colored American*, June 20, 1840, reprinted from the *Lutheran Observer*. Both use girls to teach black children about virtue and goodness. In "Forgetting God in Good Health," *Colored American*, November 14, 1840, a girl prays to restore her father to good health and explains to young readers "the very common sin among all ages, of forgetting God in times of health and prosperity."

148. "Patience and Resignation," *Colored American*, August 28, 1841, reprinted from the *Sunday-School Monitor*.

Chapter 2. Youthful Girls and Prematurely Knowing Girls

1. The dedication in Jane Chaplin Dunbar's *Songs for My Children* expresses this duality: "In the preparation of this work, it has been our aim to give to the little ones a book of *home songs*; simple and playful enough to supersede all 'mother-goose' literature, yet grave enough to instruct and profit. May it prove a source of delight in many thousands of happy homes." Another hallmark of early American texts that feature black girls is the active movement of the girls across natural landscapes. This venturing, prompted by idle exploration attributable to a lack of nurturance, teaches young readers to be courageous and steadfast during moments of adversity. In her introduction to *Helps over Hard Places*, Mary Louise "Lynde" Parker asks readers, "I wonder if nobody knows that *girls* are little pilgrims, too, and meet just as many swamps and lions as the boys? I wonder if nobody thinks that *our* feet grow tired, and that we need a little help to climb some of *our* hills, which are just as big and rough as the one that almost discouraged Dick Sterling and Sam Hardy?" (v–vi). The girls have fictional playmates who keep them company and help them. In Parker's fictional world, "Flaxy" and "Prue" and "Princess Pearlypat" carry planks to help a girl cross the worst swamps. "Dudley," "Fifine," and "Jamie," can tell where the lions are and can identify the best paths over the hills. "Little Phebe" knows what to do when it rains (vi). References to geographical landscapes as fearful and daunting places also exist in narratives by black women writers, but in these texts black girl figures often traverse such landscapes alone, without the protection of playmates.

2. Widely circulated texts include *Poems: Moral and Religious, for Children and Youth* (Greenfield, Mass: Denio and Phelps, 1821); *Tawny Girl*; *The Little Keepsake: Or Easy Lessons in Words of One Syllable* (New Haven, Conn.: Sidney Babcock, 1825); *Little Rhymes for Little Readers* (Boston: John Metcalf, 1832); *William Sanders: Or, Blessings in Disguise* (Concord, Mass.: Patriot Press, 1848); *Little Miss Consequence*, particularly the section titled "The Girl Who Inked Herself and Her Book, and How It Ended" (Boston, Mass.: McLoughlin Bros., 1880); Parker, *Helps over Hard Places*; and Dunbar, *Songs for My Children*, particularly a song titled "The Little Black Girl" (123). The American Antiquarian Society in Worcester, Massachusetts, holds first editions of several popular children's books that were written by white women and circulated throughout the northern states.

3. For background on Samuel Wood, including his Quaker identity and his abolitionist activism, see the description of the Wood Family Papers, a collection held at Swarthmore College, at http://www.swarthmore.edu/library/friends/ead/5192wofa.xml (accessed January 21, 2015).

4. Weiss, *Samuel Woods and Sons*, 3.

5. Ibid.

6. *Tawny Girl* follows the trope of the black girl who is poor and wretched but finds success through the salvific grace of community members. See *Tawny Girl*, v.

7. Ibid., 11, 10, 12, 16.

8. Ibid., 10–13, 16–17, 25–26.

9. Alexander Anderson, called "the father of wood engraving in America," was the nation's first skilled and sophisticated relief engraver. From 1791 to 1868, he illustrated more than 2,000 books, pamphlets, broadsides, and printed material in diverse fields, ranging from literature and historical illustration to children's literature and medical texts. Jane R. Pomeroy, "Anderson's Life and Introduction to His Work," in Pomeroy, *Alexander Anderson*, xxx, xxxviii.

10. Ibid., xxvi.

11. This engraving is reminiscent of the type of work Anderson would do later for American Tract Society publications. It was used in the 1850s in Troy, New York, by the Merriam and Moore firms for their children's books. Ibid., 886.

12. *Tawny Girl*, iii.

13. Chesebro, *Blessings in Disguise*.

14. "The Swing," in *The Little Keepsake*, 16.

15. The American Anti-Slavery Society published *The Slave's Friend* from 1827 to 1829. See Edson, "Slave's Friend," 408–411.

16. "Emma," *Slave's Friend* 2, no. 1 (1837): 2 4.

17. See "An Example to Children" (159), "Aspirations" (37), "Haste to School" (50), "Calling Names" (49), "Deeds of Kindness" (180), "Don't Fret" (169), and "The Little Black Girl" (123), all in Dunbar, *Songs for My Children*.

18. "The Little Black Girl," in Dunbar, *Songs for My Children*, 124.

19. Ibid.

20. Ibid., 125.

21. *Jemmy and His Mother*, 51.

22. Ibid., 64.

23. DeRosa, *Domestic Abolitionism and Juvenile Literature*, 57.

24. Eric Gardner recently discovered two examples of Stewart's writing from the 1860s. The first is a transcription of a lecture; the second is a short story. See Gardner, "Introduction: Two Texts," 156–165.

25. The *Repository* was based in Indianapolis. In 1861, the year Stewart's short story was published, its chief editor was John Mifflin Brown.

26. For context about the *Repository*, see Gardner, *Unexpected Places*, 56–91; McHenry, *Forgotten Readers*, 132–33, 137; McAndrew, "Location, Location, Location," 335; and Foster, "Frances Ellen Watkins Harper," 43.

27. See Bacon, *Freedom's Journal*, 37.

28. McHenry, *Forgotten Readers*, 138–139.

29. Ibid.

30. The *Repository* is archived in only three libraries: at Harvard, at Yale, and at the Indiana State Library. It has not been digitized and does not circulate through Interlibrary Loan. Thus, analysis of this source has only recently begun to enter the scholarly literature.

31. Stewart, "Prayer," in *Productions of Mrs. Maria W. Stewart*, 12.

32. "All Fulness in Christ," *Repository of Religion and Literature* (April 1861): 86. "Prayer for a Heathen," *Repository of Religion and Literature* (July 1861): 139. Bishop Payne, "The Duty of Children to Get Knowledge," *Repository of Religion and Literature* (October 1861): 185–186.

33. "Bad Example," *Repository of Religion and Literature* (April 1861): 86; "Sleeping without the Light," *Repository of Religion and Literature* (July 1861): 141.

34. Payne, "The Duty of Children to Get Knowledge," 185–186.

35. Gardner, "Introduction: Two Texts," 157.

36. Ball, *To Live an Antislavery Life*, 2–3.

37. See "A Daughter's Request" (July 1859); "Dialogue between a Mother and Her Children" (October 1859); "Politeness" (January 1861); "The Dress" (January 1861); and "Letters to Little Children" (July 1861).

38. The mother counsels Emma to control her passion: "You got into a passion—a bad way of spending time, and you have accused somebody, and very unjustly, too, of taking away your things and losing them. Keep your temper, my dear; when you have mislaid any article[,] keep your temper and search for it." "Keep Your Temper," *Repository of Religion and Literature* (July 1858): 95.

39. Stewart, "Proper Training of Children."

40. Ibid.

41. Ibid.

42. "Young Ladies, Read!" *Repository of Religion and Literature* (January 1860): 34. Reprinted from the *Hartford Daily Courant*.

43. "Young Ladies, Read!" *Repository of Religion and Literature* (January 1860): 34.

44. In "Conversations between a Mother and Her Children," published July 1858, a mother tells her son, Harry, and daughter, Matilda, why they should not waste bread by telling a story about a male slave in Georgia who was very thankful to receive a loaf of bread because he was starving. The conversation ends with the mother saying to Henry: "Rejoice, my boy, that you are sorry for your fault; always remember, love, that *to acknowledge a fault* is the first step to improvement." Through invoking slavery in the antebellum South, the author instructs black children on moral behavior and warns them to be thrifty or fall victim to a life of labor and suffering. "Conversations between a Mother and Her Children," *Repository of Religion and Literature* (July 1858).

45. In her September 21, 1833, farewell address presented in Boston, Maria W. Stewart revealed the hostile reactions her public speaking provoked. See "Mrs. Stewart's Farewell Address," 65–74. For a description of Stewart's difficult life circumstances at the time she wrote this story, see "Sufferings during the War," first published in 1879 in *Meditations from the Pen of Mrs. Maria W. Stewart: (Widow of the Late James W. Stewart) Now Matron of the Freedman's Hospital, and Presented in 1832 to the First African Baptist Church and Society of Boston, Mass.*, reprinted in Richardson, *Maria W. Stewart*, 98–100.

46. Stewart, "Prayer," 32.

47. Ibid.

48. Maria W. Stewart, "The First Stage of Life," *Repository of Religion and Literature* 1 (January 1861), reprinted in *PMLA* 123, no. 1 (2008): 164.

49. Ibid., 162–163.

50. Ibid., 163.

51. Bernstein, *Racial Innocence*, 185.

52. Stewart, "The First Stage of Life," 162.

53. Ibid., 165.

54. Ibid.

55. Gardner, *Unexpected Places*, 87.

56. Stewart, "The First Stage of Life," 165.

57. Santamarina, "Are We There Yet?" 310.

58. Scholars have discussed how Wilson combines autobiography with fiction in *Our Nig*. In his introduction to the 1983 edition of *Our Nig*, Henry Louis Gates Jr. writes that Wilson's discursive use of fiction and autobiography is the result of "an inexperienced author struggling with or against the received conventions of her form"; Gates, Introduction, xxxvii; and Gates's chapter on *Our Nig* in *Figures in Black*, in which he argues that in the text there exist "two parallel discursive universes: the plot structure of the text claiming to be a 'fiction' and the seemingly antithetical biographical documents published as the text's 'appendix' which claim to demonstrate that this fiction is indeed fact—'an autobiography.'" Gates, *Figures in Black*, 126. See also P. Gabrielle Foreman and Reginald H. Pitts's introduction to the 2005 Penguin Classics edition of *Our Nig*, in which they argue that "*Our Nig* is prototypical of black antebellum writing in its tendency to blend and challenge the narrative forms it incorporates, weaving together factual and fictional conventions. Indeed, *Our Nig* functions as an autobiography characterized by its complex novelistic maneuvers just as surely as it is a brilliant novel that makes autobiographical claims." Foreman and Pitt, Introduction, xxx. Priscilla Wald's chapter on *Our Nig* in *Constituting Americans* argues that "*Our Nig* tells the story of how Frado becomes Our Nig and of what happens when she tries to tell her story. From the discrepancies between Wilson and 'Our Nig' emerges the story of an author's struggle with the prescriptive conventions of form and plot." Wald, *Constituting Americans*, 168. Barbara A. White has gone through historical records and documents to show the many correlations between what Wilson wrote and her actual life story: "'Our Nig' and the She-Devil: New Information about Harriet Wilson and the 'Bellmont' Family," *American Literature* 65, no. 1 (1993): 19–52. See also Ellis, *Our Nig*, and Peterson, *"Doers of the Word."* .

59. Wilson, Preface, 3.

60. P. Gabrielle Foreman and Reginald H. Pitts discuss Wilson's request for patronage from black male readers: "By the late 1850s, black patronage for literary pursuits was certainly in place. Nearly two-thirds of black adults in northern cities were at least functionally literate. There were several well-established literary societies in nearby Boston; and though their runs often spanned only several years, a full generation of black newspapers had been launched by this time." Foreman and Pitts, Introduction, 82–83n8.

61. Foreman and Pitts note that the racism and abuse Frado endured made it impossible for her to participate in the ideals of true womanhood: "The racism documented in *Our Nig* makes it impossible for Frado to join or claim a family to fulfill the maternal

and material expectations of womanhood valued by sentimental ideology. *Our Nig* challenged domestic ideals that privilege bourgeoisie home maintenance without providing a point of entry for those who have been excluded, at least as mistresses of their own homes. In that way, *Our Nig* can be characterized as *anti*sentimental; it offers perhaps the strongest and most subversive challenge to sentimental ideology and literary conventions articulated in an antebellum woman's novel." Foreman and Pitts, Introduction, xxxi.

62. Wilson, *Our Nig*, 12–13.

63. Dudden, *Serving Women*, 195.

64. Foreman and Pitts, Introduction, xlv, note 12. R. J. Ellis, citing Joan M. Jensen, *With These Hands: Women Working the Land* (New York: McGraw-Hill, 1981), suggests that seven was a typical age when girls were bound out on farms in the mid-Atlantic states. See R. J. Ellis, *Harriet Wilson's "Our Nig,": A Cultural Biography of a "Two-Story" African American Novel* (New York: Rodopi, 2003), 105.

65. Wilson, *Our Nig*, 16.

66. Ibid., 17.

67. Ibid., 48.

68. See, in particular, Reid-Pharr, *Conjugal Union*, 89–109.

69. Bernstein, *Racial Innocence*, 33.

70. Reid-Pharr, *Conjugal Union*, 104.

71. Wilson, *Our Nig*, 23.

72. Ibid., 23.

73. Ibid., 24.

74. Ibid., 38, 30–31.

75. Discussions in a graduate-level course I taught at the University of Kentucky, "Post-Bellum, Pre-Harlem," in the spring of 2012 deepened my analysis of natural landscapes in *Our Nig*.

76. Wilson, *Our Nig*, 28.

77. Ibid., 64, 68–69.

78. I arrived at Frado's age of sixteen through markers of time in Wilson's text. In Chapter 6, we learn that Frado is fourteen: "She was now able to do all the washing, ironing, baking, and the common *et cetera* of the household duties, though but fourteen" (35). The text indicates the amount of time that passes based on James Bellmont's illness: "[T]he first of spring a letter came from James" (37). Chapter 7 reveals that "month after month passed away and brought no prospect of returning health" (40). At the end of chapter 7, Wilson writes, "The month of November was one of great anxiety on James's account" (42). In Chapter 9, "Spring opened, and James, instead of rallying, as was hoped, grew worse daily" (51). This adds approximately eighteen months to the time since Frado was identified as being fourteen years old, making her age at the time she stands up to Mrs. Bellmont fifteen or sixteen.

79. Wilson, *Our Nig*, 58.

80. Ibid., 58–59.

81. See Washington, "Meditations on History: The Slave Woman's Voice," in *Invented Lives*, 3.

82. See Carby, *Reconstructing Womanhood*; Smith, Introduction; and Sterling, *We*

Are Your Sisters. Jacobs's narrative reveals her struggle with the shame and humiliation involved in exposing her past life and her inability to follow the tenets of what historian Barbara Welter calls the "cult of true womanhood," which she defines as piety, chastity, submissiveness, and domesticity; Welter, "The Cult of True Womanhood," 151–174. Conversely, as Mary Helen Washington notes, male narrators "wrote to show that they had the qualities valued and respected by other men—courage, mobility, rationality, and physical strength." The male narrator was "under no obligation to discuss his sexuality or his sex life; he did not have to reveal the existence of children he may have fathered outside of marriage"; Washington, "Meditations on History," 4. Frances Smith Foster argues that male narrators tell stories of "humanity lost, then regained" through detailed accounts of awakening to their humanity by separating themselves from other slaves, gaining power over their masters, acquiring literacy, and, finally, fleeing to northern states—patterns that are inadequate for capturing the specifics of the slave woman's experience; Foster, *Written by Herself*, 95. Valerie Smith describes how male narrators fail to represent women's actual experiences in slavery, arguing that they "rarely feature protagonists who suffer over the separation of their families or who bring relatives North with them. More importantly, they fail to represent the slave woman's sexual vulnerability, the crucial fact that differentiated her experience from that of her male counterparts." While male-authored slave narratives often represent women as victims of sexual abuse, "rare indeed is the account that provides glimpses of the interior lives or survival strategies of women so victimized." Smith, "Introduction," xxx–xxxi.

83. Smith, Introduction, xxxi. Frances Smith Foster writes that Jacobs "modifies literary techniques familiar to her anticipated audience and invents new ones in order to accommodate her testimony as she tests her readers' abilities to accept and to act upon that testimony"; Foster, *Written by Herself*, 97. Valerie Smith notes that "Jacobs's readers were accustomed to a certain degree of propriety and circumlocution in fiction. In keeping with cultural injunctions against women's assertiveness and directness in speech, the literature they wrote and read tended to be 'exercises in euphemism' that excluded certain subjects from the purview of fiction. The tension between the decorousness of the genre and the urgency of the slave woman's situation thus underscores how inadequate the sentimental novel's techniques are in telling Jacob's story. They fail, like those of the slave narrative, to meet the demands of her situation." Smith, Introduction, xxxii–xxxiii.

84. Foreman, *Activist Sentiments*, 21; Li, *Something Akin to Freedom*, 29–39; Abdur-Rahman, *Against the Closet*, 25–50. Abdur-Rahman states, "In the U.S. cultural and political context, the most recognizable and enduring symbols of social and sexual degeneracy and of historical black victimization are the single black mother and, of course, the little black girl" (115). Foreman states that "Jacobs shields her grandmother Molly Horniblow, protecting her, in turn, from the sexual unveilings to which her protagonist is discursively subjected" (36). Like Foreman's insightful unveiling of Aunt Martha's sexual history, Jacobs's representation of Linda's girlhood seeks to uncover hidden truths.

85. Durham, "Marriageable State." See also Hollick, *The Marriage Guide*; and *Ladies' Indispensable Companion and Housekeepers' Guide*.

86. Durham,"Marriageable State," 119–120.

87. Foster, *Written by Herself*, 96.

88. Jacobs, *Incidents in the Life of a Slave Girl*, 26.

89. Ibid., 47–48.

90. A pivotal, lengthy scene in Steve McQueen's filmic adaptation of Solomon Northrup's slave narrative *Twelve Years a Slave* (1853) features an enslaved girl named Patsy who sits in the grass, hums, and makes dolls out of straw while, in a blurry backdrop, slaves are whipped for their inability to pick a daily quota of cotton. These two scenes captured in one frame—one pleasurable and the other painful, one in sharp focus and the other blurred—capture visually the inhumanity of slavery, in which children's play takes place in the context of routine acts of violence. McQueen's pairing of pleasure and pain throughout his film achieve visually what Harriet Jacobs achieves linguistically through the ironic pairing of two opposites.

91. See Noble, *Masochistic Pleasures of Sentimental Literature*; Hartman, *Scenes of Subjection*; Smith, *Self-Discovery and Authority*; and Fleischner, *Mastering Slavery*.

92. Hartman, *Scenes of Subjection*, 42–43.

93. Critics have made similar arguments that in Frederick Douglass's 1845 *Narrative*, he conditions the reader to identify with his position as a child in relation to the violence of slavery, as expressed by the gory spectacle of the whipping of Hester.

94. Jacobs, *Incidents in the Life of a Slave Girl*, 10, 18.

95. Ibid., 26, 116.

96. Ibid., 27, emphasis added.

97. Ibid., 68.

98. As Foster argues, Jacobs "writes an account of slavery that does not excuse the evil inherent in that institution but does reveal it as a condition within which some are able to develop strong family ties, develop bonds of affection and loyalty among women, and unite themselves into a viable and resourceful community of resisters." Foster, *Written by Herself*, 95.

Chapter 3. "Teach Your Daughters"

1. Mrs. N. F. Mossell, "The Fate of the Newspaper that Had Nothing in It," *Christian Recorder*, February 18, 1886.

2. Garvey, *Writing with Scissors*, 131. For Mossell's influence on scrapbooking, see 136–137.

3. Mossell, *Work of the Afro-American Woman*, 61.

4. Several scholars of nineteenth-century African American literature discuss the connection between literacy, serialization, black reading communities, and citizenship rights. McHenry, *Forgotten Readers*; Gardner, *Unexpected Places*; Tate, *Domestic Allegories of Political Desire*; Foreman, *Activist Sentiments*; Foster, "A Narrative of the Interesting Origins," 1727–728; Foster, *Love and Marriage in Early African America*; Foster, *'Til Death or Distance Do Us Part*; Peterson. *"Doers of the Word."*

5. Margaret Hope Bacon, "Learning from Sarah Douglass," *Friends Journal*, January 2002, 18; "Douglass, Sarah Mapps," 186; Streitmatter, *Raising Her Voice*, 38–39.

6. Boyle and Bunie, *Paul Robeson*, 11.

7. Ibid.

8. See Davis, "Pennsylvania State Equal Rights League," 611–634.

9. For an example of Charles Bustill's work in the Underground Railroad, see the account of the escape of Samuel Green from slavery in Maryland in 1854; "Samuel Green Jr. (b. 1829–d. 1875)," Archives of Maryland (Biographical Series), http://msa.maryland.gov/megafile/msa/speccol/sc5400/sc5496/051300/051332/html/51332bio.html (accessed March 10, 2015).

10. Still, *The Underground Rail Road*, 610–612.

11. Entry for Charles Bustill, federal manuscript census returns, population, 7th Ward, Philadelphia, Pennsylvania, Eighth Census of the United States (1860), p. 682; entry for Charles Bustill, federal manuscript census returns, population, 37th District, 13th Ward, Philadelphia, Pennsylvania, 1870, Ninth Census of the United States (1870), p. 156; entry for Charles Bustill, Philadelphia, Pennsylvania, City Directory, 1881, p. 299, all accessed at Ancestry.com.

12. Entry for David and Mary Bustill, four children, and two boarders, federal manuscript census returns, population, 2nd Ward (Northern Liberties), Philadelphia, Pennsylvania, Seventh Census of the United States (1850), p. 53, accessed at Ancestry.com.

13. "Mary W. Hicks Bustill," Find a Grave Memorial #88616877, http://www.findagrave.com/cgi-bin/fg.cgi?page=gr&GRid=88616877&ref=acom (accessed March 10, 2015).

14. Entry for household of Charles Bustill, federal manuscript census returns, population, 7th Ward, Philadelphia, Pennsylvania, Eighth Census of the United States (1860), p. 682, accessed at Ancestry.com.

15. See Perkins, "Quaker Beneficence and Black Control," 19–40; and James, "Institute for Colored Youth," 83–85.

16. Sarah Mapps Douglass's mother was Grace Bustill Douglass. Grace was a daughter of Cyrus Bustill and was thus the sister of David Bustill, Charles Hicks Bustill's father and Gertrude Bustill's grandfather. Both Grace Bustill Douglass and Sarah Mapps Douglass were prominent Philadelphia abolitionists. For more, see Yee, *Black Women Abolitionists*; and Sterling, *We Are Your Sisters*, 103–105, 114–115 (for Grace Bustill Douglass) and 110–112, 114–115, 126–133 (for Sarah Mapps Douglass).

17. Boyle and Bunie, *Paul Robeson*, 11–12.

18. Streitmatter, "Gertrude Bustill Mossell," 319.

19. Entry for Gertrude Bustill, federal manuscript census returns, population, enumeration district 481, Philadelphia, Pennsylvania, Tenth Census of the United States (1880), p. 14.

20. Various dates are cited in primary and secondary sources for the marriage of Nathan Mossell and Gertrude Bustill. However, Nathan Mossell's typescript autobiography says that he married in 1881, "a year before my graduation" from medical school. See "Nathan Francis Mossell Autobiography," typescript, Penn University Archives and Records Center, http://www.archives.upenn.edu/people/1800s/mossell_nathan_f.html (accessed March 10, 2015).

21. Aaron Mossell household, enumeration district 2, Barton township, Hamilton, Ontario, page 58, Census of Canada, 1861, accessed at Ancestry.com.

22. "Aaron Mossell Home," document 27, Niagara Falls Underground Railroad Heritage Area, http://www.niagarafallsundergroundrailroad.org/index.php/sites (accessed April 3, 2016).

23. Pride and Wilson, *History of the Black Press*, 117–118.

24. Streitmatter, "Gertrude Bustill Mossell," 320.

25. Johnson, *W. E. B. Du Bois*, 24. See 24–27 for more about Fortune's reputation in the black community and his view that editors and journalists were key shapers of opinion among blacks.

26. Streitmatter, "Gertrude Bustill Mossell," 320; Evi Heilbrunn, "A Philadelphia Story: The Lost Legacy of Dr. Nathan Mossell," *Pittsburgh Post-Gazette*, April 22, 2012. The equivalent purchasing power of Gertrude's $500 annual income was $12,500 in 2013.

27. Braxton, Introduction, xxviii.

28. Tate, *Domestic Allegories of Political Desire*, 134.

29. Braxton, Introduction, xxviii.

30. See Tate, *Domestic Allegories of Political Desire*; Braxton, Introduction, xxvii–xlii; and duCille, *Coupling Convention*, 50. See also Garvey, *Writing with Scissors*, 136–137, in which Garvey draws from one of Mossell's columns on scrapbooking.

31. Tate, *Domestic Allegories of Political Desire*, 132.

32. DuCille, *Coupling Convention*, 50.

33. Foreman, *Activist Sentiments*, 143.

34. Braxton, Introduction, xlii.

35. Ivy, "A Chapter on Our Girls: Their Position in the World—How to Educate Them," *New York Freeman*, March 20, 1886, reprinted from the *Louisiana Standard*.

36. I attribute my interest in Mossell's Acknowledgments section of her column to Eric Gardner, who encouraged scholars of black print culture to look beyond texts bound between book covers for information about black readers. As Gardner observes, the printing of acknowledgments "functioned as receipts for subscribers and may also have encouraged new subscriptions or renewals by publically commending subscribers." See Gardner, "Remembered (Black) Readers," 231, and Gardner, *Black Print Unbound*, 99–101.

37. See *Finding Aid for Novels in the Mercantile Library* (Philadelphia: Mercantile Library Association, 1878) for a brief history of the Mercantile Library of Philadelphia.

38. Weikle-Mills, "Introduction: Children's Periodicals," 117.

39. See Brazeau, "I Must Have My Gossip," 159–176; Lindey, "Boys Write Back," 72–88.

40. Foster, "Genealogies of Our Concerns," 373, 378, 374.

41. Mrs. N. F. Mossell, "An Assurance," *New York Freeman*, February 13, 1886.

42. See Mrs. N. F. Mossell, "Only a Girl," February 13, 1886; "Domestic Training for Girls," April 3, 1886; and "Teach Your Daughters," April 3, 1886, all in *New York Freeman*.

43. Mossell, "Only a Girl."

44. Extract from the *Savannah Tribune*, reprinted in the section "Choice Thoughts and Utterances of Wise Colored People," in Haley, *Afro-American Encyclopedia: Thoughts, Doings, and Sayings of the Race*, 1896), 531.

45. Quoted in Vanessa Northington Gamble, "Roots of the Black Hospital Reform Movement," in Gamble, *Making a Place for Ourselves: The Black Hospital Movement, 1920–1945* (New York: Oxford University Press, 1995), 378–379.

46. Mrs. N. F. Mossell, "Care of Children," *New York Freeman*, December 26, 1886.

47. Mossell, "Teach Your Daughters."

48. Mrs. N. F. Mossell, "Domestic Training for Girls."

49. Mrs. N. F. Mossell, "Some Recent Calculations that Deserve Notice by Economists," *New York Freeman*, February 5, 1887.

50. F. B. B., "Advice to Young Housekeepers," *New York Freeman*, January 22, 1887.

51. Mossell, "'Teach Your Daughters."

52. Greenberg and Watts, *Social History of the United States*, 65.

53. "Garment Industry," in *Encyclopedia of U.S. Labor and Working-Class History*, vol. 1, *A–F*, edited by Eric Arnesen (New York: Taylor and Francis, 2007), 496.

54. See Sacks, *Before Harlem*, 143.

55. Dabel, *A Respectable Woman*, 67 (quote), 63; see also table on page 70.

56. According to the U.S. census, the black population of Philadelphia was 22,147 in 1870 and 39,371 in 1890. "Table 3: Population of Civil Divisions Less than Counties: State of Pennsylvania," in *The Statistics of the Population of the United States . . . from the Original Returns of the Ninth Census (June 1, 1870)* (Washington, D.C.: Government Printing Office, 1872), 254; Table 19, "Population by Sex, General Nativity, and Color of Places Having Inhabitants of 2,500 or More: 1890," in Department of the Interior, Census Office, *Report on Population of the United States at the Eleventh Census: 1890*, Part I (Washington, D.C.: Government Printing Office, 1895), 478.

57. Gross, *Colored Amazons*, 43–44, quote on 44.

58. For black women and domestic work before the Civil War in Philadelphia, see Horton, *In Hope of Liberty*, 114.

59. Mrs. N. F. Mossell, "Servant Girl Question," *New York Freeman*, January 2, 1886.

60. Ibid.

61. Ibid.

62. Ibid.

63. Fannie Jackson Coppin had been educated at Oberlin College in Ohio. From 1865 to 1900, she was the principal of the Institute for Colored Youth in Philadelphia, the school Gertrude Bussill had attended in the 1860s. After the Civil War, she expanded the curriculum of the school to include industrial education. See Tillman, "Afro-American Women and Their Work," 284; and Powers, *Eyes to My Soul*, 195.

64. Mrs. N. F. Mossell, "A Woman's Pocket-Book," *New York Freeman*, February 20, 1886.

65. Ibid.

66. Ibid.

67. Ibid.

68. Ibid.

69. Mrs. N. F. Mossell, "A Word of Counsel," *New York Freeman*, February 13, 1886.

70. Ibid.

71. Ibid. Monica L. Miller argues that "dandyism functions as a symptom of changing social, political, cultural and economic conditions." The dandy figure helps readers understand the black girl figure as similarly evolving and thus resistant to normative categories of gender- and sex-defined roles. Miller, *Slaves to Fashion*, 8.

72. Mrs. N. F. Mossell, "Saving Our Women," *New York Freeman*, December 11, 1886.

73. Mrs. N. F. Mossell, "Working at Watering Places during the Summer," *New York Freeman*, April 17, 1886.

74. Mrs. N. F. Mossell, "Olive Logan's Advice to Girls," *New York Freeman*, March 13, 1886.

75. Mrs. N. F. Mossell, "Home," *New York Freeman*, December 4, 1886.

76. According to an 1847 census of blacks in Philadelphia, the females in David Bustill's household operated "stands in market." "David Bustill," Philadelphia, Pennsylvania, African-American Census, 1847, p. 11, accessed at Ancestry.com. This census is a rich source for historians, especially for those interested in tracing women's work in an antebellum urban center just before the 1850 Fugitive Slave Act. A systematic analysis of this primary source would provide information about how women's wage-earning work helped fund the work of the Underground Railroad.

77. "Grace Bustill Douglass (1782–1842)," 189.

78. Ibid. Sarah Mapps Douglass may have been the "Aunt Ruth" of Mossell's article.

79. For example, "Our Literary Women" (April 13, 1886) listed twelve black women writers and the periodicals where their work was published.

80. Mrs. N. F. Mossell, "Woman's Work," *New York Freeman*, April 3, 1886.

81. Mrs. N. F. Mossell, "Training School for Girls," *New York Freeman*, August 28, 1886; Karen DeMasters, "On the Map: Remembering a Boarding School for Black Students," *New York Times*, October 1, 2000. For more on the New Jersey Industrial and Training School for Colored Youth, see Asante, *The African American People*, 145–146.

82. Mossell, "Training School for Girls." Leon Abbett held his first term as governor of New Jersey from 1884 to 1887.

83. "Documentary Focuses on 'Tuskegee of the North,'" NPR Web site, May 24, 2010, http://www.npr.org/templates/story/story.php?storyId=127091472 (accessed March 21, 2015). The documentary, directed by Dave Davidson and hosted by Alison Keyes, is *A Place Out of Time*.

84. Mossell, "Training School for Girls."

85. Mrs. N. F. Mossell, "Women's Ways," *New York Freeman*, January 8, 1887.

86. The 1910 manuscript census recorded that Gertrude Mossell had four children but only two had survived. The four-year gap between her marriage in 1881 and the birth of her oldest surviving child in 1885 suggests that she may have lost the children in the early years of her marriage. If that was the case, this would likely have been another reason that she was cautious about travel while she was pregnant. Entry for Nathan and Gertrude Mossell, federal manuscript census, population, Philadelphia, Pennsylvania, Thirteenth Census of the United States (1910), p. 551, accessed at Ancestry.com. The birth years of her two daughters are documented in the 1900 census entry for her household; entry for Natha [*sic*] and Gertrude Mossell and two daughters, federal manuscript census returns, population, 7th Ward, Philadelphia, Pennsylvania, Twelfth Census of the United States (1900), p. 1B, accessed at Ancestry.com.

87. Mrs. N. F. Mossell, "Clippings or Notes," *New York Freeman*, August 28, 1886.

88. Mrs. N. F. Mossell, "Colored People's Grievances," *New York Freeman*, December 18, 1886.

89. For an overview of the issues related to the admission of blacks to Knights of Labor assemblies, see Kessler, "Organization of Negroes," 248–276.

90. Mossell, "Colored People's Grievances."

91. Mrs. N. F. Mossell, "Our Woman's Department," *New York Freeman*, January 9, 1886.

92. Mrs. N. F. Mossell, "Our Woman's Department," *New York Freeman*, March 6, 1886.

93. Mrs. N. F. Mossell, "Our Woman's Department," *New York Freeman*, January 23, 1886.

94. Both examples from Mrs. N. F. Mossell, "Our Woman's Department," *New York Freeman*, January 23, 1886.

95. Mrs. N. F. Mossell, "Our Woman's Department," *New York Freeman*, February 20, 1886.

96. At the time Lewis unveiled her sculpture, the *Woman's Journal* reported that the three wise men were of three races, white, Asian, and African. "Of the three, the African is given the greater prominence." *Woman's Journal*, March 10, 1883, quoted in Romare Bearden and Harry Harrison, *A History of African-American Artists: 1792 to the Present* (New York: Pantheon Books, 1993), 76. Mrs. N. F. Mossell, "Our Woman's Department," *New York Freeman*, January 9, 1886.

Chapter 4. Moving the Boundaries

1. Stancliff, Frances Ellen Watkins Harper, 114; Williams, Dividing Lines, 37.

2. Many black writers in the nineteenth century published their first longer fictional pieces in serialized newspapers. Harper's *Minnie's Sacrifice*, *Sowing and Reaping*, and *Trial and Triumph* were serialized in the *Christian Recorder*. The *Colored American* serialized three of Pauline Hopkins's novels: *Hagar's Daughter: A Story of Southern Caste Prejudice* (1901–1902), *Winona: A Tale of Negro Life in the South and Southwest* (1902), and *Of One Blood: Or, The Hidden Self* (1902–1903). Katherine Davis Chapman Tillman's *Beryl Weston's Ambition: The Story of an Afro-American Girl's Life* (1893) and *Clancy Street* (1898–1899) appeared in the *A. M. E. Church Review*. Frederick Douglass published his novella *The Heroic Slave* in the *North Star* in 1853. For more information on serialization, see Patten, "Serial Literature," 514–519.

3. Gardner, "Remembered (Black) Readers," 234, 251, 246.

4. McHenry, *Forgotten Readers*, 4–5. According to U.S. census data, the percent of the black population that was literate increased from 30 percent in 1880 to 70 percent in 1910. The low literacy rate in 1880 is explained by the fact that the population included former slaves who had been excluded from education. For Harper's involvement with the *Christian Recorder*, see Foster, "Gender, Genre and Vulgar Secularism."

5. Toohey, "A Deeper Purpose," 203.

6. Foster, Introduction, in Harper, *Trial and Triumph*, xxxiii.

7. Harper, *Trial and Triumph*, 191.

8. Ibid., 191, 184.

9. Ibid., 180.

10. Ibid., 250.

11. Still, "Frances Ellen Watkins Harper," 755. Although numerous recent works focus on the role of her uncle, William Watkins, in Harper's upbringing, Still and Elizabeth Lindsay Davis write that she lived with an aunt after the death of her mother, likely until

1839, when she began service in the home of a local minister at the age of thirteen. Thus, Harper was intimately familiar with the experience of having a surrogate mother. See also Davis, "Frances Ellen Watkins Harper," 231.

12. Still, "Frances Ellen Watkins Harper," 755–756.

13. "Frances Ellen Watkins Harper," 97.

14. Ibid., 98.

15. Logan, *We Are Coming*, 48.

16. These are the words of one of Watkins's students; see ibid.

17. Filler, "Harper, Frances Ellen Watkins," 135–139; Jackson, "Harper, Frances Ellen Watkins," 374–375.

18. Johnson quoted (without full citation) in Foster, Introduction, in *Brighter Coming Day*, 7. Johnson's later career is briefly mentioned in James A. Wind, *American Congregations*, vol. 1, *Portraits of Twelve Religious Communities* (Chicago: University of Chicago Press, 1994), 244, 283.

19. Harper published *Forest Leaves* around 1845, at the age of twenty. The volume was recently recovered at the Maryland Historical Society. Nine years later, in 1854, she published *Poems on Miscellaneous Subjects* (Boston: J. B. Yerrinton and Son), a book of antislavery poems. She also published antislavery poems and stories in *Liberator*, *Frederick Douglass' Paper*, and other antislavery papers. Filler, "Harper, Frances Ellen Watkins," 138.

20. Louis Filler's biography of Harper for *Notable American Women* said that she "went to live in the household of a Baltimore bookseller named Armstrong" in order to earn her living. Armstrong & Berry is the only bookseller I have been able to locate in Baltimore city directories of this period associated with the surname Armstrong. Ibid., 137.

21. Various sources have referred to this time as an "apprenticeship" with the bookseller for whom she worked, but Still, who doubtless got his information from Harper herself, makes clear that she was hired to do domestic work.

22. Still, "Frances Ellen Watkins Harper," 756.

23. Armstrong & Berry advertisement in *American Republican and Baltimore Daily Clipper*, November 14, 1844, 2.

24. Armstrong & Berry advertisement in *Pilot and Transcript* (Baltimore), January 21, 1841, 3.

25. Ibid.

26. Filler, "Harper, Frances Ellen Watkins," 136. Apparently no copies of this volume have survived.

27. Harper, *Trial and Triumph*, 241–242.

28. Ibid., 243.

29. Both quoted in Davis, "Frances Ellen Watkins Harper," 232.

30. Harper, *Trial and Triumph*, 197–198.

31. Ibid., 226.

32. Ibid., 189.

33. Ibid., 186.

34. For the story of the black community's challenge to the segregated system and the passage of the 1881 law, see Price, "School Segregation in Nineteenth-Century Pennsylvania," 120–137.

35. Historian Roger Lane writes that "Philadelphia's public schools, in keeping with the general decentralization of local government in the nineteenth century, were generally run at the ward level." Philadelphia did not have a superintendent of schools until 1883. Lane, *William Dorsey's Philadelphia and Ours*, 148.

36. Johnson, *Philadelphia Fels*, 1880–1900, 44.

37. Table 19, "Population by Sex, General Nativity, and Color, of Places Having 2,500 Inhabitants or More: 1890," in Department of the Interior, Census Office, *Report on Population of the United States at the Eleventh Census: 1890*, Part 1 (Washington, D.C.: Government Printing Office, 1895), 478. Harper's Philadelphia address is mentioned in Foster, "Introduction," in *Brighter Coming Day*, 20.

38. Dinwiddie, *Housing Conditions in Philadelphia*, 1, 4.

39. Harper, *Trial and Triumph*, 190.

40. Ibid., 255.

41. Ibid., 212.

42. Mr. Thomas tells Rev. Lomax, "My father is a wealthy Southerner; he has several other sons who are inheritors of his name and heirs of his wealth. They are educated, cultured and occupy high social positions. Had I not as good a right to be well born as any of them? And yet, through my father's crime, I was doomed to the status of a slave with its heritage of ignorance, poverty and social debasement." Ibid., 235.

43. Ibid., 225.

44. Ibid., 245.

45. Ibid., 181, 226.

46. Ibid., 236.

47. Ibid., 245.

48. Ibid., 207.

49. Alexander, *History of the Colored Race*, 20.

50. Lane, *William Dorsey's Philadelphia and Ours*, 26, 66; Dickson T. Bruce, *Black American Writing from the Nadir: The Evolution of a Literary Tradition, 1877–1915* (Baton Rouge: Louisiana State University Press, 1992), 32, quoted in Tate, *Domestic Allegories of Political Desire*, 112.

51. Matthews, *The Value of Race Literature*, 172–175.

52. Harper, *Trial and Triumph*, 180.

53. Ibid., 181.

54. Ibid., 185.

55. Ibid.

56. Ibid., 186.

57. Ibid., 185.

58. Ibid., 219–220.

59. Ibid., 214–215.

60. Ibid., 220.

61. Haven, *The Pilgrim's Wallet*, 205.

62. Ibid., 201–202.

63. Harper, *Trial and Triumph*, 220.

64. Gold, "The Death of Cleopatra," 320. See also Woods, "An African Queen," 62–82.

65. Ibid.

66. Chaney, *Fugitive Vision*, 19.

67. Harper, *Trial and Triumph*, 202.

68. Ibid., 229.

69. Ibid., 228. The term *upper tens* appeared sometime in the 1870s to describe the black economic elite. Other terms, such as *colored aristocracy* and the *black 400* (in Washington, D.C.) were also used in the late nineteenth century to describe this stratum of the black community. Gatewood, *Aristocrats of Color*, 97. The term *talented tenth* was not used to describe black elites until W. E. B. Du Bois used it in the 1903 book *The Negro Problem*.

70. Ibid., 184, 228.

71. Ibid., 228.

72. Ibid., 227.

73. Ibid.

74. Ibid., 228.

75. Ibid., 254.

76. Ibid., 256. It seems that Dr. Harcourt's home is closer to the Lasette residence in the 19th Ward than it is to Annette's former home in the Tennis Court neighborhood, because when Mrs. Lasette hears what the aunt has said, she asks her daughter "who has been gossipping to you about your neighbors?" Ibid.

77. Ibid., 258. In the third chapter of the novel, Harper said that Lucy "had gone from home to teach school in a distant city as there were no openings of the kind for her at her own home" (190). By the fifteenth installment, Harper had evidently decided that a cautionary tale about a domestic worker would have more resonance with her readership.

78. Ibid., 265.

79. Ibid., 265–266.

80. Ibid., 280.

81. Ibid.

82. Ibid., 281.

83. Ibid., 229.

84. Ibid., 282.

85. Harper, "We Are All Bound Up Together," 217–219.

86. Frances E. W. Harper to William Still, n.d., quoted in Still, "Frances Ellen Watkins Harper," 778.

87. Frances E. W. Harper, Darlington, S.C., to William Still, May 13, 1867, quoted in ibid., 768.

88. Frances E. W. Harper, Kingstree, S.C., to William Still, July 11, 1867, quoted in ibid., 770.

89. In May 1867, while traveling in South Carolina, Harper wrote to William Still that "There had been some violence in the district, and some of my friends did not wish me to go, but I had promised, and, of course, I went." Quoted in ibid., 768.

90. Frances Harper, Greenville, Ga., to William Still, March 29, no year [1870?], quoted in ibid., 773.

91. Still, "Frances Ellen Watkins Harper," 767.

92. Ibid., 772.

93. Ibid., 767.

94. Editorial by Col. J. W. Forney, of "The Press" (Mobile, Ala.), July 12, 1871, quoted in ibid., 774.

95. Newspaper clipping enclosed in Frances E. W. Harper to William Still, Mobile, Ala., July 5, 1871, quoted in ibid., 775–776.

96. Harper, "Coloured Women of America," quote on 11.

97. Frances Harper to William Still, n.d., quoted in Still, "Frances Ellen Watkins Harper," 778.

98. Frances Harper, Eufaula, Ala., to William Still, December 9, 1870, quoted in ibid., 771.

99. Harper, *Trial and Triumph*, 285.

100. Ibid., 250.

101. Harper, "Enlightened Motherhood," 287, 286, 292.

102. Harper, *Trial and Triumph*, 284.

103. Ibid.

104. Ibid.

105. Ibid., 284–285.

106. Ibid., 285.

107. Ibid., 284.

108. Ibid., 285.

Chapter 5. Black Girlhood in Early-Twentieth-Century Black Conduct Books

1. Du Bois, "Of the Meaning of Progress," in *The Souls of Black Folk*, 50.

2. Ibid., 51.

3. Ibid.

4. Ibid., 50.

5. Ibid.

6. Ibid., 53.

7. Ibid., 55.

8. Williams, "The Colored Girl," 63.

9. Ibid.

10. Ibid., 66.

11. Ibid.

12. Logan, *Negro in American Life and Thought*.

13. Claudia Tate argues that after emancipation African American women writers wrote novels that portrayed courtships and wedded bliss as resources that enabled African Americans to enter areas of civic life from which they were largely excluded. Tate, *Domestic Allegories of Political Desire*, 5.

14. Gates, "The Trope of the New Negro," 130–131.

15. Gates's definition of the New Negro is specific to these dates. The meaning of the term *New Negro* fluctuates from the late nineteenth to the early twentieth centuries.

16. Floyd, *Floyd's Flowers*; Floyd, *Charming Stories for Young and Old*. Other editions of *Floyd's Flowers* include *Short Stories for Colored People* and *New Floyd's Flowers*.

17. Wright, "Black Girls and Representative Citizenship."

18. Dyer, "An Early Black Textbook," 359.

19. Ibid., 360.

20. Gates and Jarrett, *The New Negro*, 7.

21. Floyd, Preface, *Floyd's Flowers*, 7.

22. Foster, "Creative Collaboration." For other scholarship on visual representation and the New Negro, see Sherrard-Johnson, *Portraits of the New Negro Woman*; Carroll, *Word, Image, and the New Negro*; and Goeser, *Picturing the New Negro*.

23. Smith, "The Emblematic Black Child," chapter 1 of Smith, *Children's Literature of the Harlem Renaissance*.

24. Du Bois, *Morals and Manners among Negro Americans*, 5. At a conference that addressed the moral improvement of the black race, Du Bois countered the stereotype, crediting the work of the National Association of Colored Women with uplifting the race. He said that he was "pleased to call the attention of the country to the fact that much of the real work of social uplift and moral awakening is being carried on by Negro women in their clubs and institutions" (7).

25. In "Industrial Education for the Negro," Washington stated, "I would teach the race that in industry the foundation must be laid—that the very best service which any one can render to what is called the higher education is to teach the present generation to provide a material or industrial foundation. On such a foundation as this will grow habits of thrift, a love of work, economy, ownership of property, bank accounts. Out of it in the future will grow practical education, professional education, positions of public responsibility. Out of it will grow moral and religious strength. Out of it will grow wealth from which alone can come leisure and the opportunity for the enjoyment of literature and the fine arts." Washington, "Industrial Education for the Negro," 18. Washington argued that "it has been necessary for the Negro to learn the difference between being worked and working—to learn that being worked meant degradation, while working means civilization; that all forms of labor are honorable, and all forms of idleness disgraceful" (9).

26. Gaines, *Uplifting the Race*. Katharine Capshaw Smith claims that "an anxiety about crude public behavior courses through most conduct material, as elites betrayed their fears that blacks would be judged as a whole through the behavior of the lower classes among them. For the black aristocracy, race solidarity resulted from political necessity as well as moral obligation." Smith, "Childhood, the Body, and Race Performance," 798. Saidiya Hartman argues that "the majority of the violence committed against the freed in the aftermath of slavery was incited by charges of unbecoming conduct, which included one's dress, demeanor, movement through public space, tone of voice, and companions." Hartman, *Scenes of Subjection*, 148.

27. See other instructional manuals such as *The New England Offering* (1847–1850), which discusses sexuality, reproduction, and health for girls. Lydia Maria Child's *The Juvenile Miscellany: For the Instruction and Amusement of Youth (1826–1836)* is said to be the first American children's magazine that included information geared for children, including discussions of proper behavior, essays on virtue, and biographical sketches of notable figures.

28. Gibson and Gibson, *Golden Thoughts on Chastity and Procreation*, 74.

29. Mitchell, *Righteous Propagation*, 121.

30. Ibid.

31. Ibid., 122. Benjamin was not the first to offer this advice. Almost forty years earlier, Frances E. W. Harper had promoted "spinsterhood" in "The Two Offers," *Anglo-African Magazine*, September-October 1859, 288–291, 311–313; and "Fancy Sketches," *Anglo-African Magazine*, November 1859, 340–343. The latter is short fiction that Harper published under the name Jane Rustic.

32. Wood-Allen, *What a Young Woman Ought to Know*.

33. Ibid., 16.

34. Ibid., 21.

35. Ibid., 112.

36. Ibid.

37. Toward the end of the story, readers learn that a boy from Piney Grove "had gone to school at T——one year after Grace went." He had studied agriculture at Tuskegee and had returned home to establish a successful poultry and dairy business. Floyd, "Thanksgiving at Piney Grove," in *Floyd's Flowers*, 45.

38. In his autobiography *Up from Slavery*, Booker T. Washington wrote of the importance of the toothbrush as a civilizing agent for the students at Tuskegee Institute: "In all my teaching I have watched carefully the influence of the tooth-brush, and I am convinced that there are few single agencies of civilization that are more far-reaching." Washington, *Up from Slavery*, 110.

39. Floyd, "Thanksgiving at Piney Grove," 39.

40. Ibid., 40–41.

41. See Yarborough, Introduction, xxxv.

42. Scholars maintain that an "emphasis on hygiene expresses larger concerns about national well-being since hygiene legitimated, if not invited, the policing of dwellings but also the setting of guidelines for marriage and other forms of social association, particularly those considered dangerous or destabilizing of social order." See Hartman, *Scenes of Subjection*, 158. Katherine Capshaw Smith notes that in Floyd's books, "the child's body becomes the site on which the character of the new black identity can be staged." Floyd believed that "through education and uplift, the supposedly fixed nature of public identity [could] change and be witnessed in the new, cultured body of the black child." Smith, "Childhood, the Body, and Race Performance," 799, 806.

43. Smith, *Children's Literature of the Harlem Renaissance*, x; Floyd, "Thanksgiving at Piney Grove," 41.

44. Smith, *Children's Literature of the Harlem Renaissance*, x.

45. Smith, "Childhood, the Body, and Race Performance," 799.

46. Floyd, "Thanksgiving at Piney Grove," 46.

47. Adams, "Rough Sketches," 238–241. The quote I used is from a caption to a picture accompanying the article.

48. Washington, "Industrial Education for the Negro," 16–17.

49. Washington, *Working with the Hands*, 122. This text contains illustrations and photographs by Frances Benjamin Johnson.

50. Floyd, "Mary and Her Dolls," in *Floyd's Flowers*, 76–77.

51. Ibid., 76.

52. Ibid., 77.

53. Mitchell, *Righteous Propagation*, 178.

54. Ibid., 195.

55. For more information on dolls in American culture, see Formanek-Brunell, *Dolls and the Commercialization of American Culture*; and Bernstein, *Racial Innocence*.

56. Floyd, "Directions for Little Ladies," in *Floyd's Flowers*, 264–265.

57. Floyd, "The Don't-Care Girl," in *Floyd's Flowers* (1905), 49–51.

58. Ibid.

59. Floyd, "The Don't-Care Girl," 310–311.

60. Ibid., 311.

61. Ibid.

62. Floyd, "The Loud Girl," in *Floyd's Flowers* (1905), 47–48.

63. Hopkins, *Contending Forces*, 110–111, Hopkins's italics.

64. See Wells, *Crusade for Justice*; and Higginbotham, *Righteous Discontent*.

65. Floyd, "The Don't-Care Girl," 49.

66. Floyd, "The Rowdy Boy," in *Floyd's Flowers* (1905), 53.

67. Ibid., 51.

68. Ibid., 53.

69. Ibid., 49.

70. Smith, *Photography on the Color Line*, 109.

71. Floyd, "Keeping School," in *Floyd's Flowers*, 93.

72. Ibid.

73. Ibid., 94.

74. Ibid., 95.

75. Willis, "Picturing the New Negro Woman," 227.

76. Ibid., 228.

77. Wallace and Smith, *Pictures and Progress*, 4.

78. Wells, *A Red Record*, 77.

79. Mitchell, *Living with Lynching*, 1.

80. Ibid., 2.

81. Dunbar-Nelson, "Mine Eyes Have Seen," 239–249.

82. Burrill, *Aftermath*, 79.

83. Ibid.

84. Mitchell, *Living with Lynching*, 2.

85. Ibid.

86. Hackley, *The Colored Girl Beautiful*, 102.

87. Mossell, *Little Dansie's One Day*. A page-image version is available at http://digitalcollections.nypl.org/items/987ae9ee-b010-d56a-e040-e00a18064dbe (accessed October 25, 2015).

88. Ibid., 1.

89. Ibid.

90. Ibid., 2.

91. Ibid.

92. Ibid., 4.

93. Ibid., 4–5.

94. Ibid., 5–6.

95. Ibid., 7.

96. Ibid., 9.

97. Ibid., 9–10.

Epilogue

1. Jones, "The Changing Same," 208.

2. McDowell, "*The Changing Same.*" As Deborah McDowell argues, recurring patterns in contemporary literary depictions of womanhood—and in this case black girlhood—"had not emerged *in vacuo*, but were preceded by an earlier generation of women writers, albeit those with limited popular appeal," xii.

3. "Commitment: Toni Cade Bambara Speaks," 247.

4. Morrison, "Afterword," 210.

5. Ibid., 211.

6. Rosenberg, "Seeds in Hard Ground," 435–445.

7. Wall quoted in Sarah Projansky, *Spectacular Girls: Media Fascination and Celebrity Culture* (New York: New York University Press, 2014), 77.

8. "Fox News' Andrea Tantaros Asks if Malia Obama Will Take Birth Control," *Inquisitr*, May 3, 2013, http://www.inquisitr.com/647457/fox-news-andrea-tantaros-asks-if-malia-obama-will-take-birth-control-audio/ (accessed October 10, 2015).

9. Demetria Lucas D'Oyley, "Picking on the Obama Girls Isn't Smart, Especially if You Work for a GOP Congressman," *Root*, November 29, 2014, http://www.theroot.com/articles/culture/2014/11/elizabeth_lauten_faces_backlash_after_scolding_sasha_and_malia_on_facebook.html (accessed October 10, 2015). For footage of the press conference, see "National Thanksgiving Turkey Pardon," C-Span, November 26, 2014, http://www.c-span.org/video/?322965-1/national-thanksgiving-turkey-pardon (accessed October 10, 2015).

10. Juliet Macur, "A Very Long Journey Was Very Swift," *New York Times*, August 2, 2012.

11. Natalie Hawkins's decision to allow her daughter to live with the Partons came with much difficulty. She is the single mother of four children and works as a debt collector. Struggling to make ends meet, she filed for Chapter 13 Bankruptcy. Gabrielle saw her mother only four times during the two years she trained in Iowa. Ibid.

12. Ibid.

13. Ibid.

14. Ibid.

15. Gabrielle's mother elaborated on this cultural dissonance in several interviews:

"She lives with a white host family and they don't know anything about taking care of her hair," Hawkins told one news source. "And there's no black salons in their area [in Iowa] not one. We had to work really hard to find a stylist to come and do her hair." Cheryl Wischover, "Gabby Douglas's Mom Takes On Her Daughter's Hair Haters: 'If She Feels Good about Herself, Who Are You to Criticize Her?'" *Fashionista*, August 6, 2012.

16. "'They Don't Know Anything about Taking Care of Her Black Hair': Mother of Olympic Star Gabby Douglas Blames Star's White Host Family for Controversial Pony-

tail," *The Daily Mail*, August 2, 2012, http://www.dailymail.co.uk/femail/article-2182815/Gabby-Douglas-hair-Mother-Olympic-star-attacks-white-host-family-controversial-ponytail.html (accessed January 28, 2015).

17. The youngest actress ever to win any kind of Oscar was Shirley Temple, who received the Juvenile Academy Award in 1935, when she was just six years old. Ten other youngsters between the ages of 7 and 17 accepted that award—a miniature statuette standing just seven inches tall—between 1945 and 1961, when Hayley Mills (*Pollyanna*) became the last recipient. *Beasts of the Southern Wild* was nominated for a total of four awards. In addition to Wallis's nomination for Best Actress, the film was nominated for Best Picture, Best Director (Benh Zeitlin), and Best Adapted Screenplay. Madeline Boardman, "Quvenzhané Wallis & Oscars: 9-Year-Old Is Youngest Best Actress Nominee Ever," *The Huffington Post*, January 10, 2013, http://www.huffingtonpost.com/2013/01/10/quvenzhane-wallis-oscars-best-actress_n_2446855.html (accessed October 25, 2015).

18. Since her breakout role and award-winning performance in *Beasts of the Southern Wild*, Wallis has lined up a number of leading roles for upcoming films, including *Twelve Years a Slave*, which stars Paul Giamatti, Brad Pitt, and Michael Fassbender.

19. A. J. Verdelle, "Quvenzhané and the Tweet," *The Huffington Post*, February 27, 2013, http://www.huffingtonpost.com/aj-verdelle/quvenzhane-wallis-onion-tweet_b_2773557.html (accessed October 25, 2015).

20. "Everyone else seems afraid to say it, but that Quvenzhane Wallis is kind of a cunt right?" Mark Memmott, "*The Onion* Apologizes for Offensive Tweet about 9-Year-Old Quevenzhane Wallis," NPR, February 25, 2013, http://www.npr.org/sections/thetwo-way/2013/02/25/172884045/the-onion-apologizes-for-offensive-tweet-about-9-year-old-quvenzhane-wallis (accessed October 25, 2015).

21. Tricia Romano, "The Onion Tweets that Quvenzhané Wallis Is the C-Word," *The Daily Beast*, February 25, 2013, http://www.thedailybeast.com/articles/2013/02/25/the-onion-tweets-that-quvenzhan-wallis-is-a-cunt.html (accessed October 25, 2015).

22. For the text of the apology, see Memmot, "'The Onion' Apologizes for Its Offensive Tweet about Quvenzhané Wallis." See also Sarah Ditum, "The Onion's Apology for Its Quvenzhané Wallis Tweet—Well, This Is Awkward," *The Guardian*, February 26, 2013, http://www.theguardian.com/commentisfree/2013/feb/26/onion-c-word-tweet-quvenzhane-wallis (accessed October 25, 2015).

23. Verdelle, "Quvenzhané and the Tweet."

24. African American Policy Institute, *Black Girls Matter*, 6–7.

25. Khadijah Costley White, "On Being a Little Black Girl," *Role Reboot*, February 19, 2015, http://www.rolereboot.org/culture-and-politics/details/2015-02-little-black-girl/ (accessed October 25, 2015).

26. Gates, *Trials of Phillis Wheatley*, 26–27.

27. Ibid., 30.

28. Brown, *Black Girlhood Celebration*, 2.

Bibliography

Abdur-Rahman, Aliyyah I. *Against the Closet: Black Political Longing and the Erotics of Race*. Durham: Duke University Press, 2012.

Adams, John Henry. "Rough Sketches: A Study of the Features of the New Negro Woman." *Voice of the Negro* (June 1907): 238–241.

African American Policy Institute. *Black Girls Matter: Pushed Out, Overpoliced, and Underprotected*. New York: African American Policy Forum, 2015.

Alexander, William T. *History of the Colored Race in America*. Kansas City: Palmetto Publishing Co., 1888.

Anderson, Benedict. *Imagined Communities: Reflections on the Origins and Spread of Nationalism*. London: Verso, 2006.

Andrews, Charles C. *The History of the New-York African Free Schools: From Their Establishment in 1787 to the Present Time; Embracing a History of More than Forty Years*. New York: M. Day, 1830.

Asante, Molefi Kete. *The African American People: A Global History*. New York: Routledge, 2013.

Bacon, Jacqueline. *Freedom's Journal: The First African American Newspaper*. New York: Lexington Books, 2007.

Ball, Erica L. *To Live an Antislavery Life: Personal Politics and the Antebellum Black Middle Class*. Athens: University of Georgia Press, 2012.

Ballou, Giddings Hyde. *The Rose of Sharon: A Religious Souvenir, for MDCCCL*, edited by Mrs. C. M. Sawyer. Boston: A. Tompkins and B. B. Mussey and Co., 1849.

Bancroft, Frederic. *Slave Trading in the Old South*. Columbia: University of South Carolina Press, 1996.

Baym, Nina. *American Women Writers and the Work of History, 1790–1860*. New Brunswick: Rutgers University Press, 1995.

Bernstein, Robin. *Racial Innocence: Performing American Childhood from Slavery to Civil Rights*. New York: New York University Press, 2011.

Boyle, Sheila Tully, and Andrew Bunie. *Paul Robeson: The Years of Promise and Achievement*. Amherst: University of Massachusetts Press, 2005.

Braxton, Joanne. Introduction. In Mrs. N. F. Mossell, *The Work of the Afro-American Woman*. New York: Oxford University Press, 1988.

Brazeau, Alicia. "I Must Have My Gossip with the Young Folks": Letter Writing and Literacy in The Boys' and Girls' Magazine and Fireside Companion." *Children's Literature Association Quarterly* 38, no. 2 (2013): 159–176.

Brooks, Joanna. "The Unfortunates: What the Life Spans of Early Black Books Tell Us about Book History." In *Early African American Print Culture*, edited by Lara Langer Cohen and Jordan Alexander Stein, 40–52. Philadelphia: University of Pennsylvania Press, 2012.

Brown, Ruth Nicole. *Black Girlhood Celebration: Toward a Hip-Hop Feminist Pedagogy*. New York: Peter Lang Publishing, 2009.

Burrill, Mary Powell. *Aftermath*. In *Strange Fruit: Plays on Lynching by American Women*, edited by Kathy A. Perkins and Judith Stephens, 79–91. Bloomington: Indiana University Press, 1998.

Capshaw, Katharine. *Civil Rights Childhood: Picturing Liberation in African American Photobooks*. Minneapolis: University of Minnesota Press, 2014.

Carby, Hazel. *Reconstructing Womanhood: The Emergence of the Afro-American Woman Novelist*. New York: Oxford University Press, 1987

Carroll, Anne Elizabeth. *Word, Image, and the New Negro: Representation and Identity in the Harlem Renaissance*. Bloomington: Indiana University Press, 2005.

Chaney, Michael. *Fugitive Vision: Slave Image and Black Identity in Antebellum Narrative*. Bloomington: Indiana University Press, 2008.

Chesebro, Caroline. *Blessings in Disguise: Or, Pictures of Some of Miss Haydon's Girls*. New York: Carlton and Porter, 1863.

Cohen, Lara Langer, and Jordan Alexander Stein. Introduction. In *Early African American Print Culture*, edited by Lara Langer Cohen and Jordan Alexander Stein, 1–18. Philadelphia: University of Pennsylvania Press, 2012.

"Commitment: Toni Cade Bambara Speaks." In *Sturdy Black Bridges: Visions of Black Women in Literature*, edited by Roseanne P. Bell, Bettye J. Parker, and Beverly Guy-Sheftall, 231–250. Garden City: Anchor Press, 1979.

Cooper, Anna Julia. "Womanhood: A Vital Element in the Regeneration and Progress of a Race" (1886). In *The Voice of Anna Julia Cooper, Including* A Voice from the South *and Other Important Essays, Papers, and Letters*, edited by Charles Lemart and Esme Bhan, 53–71. Lanham, Md.: Rowman and Littlefield Publishers, 1998.

Crummell, Alexander. "The Black Woman of the South: Her Neglects and Her Needs." In *Civilization and Black Progress: Selected Writings of Alexander Crummell on the South*, edited by Oldfield, 101–113. Charlottesville: University of Virginia Press, 1995.

Dabel, Jane E. *A Respectable Woman: The Public Roles of African American Women in 19th-Century New York*. New York: New York University Press, 2007.

Dann, Martin, comp. *The Black Press, 1827–1890: The Quest for National Identity*. New York: G. P. Putnam, 1971.

Davis, Elizabeth Lindsay. "Frances Ellen Watkins Harper." In Davis, *Lifting as They Climb*, 231–232. Washington, D.C.: National Association of Colored Women, 1933.

Davis, Hugh. "The Pennsylvania State Equal Rights League and the Northern Black Struggle for Legal Equality, 1864–1877." *Pennsylvania Magazine of History and Biography* 126, no. 4 (2002): 611–634.

Dawson, Melanie. "The Miniaturizing of Girlhood: Nineteenth-Century Playtime and Gendered Theories of Development." In *The American Child: A Cultural Studies Reader*, edited by Caroline Levander and Carol Singley, 63–84. New Brunswick: Rutgers University Press, 2003.

Delany, Martin. "The Condition, Elevation, Emigration and Destiny of the Colored People of the United States" (1852). Reprinted in *The Norton Anthology of African American Literature*, 2nd ed., edited by Henry Louis Gates Jr. and Nellie McKay, 258–278. New York: W. W. Norton and Co., 2004.

DeRosa, Deborah. *Domestic Abolitionism and Juvenile Literature, 1830–1865*. Albany: State University of New York Press, 2003.

Dinwiddie, Emily P. *Housing Conditions in Philadelphia: An Investigation Made by Emily W. Dinwiddie under the Direction of a Committee of the Octavia Hill Association*. Philadelphia: n.p., 1904.

"Douglass, Sarah Mapps." In *Dictionary of American Negro Biography*, edited by Rayford W. Logan and Michael R. Winston. New York: W. W. Norton and Company, 1982.

Driscoll, Catherine. *Girls: Feminine Adolescence in Popular Culture and Cultural Theory*. New York: Columbia University Press, 2002.

Duane, Anna Mae. *Suffering Childhood in Early America: Violence, Race, and the Making of the Child Victim*. Athens: University of Georgia Press, 2010.

Du Bois, W. E. B. *Morals and Manners among Negro Americans*, edited by W. E. Burghardt Du Bois and Augustus Granville Dill. Atlanta: Atlanta University Press, 1914.

———. *The Souls of Black Folk*, edited by John Edgar Wideman. New York: Vintage Books, 1990.

duCille, Ann. *The Coupling Convention: Sex, Text, and Tradition in Black Women's Fiction*. New York: Oxford University Press, 1993.

Dudden, Faye E. *Serving Women: Household Service in the Nineteenth-Century America*. Middletown, Conn.: Wesleyan University Press, 1985.

Dunbar, Erica Armstrong. *A Fragile Freedom: African American Women and Emancipation in the Antebellum City*. New Haven: Yale University Press, 2008.

Dunbar, Jane Chaplin. *Songs for My Children*. Boston: American Tract Society, 1861.

Dunbar-Nelson, Alice. "Mine Eyes Have Seen: A Play in One Act." In *The Works of Alice Dunbar-Nelson*, vol. 3, edited by Gloria T. Hull, 239–249. New York: Oxford University Press, 1988.

Durham, J. X. "Marriageable State." In *Ladies' Physo Medical Companion: Containing the Causes and Preventatives of a Premature Decline, with a Review of the Various Changes and Derangements of the Female Constitution*. Canton, Ohio: Gotshall and Martin Printers, 1850.

Dyer, Thomas G. "An Early Black Textbook: *Floyd's Flowers or Duty and Beauty for Colored Children*." *Phylon* 37, no. 4 (1976): 359–361.

Edson, John R. "Slave's Friend." In *Children's Periodicals of the United States: Historical Guides to the World's Periodicals and Newspapers*, edited by R. Gordon Kelly, 408–411. Westport, Conn.: Greenwood Press, 1984.

Ellis, R. J. *Our Nig: A Cultural Biography of a "Two-Story" African American Novel*. New York: Rodopi BV, 1993.

Ernest, John. *Chaotic Justice: Rethinking African American Literary History*. Chapel Hill: University of North Carolina Press, 2009.

Fagan, Benjamin. "'Americans as They Really Are': The *Colored American* and the Illustration of National Identity." *American Periodicals* 21, no. 2 (2011): 97–119.

Field, Corinne. *The Struggle for Equal Adulthood: Gender, Race, and the Fight for Citizenship in Antebellum America*. Chapel Hill: University of North Caroline Press, 2014.

Filler, Louis. "Harper, Frances Ellen Watkins." In *Notable American Women, 1607–1950*, vol. 2, *G–O*, edited by Edward T. James, Janet Wilson James, and Paul S. Boyer, 137–139. Cambridge: Harvard University Press, 1971.

Fleischner, Jennifer B. *Mastering Slavery: Memory, Family, and Identity in Women's Slave Narratives*. New York: New York University Press, 1996.

Fletcher, Holly Berkely. *Gender and the American Temperance Movement of the Nineteenth Century*. New York: Routledge, 2008.

Floyd, Silas X. *Charming Stories for Young and Old*. Washington, D.C.: Austin Jenkins, 1925.

———. *Floyd's Flowers: Or, Duty and Beauty for Colored Children*, illustrated by John Henry Adams. Atlanta: Hertel, Jenkins, 1905.

———. *The New Floyd's Flowers: Short Stories for Colored People Old and Young*. Washington, D.C.: Austin Jenkins, 1922.

———. *Short Stories for Colored People Both Old and Young*. Washington, D.C.: Austin Jenkins, 1920.

Foreman, P. Gabrielle. *Activist Sentiments: Reading Black Women in the Nineteenth Century*. Urbana: University of Illinois Press, 2009.

———. "'Reading Aright': White Slavery, Black Referents, and the Strategy of Histotextuality in *Iola Leroy*." *Yale Journal of Criticism* 10, no. 2 (1997): 327–354.

Foreman, P. Gabrielle, and Reginald H. Pitts. Introduction. In *Our Nig: Or, Sketches from the Life of a Free Black*, edited by P. Gabrielle Foreman and Reginald H. Pitts, xxii–l. New York: Penguin Books, 2005.

Formanek-Brunell, Miriam. *Dolls and the Commercialization of American Culture*. New Haven: Yale University Press, 1993.

Foster, Frances Smith. "Creative Collaboration: As African American as Sweet Potato Pie." In *Post-Bellum, Pre-Harlem: African American Literature and Culture, 1877–1919*, edited by Barbara McCaskill and Caroline Gebhard, 17–56. New York: New York University Press, 2006.

———. "Frances Ellen Watkins Harper (1825–1911)." In *Kindred Hands: Letters on Writing by British and American Women Authors, 1865–1935*, edited by Jennifer Cognard-Black and Elizabeth MacLeod Walls, 43–47. Ames: University of Iowa Press, 2006.

———. "Gender, Genre and Vulgar Secularism: The Case of Frances Ellen Watkins Harper and the AME Press." In *Recovered Writers/Recovered Texts*, edited by Dolan Hubbard, 46–59. Knoxville: University of Tennessee Press, 1997.

———. "Genealogies of Our Concerns, Early (African) American Print Culture, and Transcending Tough Times." *American Literary History* 22, no. 2 (2010): 368–380.

———. "How Do You Solve a Problem like Theresa?" *African American Review* 40, no. 4 (2006): 631–645.

———. Introduction. In *A Brighter Coming Day: A Frances Ellen Watkins Harper Reader*, edited by Frances Smith Foster, 3–40. New York: Feminist Press, 2000.

———. Introduction. In Frances E. W. Harper, *Trial and Triumph*, in *Minnie's Sacrifice, Sowing and Reaping, and Trial and Triumph: Three Rediscovered Novels by Frances E. W. Harper*, edited by Frances Smith Foster, xi–xxxvii. Boston: Beacon Press, 1994.

———, ed. *Love and Marriage in Early African America*. Boston: Northeastern University Press, 2008.

———. "A Narrative of the Interesting Origins and (Somewhat) Surprising Developments of African-American Print Culture." *American Literary History* 17, no. 4 (2005): 714–740.

———. *'Til Death or Distance Do Us Part: Love and Marriage in African America*. New York: Oxford University Press, 2010.

———. *Written by Herself: Literary Productions by African American Women, 1746–1892*. Bloomington: Indiana University Press, 1993.

"Frances Ellen Watkins Harper." In Hallie Quinn Brown, *Homespun Heroines and Other Women of Distinction*, 97–103. Xenia, Ohio: Aldine Publishing Co., 1926.

Gaines, Kevin. *Uplifting the Race: Black Leadership, Politics, and Culture in the Twentieth Century*. Chapel Hill: University of North Carolina Press, 1996.

Gardner, Eric. "Children's Literature in the AME *Christian Recorder*: An Initial Comparative Bio-Bibliography for May 1862 and April 1873." In Gardner, *Impossible Publics*. Forthcoming.

———. "Early African American Print Culture and the American West." In *Early African American Print Culture*, edited by Lara Langer Cohen and Jordan Alexander Stein, 75–92. Philadelphia: University of Pennsylvania Press, 2012.

———. "Introduction: Two Texts on Children and Christian Education." *PMLA* 123, no. 1 (2008): 156–165.

———. "Remembered (Black) Readers: Subscribers to the *Christian Recorder*, 1864–1865." *American Literary History* 23, no. 2 (2011): 229–259.

———. "'This Attempt of Their Sister': Harriet Wilson's *Our Nig* from Printer to Readers." *New England Quarterly* 66, no. 2 (1993): 226–246.

———. *Unexpected Places: Relocating Nineteenth-Century African American Literature*. Jackson: University of Mississippi Press, 2010.

Garvey, Ellen Gruber. *Writing with Scissors: American Scrapbooks from the Civil War to the Harlem Renaissance*. New York: Oxford University Press, 2013.

Gates, Henry Louis, Jr. *Figures in Black: Words, Signs, and the "Racial" Self*. New York: Oxford University Press, 1989.

———. Introduction. In Harriet Wilson, *Our Nig: Or, Sketches from the Life of a Free*

Black, in a Two-Story White House, North. Showing that Slavery's Shadows Fall Even There. New York: Random House, 1983.

———. *The Trials of Phillis Wheatley: America's First Black Poet and Her Encounter with the Founding Fathers*. New York: Basic Books, 2003.

———. "The Trope of the New Negro and the Reconstruction of the Image of the Black." *Representations* 24 (Fall 1988): 129–156.

Gates, Henry Louis, Jr., and Gene Andrew Jarrett. *The New Negro: Race, Representation and African American Culture*. New York: Columbia University Press, 2007.

Gatewood, Willard B. *Aristocrats of Color: The Black Elite, 1890–1920*. Little Rock: University of Arkansas Press, 1990.

Gibson, Prof. and Mrs. John William. *Golden Thoughts on Chastity and Procreation: Including Heredity, Prenatal Influences, etc.* Naperville, Ill: J. L. Nichols, 1903.

Goeser, Caroline. *Picturing the New Negro: Harlem Renaissance Print Culture and Modern Identity*. Lawrence: University Press of Kansas, 2007.

Gold, Susanna W. "The Death of Cleopatra/The Birth of Freedom: Edmonia Lewis at the New World's Fair." *Biography* 35, no. 2 (2012): 318–341.

"Grace Bustill Douglass (1782–1842)." In *Notable Black American Women*, Book 2, edited by Jessie Carney Smith, 189–190. Detroit: Gale Research, 1996.

Graff, Harvey J. *Conflicting Paths: Growing Up in America*. Cambridge: Harvard University Press, 1995.

Greenberg, Brian, and Linda S. Watts. *The Social History of the United States: The 1900s*. Santa Barbara, Calif.: ABC-CLIO, 2009.

Gross, Kali N. *Colored Amazons: Crime, Violence, and Black Women in the City of Brotherly Love, 1880–1910*. Durham: Duke University Press, 2006.

Hackley, E. Azalia. *The Colored Girl Beautiful*. Kansas City, Mo.: Burton Publishing Company, 1916.

Haley, James T., ed. *Afro-American Encyclopedia: Thoughts, Doings, and Sayings of the Race*. Nashville, Tenn.: Haley and Florida, 1896.

Harley, Sharon. "Anna J. Cooper: A Voice for Women." In *The Afro-American Woman: Struggles and Images*, 87–96. 1987; repr., Baltimore, Md.: Black Classic Press, 1997.

Harper, Frances. "Enlightened Motherhood." In *A Brighter Coming Day: A Frances Ellen Watkins Harper Reader*, edited by Frances Smith Foster, 285–292. New York: Feminist Press, 1990.

Harper, Frances E. W. "Coloured Women of America." *The Englishwoman's Review of Social and Industrial Questions* 9, no. 57 (January 18, 1878): 10–15.

———. *Trial and Triumph*. In *Minnie's Sacrifice, Sowing and Reaping, and Trial and Triumph: Three Rediscovered Novels by Frances E. W. Harper*, edited by Frances Smith Foster. Boston: Beacon Press, 1994.

Harper, Frances Watkins. "We Are All Bound Up Together." In *Proceedings of the Eleventh Woman's Rights Convention, New York, May 1866*. Reprinted in *A Brighter Coming Day: A Frances Ellen Watkins Harper Reader*, edited by Frances Smith Foster, 217–219. New York: The Feminist Press at the City University of New York, 1990.

Harris, Leslie M. *In the Shadow of Slavery: African Americans in New York City, 1626–1863*. Chicago: University of Chicago Press, 2003.

Hartman, Saidiya V. *Scenes of Subjection: Terror, Slavery, and Self-Making in Nineteenth-Century America.* New York: Oxford University Press, 1997.

Haven, Gilbert. *The Pilgrim's Wallet: Or, Scraps of Travel Gathered in England, France, and Germany.* 1864; repr., New York: Hurd and Houghton, 1869.

Higginbotham, Evelyn. *Righteous Discontent: The Black Woman's Club Movement in the Black Baptist Church, 1880–1920.* Cambridge: Harvard University Press, 1993.

Hollick, Frederick. *The Marriage Guide, or Natural History of Generation: A Private Instructor for Married Persons and Those About to Marry Both Male and Female; in Every Thing Concerning the Physiology and Relations of the Sexual System and the Production or Prevention of Offspring—Including All the New Discoveries, Never Before Given in the English Language.* New York: T. W. Strong, 1850.

hooks, bell. *Bone Black: Memories of Girlhood.* New York: Henry Holt and Company, 1996.

Hopkins, Pauline. *Contending Forces: A Romance Illustrative of Negro Life North and South.* New York: Oxford University Press, 1988.

———. "Prospectus of the New Romance of Colored Life, *Contending Forces.*" *Colored American Magazine* 1 (September 1900).

Horton, James O. *In Hope of Liberty: Culture, Community and Protest among Northern Free Blacks, 1700–1860.* Oxford: Oxford University Press, 1996.

Hutchinson, George. *The Harlem Renaissance in Black and White.* Cambridge: Harvard University Press, 1995.

Hutton, Frankie. *The Early Black Press in America, 1827 to 1860.* Westport, Conn.: Greenwood Press, 1993.

Jackson, Cassandra. "Harper, Frances Ellen Watkins." In *African American Lives,* edited by Henry Louis Gates Jr. and Evelyn Brooks Higginbotham, 374–376. Oxford: Oxford University Press, 2004.

Jackson, Holly. "Another Long Bridge: Reproduction and Reversion in Hagar's Daughter." In *Early African American Print Culture,* edited by Lara Langer Cohen and Jordan Alexander Stein, 192–202. Philadelphia: University of Pennsylvania Press, 2012.

Jackson, Leon. "The Talking Book and the Talking Book Historian: African American Cultures of Print—The State of the Discipline." *Book History* 13 (2010): 251–308.

Jacobs, Harriet. *Incidents in the Life of a Slave Girl.* 1861; repr., New York: Dover Publications, 2001.

James, Milton. "Institute for Colored Youth." *Negro History* 21 (January 1958): 83–85.

Jemmy and His Mother: A Tale for Children: and Lucy: Or, The Slave Girl of Kentucky. Cincinnati: American Reform Tract and Book Society, 1858.

Jeynes, William H. *American Educational History: School, Society, and the Common Good.* Thousand Oaks, Calif.: Sage Publications, 2007.

Johnson, Brian L. *W. E. B. Du Bois: Toward Agnosticism, 1868–1934.* Lanham, Md.: Rowman and Littlefield, 2008.

Johnson, Evelyn Bodek. *The Philadelphia Fels, 1880–1900: A Social Portrait.* Cranbury, N.J.: Associated University Presses, 2000.

Jones, Jacqueline. *American Work: Four Centuries of Black and White Labor.* New York: W. W. Norton, 1999.

Jones, LeRoi. "The Changing Same (R&B and the New Black Music)" (1966). In *The Leroi Jones/Amiri Baraka Reader*, edited by William J. Harris in collaboration with Amiri Baraka, 186–209. New York: Thunder's Mouth Press, 1995.

Keckley, Elizabeth. *Behind the Scenes: Thirty Years a Slave, or Four Years in the White House*. Reprinted in *The Norton Anthology of African American Literature*, edited by Henry Louis Gates Jr. and Nellie McKay, 366–384. New York: W. W. Norton, 2004.

Kerber, Linda. *Women of the Republic: Intellect and Ideology in Revolutionary America*. Chapel Hill: University of North Carolina Press, 1980.

Kessler, Sidney H. "The Organization of Negroes in the Knights of Labor." *Journal of Negro History* 37, no. 3 (1952): 248–276.

King, Wilma. *African American Childhoods: Historical Perspectives from Slavery to Civil Rights*. New York: Palgrave Macmillan, 2005.

The Ladies' Indispensable Companion and Housekeepers' Guide: Embracing Rules of Etiquette; Rules for the Formation of Good Habits; and a Great Variety of Medical Recipes. New York: H. Dayton, 1859.

Lane, Roger. *William Dorsey's Philadelphia and Ours: On the Past and Future of the Black City in America*. Oxford: Oxford University Press, 1991.

Larsen, Nella. *Quicksand and Passing*. New Brunswick: Rutgers University Press, 2004.

Levine, Robert S. "Circulating the Nation: David Walker, the Missouri Compromise, and the Rise of the Black Press." In *The Black Press: New Literary and Historical Essays*, edited by Todd Vogel, 17–36. New Brunswick: Rutgers University Press, 2001.

Lewis, Jan. "The Republican Wife: Virtue and Seduction in the Early Republic," *William and Mary Quarterly* 44, no. 4 (Oct. 1987): 689–721.

Li, Stephanie. *Something Akin to Freedom: The Choice of Bondage in Narratives by African American Women*. Albany: State University of New York Press, 2010.

Lindey, Sara. "Boys Write Back: Self-Education and Periodical Authorship in Late-Nineteenth-Century Story Papers." *American Periodicals* 21, no. 1 (2011): 72–88.

Logan, Rayford. *The Negro in American Life and Thought: The Nadir, 1877–1901*. New York: Dial, 1954.

Logan, Shirley Wilson. *We Are Coming: The Persuasive Discourse of Nineteenth-Century Black Women*. Carbondale: Southern Illinois University Press, 1999.

Lorde, Audre. "Age, Race, Class, and Sex: Women Redefining Difference." In Lorde, *Sister Outsider: Essays and Speeches*, 114–123. Berkeley: Crossing Press, 1984.

MacLeod, Anne Scott. *American Childhood: Essays on Children's Literature of the Nineteenth and Twentieth Centuries*. Athens: University of Georgia Press, 1994.

Matthews, Victoria Earle. *The Value of Race Literature: An Address Delivered at the First Congress of Colored Women of the United States, at Boston, Mass., July 30th, 1895*. Boston: n.p., 1895. Reprinted in *The Massachusetts Review* 27, no. 2 (1986): 172–175.

McAndrew, Quentin Story. "Location, Location, Location: Remapping African American Print Culture in the Nineteenth-Century United States." *Criticism* 53, no. 2 (2011): 331–336.

McDowell, Deborah. *"The Changing Same": Black Women's Literature, Criticism, and Theory*. Bloomington: Indiana University Press, 1995.

McGill, Meredith. "Frances Ellen Watkins Harper and the Circuits of Abolitionist Poetry." In *Early African American Print Culture*, edited by Lara Langer Cohen and Jordan Alexander Stein, 53–74. Philadelphia: University of Pennsylvania Press, 2012.

McGill, Meredith L. *American Literature and the Culture of Reprinting, 1834–1853*. Philadelphia: University of Pennsylvania Press, 2003.

McHenry, Elizabeth. *Forgotten Readers: Recovering the Lost History of African American Reading Societies*. Durham: Duke University Press, 2005.

Miller, Monica L. *Slaves to Fashion: Black Dandyism and the Styling of Black Diasporic Identity*. Durham: Duke University Press, 2009.

Mintz, Steven. *Huck's Raft: A History of American Childhood*. Cambridge: Belknap Press of Harvard University Press, 2004.

Mitchell, Koritha. *Living with Lynching: African American Lynching Plays, Performance, and Citizenship, 1890–1930*. Urbana: University of Illinois Press, 2011.

Mitchell, Michelle. *Righteous Propagation: African Americans and the Politics of Racial Destiny after Reconstruction*. Chapel Hill: University of North Carolina Press, 2004.

Morrison, Toni. Afterword. In Morrison, *The Bluest Eye*, 207–216. New York: Penguin Books, 1994.

———. *Sula*. New York: Alfred A. Knopf, 1973.

Moss, Hilary J. *Schooling Citizens: The Struggle for African American Education in Antebellum America*. Chicago: University of Chicago Press, 2009.

Mossell, Mrs. N. F. *Little Dansie's One Day at Sabbath School*. Germantown, Pa.: Philander V. Baugh, 1902.

———. *The Work of the Afro-American Woman*. 2nd ed. Philadelphia: Geo. S. Ferguson Company, 1894.

Mott, Abigail. Preface. In Olaudah Equiano, *The Life and Adventures of Olaudah Equiano: Or Gustavus Vassa, the African. From an Account Written by Himself, Abridged by A. Mott, to Which Is Added Some Remarks on the Slave Trade*. New York: Samuel and Sons, 1829.

Newman, Richard, Patrick Rael, and Phillip Lapsansky. *Pamphlets of Protest: An Anthology of Early African American Protest Literature, 1790–1860*. New York: Routledge, 2001.

Noble, Marianne. "The Ecstasies of Sentimental Wounding in Uncle Tom's Cabin." *Yale Journal of Criticism* 10, no. 2 (1997): 295–320.

———. *The Masochistic Pleasures of Sentimental Literature*. Princeton: Princeton University Press, 2000.

Norton, Mary Beth. *Liberty's Daughters: The Revolutionary Experience of American Women, 1750–1800*. Boston: Little, Brown and Company, 1980.

Parker, Mary Louise. *Helps over Hard Places: Stories for Girls*. Boston: American Tract Society, 1861.

Patten, Robert. "Serial Literature." In *Oxford Reader's Companion to Dickens*, edited by Paul Schlicke, 514–519. Oxford: Oxford University Press, 1999.

Perkins, Linda M. "Quaker Beneficence and Black Control: The Institute for Colored Youth, 1852–1903." In *New Perspectives on Black Educational History*, edited by Vincent P. Franklin and James D. Anderson, 61–96. Boston: G. K. Holland, 1978.

Peterson, Carla L. *"Doers of the Word": African-American Women Writers and Speakers in the North (1830–1880)*. New York: Oxford University Press, 1995.
Pomeroy, Jane R. "Anderson's Life and Introduction to His Work." In Jane R. Pomeroy, *Alexander Anderson: Wood Engraver and Illustrator: An Annotated Bibliography*, vol. 1. New Castle, Del.: Oak Knoll Press; and Worcester, Mass.: American Antiquarian Society, 2005.
Powers, Tyrone. *Eyes to My Soul: The Rise or Decline of a Black FBI Agent*. Dover, Mass.: The Majority Press, 1996.
Price, Edward J., Jr. "School Segregation in Nineteenth-Century Pennsylvania." *Pennsylvania History* 43, no. 2 (1976): 120–137.
Pride, Armistead Scott, and Clint C. Wilson II. *A History of the Black Press*. Washington, D.C.: Howard University Press, 1997.
Rael, Patrick. *Black Identity and Black Protest in the Antebellum North*. Chapel Hill: University of North Carolina Press, 2002.
Reid-Pharr, Robert. "Black, White, and Yeller." In *Conjugal Union: The Body, the House, and the Black American*. New York: Oxford University Press, 1999.
Roethler, Jacques. "Reading in Color: Children's Book Illustrations and Identity Formation for Black Children in the United States." *African American Review* 32, no. 1 (1998): 95–105.
Rohrbach, Augusta. *Truth Stranger than Fiction: Race, Realism and the U.S. Literary Marketplace*. New York: Palgrave, 2002.
Rosenberg, Ruth. "Seeds in Hard Ground: Black Girlhood in *The Bluest Eye*." *Black American Literature Forum* 21, no. 4 (1987): 435–445.
Rury, John L. "The New York African Free School, 1827–1836: Conflict over Community Control of Black Education." *Phylon* 44, no. 3 (1983): 187–197.
Ryan, Susan. *The Grammar of Good Intentions: Race and the Antebellum Culture of Benevolence*. Ithaca, N.Y.: Cornell University Press, 2003.
Sacks, Marcy S. *Before Harlem: The Black Experience in New York City before World War I*. Philadelphia: University of Pennsylvania Press, 2006.
Sanborn, Geoffrey. "The Plagiarist's Craft: Fugitivity and Theatricality in *Running a Thousand Miles for Freedom*." *PMLA* 128, no. 4 (2013): 907–922.
Sánchez-Eppler, Karen. *Dependent States: The Child's Part in Nineteenth-Century American Culture*. Chicago: University of Chicago Press, 2005.
Sander, Valerie. *Records of Girlhood*, vol. 2, *An Anthology of Nineteenth-Century Women's Childhoods*. Surrey: Ashgate, 2012.
Santamarina, Xiomara. "'Are We There Yet?' Archives, History, and Specificity in African-American Literary Studies." *American Literary History* 20, nos. 1–2 (2008): 304–316.
———. *Belabored Professions: Narratives of African American Working Womanhood*. Chapel Hill: The University of North Carolina Press, 2005.
Scruggs, Dalila. "Photographs to Answer Our Purposes": Representations of the Liberian Landscape in Colonization Print Culture." In *Early African American Print Culture*, edited by Lara Langer Cohen and Jordan Alexander Stein, 203–230. Philadelphia: University of Pennsylvania Press, 2012.

Sherrard-Johnson, Cherene. *Portraits of the New Negro Woman: Visual and Literary Culture in the Harlem Renaissance*. New Brunswick: Rutgers University Press, 2007.

Smith, Katharine Capshaw. "Childhood, the Body, and Race Performance: Early Twentieth-Century Etiquette Books for Black Children." *African American Review* 40, no. 4 (2006): 795–811.

———. *Children's Literature of the Harlem Renaissance*. Bloomington: Indiana University Press, 2004.

Smith, Shawn Michelle. *Photography on the Color Line: W. E. B. DuBois, Race, and Visual Culture*. Durham: Duke University Press, 2004.

Smith, Valerie. Introduction. In Harriet Jacobs, *Incidents in the Life of a Slave Girl*. New York: Oxford University Press, 1988.

———. *Self-Discovery and Authority in Afro-American Narrative*. Cambridge: Harvard University Press, 1991.

Spillers, Hortense. "Mama's Baby, Papa's Maybe: An American Grammar Book." In *Within the Circle: An Anthology of African American Literary Criticism*, edited by Angelyn Mitchell, 454–481. Raleigh: Duke University Press, 1994.

Stancliff, Michael. *Frances Ellen Watkins Harper: African American Reform Rhetoric and the Rise of a Modern Nation State*. New York: Taylor and Francis, 2011.

Steedman, Carolyn. *Strange Dislocations: Childhood and the Idea of Human Interiority, 1780–1930*. Cambridge: Harvard University Press, 1998.

Sterling, Dorothy, ed. *We Are Your Sisters: Black Women in the Nineteenth Century*. New York: W. W. Norton, 1984.

Stewart, Maria W. "Lecture Delivered at the Franklin Hall." *The Liberator*, November 17, 1832. Reprinted in *Words of Fire: An Anthology of African American Feminist Thought*, edited by Beverly Guy-Sheftall, 30–34. New York: The New Press, 1995.

———. "Mrs. Stewart's Farewell Address to Her Friends in Boston." *The Liberator*, September 28, 1833. Reprinted in *Maria W. Stewart: American's First Black Woman Political Writer: Essays and Speeches*, edited by Marilyn Richardson, 65–74. Bloomington: Indiana University Press, 1987.

———. *Productions of Mrs. Maria W. Stewart: Presented to the First African Baptist Church and Society of the City of Boston*. Boston: Friends of Freedom and Virtue, 1835.

——— "The Proper Training of Children," speech delivered November 21, 1860, at the Ladies Literary Festival in St. James' Protestant Episcopal Church in Baltimore.

Still, William. "Frances Ellen Watkins Harper." In William Still, *The Underground Rail Road: A Record of Facts, Authentic Narratives, Letters, &c., Narrating the Hardships Hair-Breadth Escapes and Death Struggles of the Slaves in Their Efforts for Freedom*. Philadelphia: Porter and Coates, 1872.

———. *The Underground Rail Road: A Record of Facts, Authentic Narratives, Letters, &c., Narrating the Hardships Hair-Breadth Escapes and Death Struggles of the Slaves in Their Efforts for Freedom*. Philadelphia: Porter and Coates, 1872.

Streitmatter, Roger. "Gertrude Bustill Mossell: Guiding Voice for Newly Freed Blacks." *Howard Journal of Communications* 4, no. 4 (1993): 317–328.

———. *Raising Her Voice: African American Women Journalists Who Changed History*. Lexington: University of Kentucky, 1996.

Tate, Claudia. *Domestic Allegories of Political Desire: The Black Heroine's Text at the Turn of the Century*. New York: Oxford University Press, 1992.

The Tawny Girl: Or The History of Margaret Russel, Illustrating the Benefits of Education on the Most Degraded Classes of Society. New York: Samuel Wood and Sons, 1823.

Tillman, Katherine. "Afro-American Women and Their Work." In *The New Negro: Readings on Race, Representation, and African American Culture*, edited by Henry Louis Gates Jr. and Gene Andrew Jarrett, 277–286. Princeton: Princeton University Press, 2007.

Tompkins, Jane. *Sensational Designs: The Cultural Work of American Fiction, 1790–1860*. New York: Oxford University Press, 1985.

Toohey, Michelle Campbell. "'A Deeper Purpose' in the Serialized Novels of Frances Ellen Watkins Harper." In *"The Only Efficient Instrument": American Women Writers and the Periodical, 1837–1916*, edited by Aleta Feinsod Cane and Susan Alves, 202–215. Iowa City: University of Iowa Press, 2001.

Townsend, John. *Faith in Their Own Color: Black Episcopalians in Antebellum New York City*. New York: Columbia University Press, 2012.

Vogel, Todd, ed. *The Black Press: New Literary and Critical Essays*. New Brunswick: Rutgers University Press, 2001.

Wald, Priscilla. *Constituting Americans: Cultural Anxiety and Narrative Form*. Durham: Duke University Press, 2004.

Wall, Cheryl. "On Dolls, Presidents, and Little Black Girls." *Signs* 35, no. 4 (2010): 796–801.

Wallace, Maurice O., and Shawn Michelle Smith. Introduction. In *Pictures and Progress: Early Photography and the Making of African American Identity*, edited by Maurice O. Wallace and Shawn Michelle Smith, 1–17. Durham: Duke University Press, 2012.

Washington, Booker T. "Industrial Education for the Negro." In *The Negro Problem: A Series of Articles by Representative Negroes of To-Day*, 1903; repr., New York: Humanity Books, 2003.

———. *Up from Slavery: An Autobiography*. New York: Doubleday, 1901.

———. *Working with the Hands: Being a Sequel to "Up from Slavery," Covering the Author's Experiences in Industrial Training at Tuskegee*. New York: Doubleday, Page and Co., 1904.

Washington, Mary Helen. Introduction. In Washington, *Black-Eyed Susans: Classic Stories by and about Black Women*. New York: Anchor Books, 1975.

———. *Invented Lives: Narratives of Black Women, 1860–1960*. New York: AnchorBooks Doubleday, 1987.

Weikle-Mills, Courtney. Introduction: Children's Periodicals. *American Periodicals* 22, no. 2 (2012): 117–120.

Weiss, Harry B. *Samuel Woods & Sons: Early New York Publisher of Children's Books*. New York: New York Public Library, 1942.

Wells, Ida B. *Crusade for Justice: Autobiography of Ida B. Wells*, edited by Alfreda M. Duster. Chicago: University of Chicago Press, 1978.

———. *A Red Record: Tabulated Statistics and Alleged Causes of Lynchings in the United States, 1892–1893–1894* (1895). In *Southern Horrors and Other Writings: The Anti-Lynching Campaign of Ida B. Wells, 1892–1900*, edited by Jacqueline Jones Royster, 73–157. Boston: Bedford St. Martins, 1997.

Welter, Barbara B. "The Cult of True Womanhood: 1820–1860." *American Quarterly* 18, no. 2, part 1 (1966): 151–174.

Wheatley, Phillis. *Poems on Various Subjects, Religious and Moral*, edited by John Shields. New York: Oxford University Press, 1988.

Wilder, Craig Steven. "Black Life in Freedom: Creating a Civic Culture." In *Slavery in New York*, edited by Ira Berlin and Leslie Harris, 215–239. New York: New Press, 2005.

"William Watkins (b. circa 1803–d. circa 1858)," Archives of Maryland, http://msa.maryland.gov/megafile/msa/speccol/sc5400/sc5496/002500/002535/html/002535bio.html (accessed March 29, 2016).

Williams, Andreá N. *Dividing Lines: Class Anxiety and Postbellum Black Fiction*. Ann Arbor: University of Michigan Press, 2013.

Williams, Fannie Barrier. "The Colored Girl." In *The New Woman of Color: The Collected Writings of Fannie Barrier Williams, 1893–1918*, edited by Mary Jo Deegan, 63–66. DeKalb: Northern Illinois University Press, 2002.

Willis, Deborah. "Picturing the New Negro Woman." In *Black Womanhood: Images, Icons, and Ideologies of the African Body*, edited by Barbara Thompson, 227–245. Seattle: University of Washington Press, 2008.

Wilson, Harriet E. *Our Nig: Or, Sketches from the Life of a Free Black*, edited by P. Gabrielle Foreman and Reginald H. Pitts. New York: Penguin Books, 2005.

Winch, Julie. *The Elite of Our People: James Willson's Sketches of Black Upper-Class Life in Antebellum Philadelphia*. University Park: Pennsylvania State University Press, 2000.

Wood-Allen, Mary. *What a Young Woman Ought to Know*. Philadelphia: Vir, 1905.

Woods, Naurice Frank, Jr. "An African Queen at the Philadelphia Centennial Exposition 1876: Edmonia Lewis's *The Death of Cleopatra*." *Meridians: Feminism, Race, Transnationalism* 9, no. 1 (2008): 62–82.

Wright, Nazera Sadiq. "Black Girls and Representative Citizenship." In *From Bourgeois to Boojie: Black Middle-Class Performances*, edited by Vershawn Ashanti Young and Bridget Harris Tsemo, 91–110. Detroit, Mich.: Wayne State University Press, 2011.

Yarborough, Richard. Introduction. In Pauline Hopkins, *Contending Forces: A Romance Illustrative of Negro Life North and South*, xxviii–xlviii. New York: Oxford University Press, 1988.

Yee, Shirley J. *Black Women Abolitionists: A Study in Activism, 1828–1860*. Knoxville: University of Tennessee Press, 1992.

Young, R. J. *Antebellum Black Activists: Race, Gender, and Self*. New York: Garland Publishing, 1996.

Index

Abett, Leon, 111, 208n82
abolitionist activism: and black women writers' treatment of black girls, 85, 90; in Britain, 43; of Frances E. W. Harper, 122, 124, 143–144; and Harriet Jacobs, 84; and hypocrisy of white activists, 19; of Maria W. Stewart, 71, 76; mentioned, 2, 21, 28, 79; of the Mossell family, 109; and northern free blacks, 23, 26; of Philip Alexander Bell, 47; and presentation of white women as benevolent rescuers of black girls, 28; and *Uncle Tom's Cabin*, 39, 41; whites' treatments of black girls in print, 28, 58, 63, 67–70, 76, 91; of William Watkins, 122. *See also* American Convention for Promoting the Abolition of Slavery; antislavery activism; Plymouth Committee for the Abolition of Slavery; Underground Railroad
absent mothers: because of educational needs of daughters, 183; because of extreme poverty, 80–81, 153; because of slavery, 67, 69, 74–77, 84, 86–88; because of waged work, 28, 47, 58, 61, 121; through death, 14, 52–53, 61, 64–65, 96–97, 121, 137, 183, 209n11; and young girls' household labor, 19. *See also* mothers; surrogate mothers; surrogate parents
Adams, John Henry, 153
African American Policy Institute, 185–186
African Free Schools, 30, 40–45, 47, 58, 195n84
African Methodist Episcopal Church, 116, 118, 122, 133
alcoholism, 18, 20, 52–53, 129, 196–197n130
AME Church Review, 98
American Convention for Promoting the Abolition of Slavery, 30
American Frugal Housewife, 49
American Mercury, 43
American Tract Society, 67, 199n11
Anderson, Alexander, 199n9
Anderson, Caroline, 129
antilynching plays, 172–173
antislavery activism: of Abigail Mott Moore, 43–44; of the American Tract Society, 67; in *Freedom's Journal*, 29, 32, 34; in *The Liberator*, 11; mentioned, 69, 91; of Philadelphia free black community, 205n16; of Samuel Wood, 44–45, 63–65, 198n3. *See also* abolitionist activism; American Convention for Promoting the Abolition of Slavery; Plymouth Committee for the Abolition of Slavery; Underground Railroad
aunts: and attempts to protect enslaved black girls, 191n40; black press presents as socializers of white children about slavery, 69; and care of Frances E. W. Harper, 121–122, 209n11; and care of Gertrude Bustill Mossell, 110, 208n78; and care of Linda Brent, 90; Linda Brent's grandmother described as in *Incidents in the Life of a Slave Girl*, 87, 203n84; in *Trial and Triumph*, 135–136, 212n76
autobiography in black women's writing: in "The First Stage of Life," 75–77; and Frances E. W. Harper, 120–121, 123–124, 131, 135, 144–145; and Harriet Jacobs, 84, 120,

203n83; Harriet Wilson, 79, 120, 201n58; Maria W. Stewart, 74–75, 120

Baltimore, Maryland: Frances E. W. Harper's childhood in, 121–122, 210n20, 210n21; free black men's self-employment in, 24, 190n11; literacy rates in, 9; Maria W. Stewart speaks in, 73; site of Edmonia Lewis sculpture, 116; slavery in, 45, 121
Bambara, Toni Cade, 180
Baraka, Amiri, 179
Bell, Philip Alexander, 47
B. F. Hughes's School for Colored Children, 40–41
black boys: education of, 42, 48–49, 139, 153, 166, 185; in *Floyd's Flowers*, 149, 153, 158, 161, 165–166, 215n37; intemperance and, 72, 129; as laborers, 25; mentioned, 3–4, 66, 180, 198n1; relationships with mothers, 26, 72, 135, 200n44, 204n93
black child labor: Frances E. W. Harper and, 122–123, 210n21; in "The Little Black Girl" (1834), 46; Maria W. Stewart and, 74; in New York City, 25; in *Our Nig*, 80–81, 83 *See also* black girls as servants; indentured servitude
black female sexuality: dangers of not preparing daughters in *Trial and Triumph*, 137; discussed in conduct books, 85, 109, 152, 162, 214n27; mentioned, 60, 144; and stages of girlhood, 14, 19, 61; stereotypes about, 11, 150; violated during slavery, 11–13, 27, 37, 83, 85, 87–90
black girls as servants: black women writers describe, 91; in *Freedom's Journal*, 31–32, 34; Gertrude Bustill Mossell writes about, 105–106; Henry George Assembly of the Knights of Labor and, 114; in *Incidents in the Life of a Slave Girl*, 87; in the *Liberator*, 46–47; and Maria Stewart, 5, 13–14; and obstacles to better employment, 5, 105; in *Our Nig*, 80. *See also* indentured servitude
black girls as waged domestic workers, 104–107, 109
black girls' conversation discouraged: in black press, 35–36; in *Floyd's Flowers*, 161–163, 165
Black Girls Matter, 185
black girls use cramped quarters as regenerative spaces, 15, 81, 91–92, 145
black hair: Gabrielle Douglas and, 183, 217n15; in "Thanksgiving at Piney Grove," 153, 155, 169; in "The Little Black Girl," 67–69
black literary societies, 9–10, 71, 119, 201n60
black male newspaper editors: belief of in republican values, 27–28; encourage black girls to be responsible for fathers, 52–53; influence of in black community, 98; present idealized versions of black girls, 3, 6, 8–19, 58, 60; promote domesticity for black girls, 4, 20, 26, 49–50
black males' efforts to protect black girls, 27, 31–32
black manhood, 8, 24, 27, 90, 100, 133
black migration north, 105–107, 149
black newspapers: and black literacy, 9; female columnists for, 98–101, 116–117; layout of articles conveys content, 99, 107; promote marriage for black girls, 35–37; unite scattered free black population, 26, 30. See also *Colored American* (1837–1841); *Freedom's Journal* (1827–1829); Mossell, Gertrude Bustill
black women educators: Alice Dunbar-Nelson, 177; Fannie Barrier Williams, 147; Frances E. W. Harper, 121; in *Floyd's Flowers*, 155; Gertrude Bustill Mossell, 97; Sarah Mapps Douglass, 110, 205n16; in *Trial and Triumph*, 139
Blessings in Disguise: Or, Pictures of Some of Miss Haydon's Girls, 65
Bordentown School, 111–112
Boston Mercantile Advertiser, 52
Boys' and Girls' Magazine, 101
Brent, Linda (*Incidents in the Life of a Slave Girl*): as an example of a prematurely knowing girl, 12–14, 84–85, 88–90; as an example of a youthful girl, 61, 84–88; uses restricted space to advantage, 15
Brooks, Gwendolyn, 14
Brown, John, 121
Brownies' Book, The (1921–1922), 151
Burrill, Mary P., 173
Bustill, Charles, 96, 205n9
Bustill family history, 95–97

Child, Lydia Maria, 49, 84
childhood innocence: Alexander Crummell criticizes whites for denying to black girls, 5; antebellum black girls do not experience, 19; black males unable to ensure, 27; *Colored American* and, 54; denied to black girls in contemporary culture, 181–184; in "The First Stage of Life," 75, 78; in *Incidents in the Life of a Slave Girl*, 84; and interracial playdates, 66–67, 87; Maria W. Stewart calls for for black girls, 5, 72; in *Maud Mar-*

tha, 14; mentioned, 14; in *Our Nig*, 81–82; seen as the privilege of white children, 18, 61, 63, 69–70, 81–82; and sexuality, 61; in "Theresa-A Haytien Tale," 38. *See also* youthful girls
Christian Intelligencer, 51, 57
Christian Recorder: employs Gertrude Bustill Mossell, 93–94; serializes Frances E. W. Watkins's novels, 21, 118–119, 209n2; subscribers to, 119
Christian Watchman, 52
citizenship: antebellum free blacks strategize to obtain in antebellum years, 2, 19, 28–30, 189n1; antislavery activism and, 44; black girls and, 10, 18, 29, 51, 54, 57; and parenting advice, 19; postbellum models of within black community, 94, 100, 106, 147, 149, 151; and republican motherhood, 25, 29, 143, 200n44; and republican values, 23–25, 46; rights of violated by Jim Crow, 172
Cleopatra, 133–135
Cold Water Army, 53
colonization movement, 42. *See also* Manumission Society
Colored American, The (1837–1841): Children's Department of, 54, 57; distribution of, 195n111; history of, 47–48; mentioned, 18, 21, 41; presents black women as republican mothers, 29, 49–50; promotes domestic education for black girls, 49–50; publication history of, 47–48; reveals difficulties of black families in antebellum years, 18; socializes black children to be good citizens, 57; Youth's Department of, 54–56
"Colored Girl, The" (1905), 22, 147
Colored Reading Society (Philadelphia), 30, 74
community networks: and Gertrude Bustill Mossell's childhood, 96–97; in "The First Stage of Life," 74; in *Incidents in the Life of a Slave Girl*, 90; in *The Tawny Girl*, 64; in *Trial and Triumph*, 128, 131–135, 143–144. *See also* Mrs. Lasette (*Trial and Triumph*)
Condition, Elevation, Emigration and Destiny of the Colored People of the United States (1852), 6
conduct books, 148–150
conduct of black girls: criticized in conduct books, 148, 151–152, 161–163; Gertrude Bustill Mossell criticizes, 112; Pauline Hopkins criticizes, 164
Congress of Colored Women of the United States, 129
Contending Forces: A Romance Illustrative of Negro Life North and South (1901), 164
Cooper, Anna Julia, 7–8, 95
Coppin, Fannie Jackson, 107, 207n63
Cornish, Samuel, 48, 56
Crummell, Alexander, 6–7

dark-skinned girls: Fannie Barrier Williams champions, 22; in *Floyd's Flowers*, 166; mentioned, 19
David Walker's Appeal to the Coloured Citizens of the United States (1829), 27–28
Despotism in America: Or, an Inquiry into the Nature and Results of the Slave-Holding System in the United States (1840), 55
"Directions for Little Ladies" (*Floyd's Flowers*), 160
disenfranchisement of black men, 24
dolls for black girls, 57, 76, 157–160, 166, 170, 204n90
Don't! A Book for Girls (1891), 152
"Don't-Care Girl, The" (*Floyd's Flowers*), 161–163
Douglas, Gabrielle, 182–183
Douglass, Frederick, 4, 135, 156
Douglass, Grace Bustill, 110, 205n16
Douglass, Sarah Mapps, 96, 110, 205n16, 208n78
Du Bois, W. E. B., 20, 111, 146–147, 212n69
Dunbar, Paul Lawrence, 156
Dunbar-Nelson, Alice, 173, 177
Dwight, Timothy, 193n80

education of black girls: in African Free Schools, 40–45; in the antebellum North, 25–26, 40–41; in black-run schools, 40–41, 194n83, 194n86; Booker T. Washington's views on, 157; at Bordentown School, 111–112; in the *Colored American*, 49, 52; of Frances E. W. Harper, 12; of Gertrude Bustill Mossell, 96–97; in industrial schools, 153; at the Institute for Colored Youth, 96, 107, 207n63; of Maria W. Stewart, 74; in normal schools, 139, 155, 177; in *Our Nig*, 82; in public schools, 125–126; and racial violence, 46; in *The Tawny Girl*, 63–65; in *Trial and Triumph*, 120, 125, 132–136; at the Watkins Academy for Negro Youth, 122; in white schools, 45, 51–52. *See also* literacy in black communities
"Emma" (1837), 67–*68*
employment: of northern blacks in the 1820s, 23–24; optimism about after the Civil War,

102, 110–111, 115, 127–130. *See also* obstacles to black employment
Equiano, Olaudah, 27, 41, 43–45

"Fate of the Newspaper that Had Nothing in It, The" (1886), 93–94
Female Literary Association of Philadelphia, 45
"First Stage of Life, The" (1861), xi, 12, 71–72, 74–79
Floyd, Silas X.: biography of, 22, 149; mentioned, 130; views of on girls' education, 20, 22
Floyd's Flowers: analysis of, 155–173; literary context for, 150–152; mentioned, 2, 22, 103, 177, 182; and reading "aright," 9, 20, 149–150. *See also* "The Don't-Care Girl" (*Floyd's Flowers*); "The Loud Girl" (*Floyd's Flowers*); "Thanksgiving at Piney Grove" (*Floyd's Flowers*)
Forten, Sarah, 45, 195n101
Frado (*Our Nig*): cramped quarters of, 15, 81; mentioned, 2, 88, 183; physical abuse of, 81, 192n58, 201n61; as a prematurely knowing girl, 12, 80, 183, 202n78; survival strategies of, 82, 165; as a youthful girl, 61, 80, 82
Freedom's Journal (1827–1829): advertises schools for black children, 194n83; discusses violence against black girls, 31–34; and evidence that black mothers worked outside the home, 28; founding of, 29; mentioned, 11, 21, 23, 29, 41, 47–48, 52, 71; parenting advice in, 193–194n81; portrays black servant girls as smart and canny, 34; promotes marriage for black girls, 35–37, 102; readership of, 190n29, 191n36; and republican values, 23, 28–30; reveals struggles of black men, 18; roles of in black community, 30
Fugitive Slave Act (1850), 34, 74, 208n76

Garrison, William Lloyd, 41, 47, 191n36
genealogy of black girlhood, 12–14, 18. *See also* prematurely knowing girls; youthful girlhood
Golden Thoughts on Chastity and Procreation (1903), 151
Grace ("Emma," 1837), 67
Great Migration, 148, 151
Grimké, Angelina Weld, 172, 177

Haitian Revolution, 37–39
Harcourt, Annette (*Trial and Triumph*), 12–13, 119–121, 123–124, 130, 132–135
Harper, Frances E. W.: career as antislavery lecturer, 122, 125; childhood of, 121–122, 209–210n11, 210n20, 210n21; delivers "Enlightened Motherhood" speech to Brooklyn Literary Society, 143; early publications of, 209n19; focus on interiority in *Trial and Triumph*, 130, 135, 138, 173; mentioned, 8, 12; networks with Gertrude Bustill Mossell, 101; optimism of about racial progress in 1880s, 129, 135, 143, 145; republican values of, 133, 141, 143; and temperance movement, 125; tours South after Civil War, 139–141; and Underground Railroad, 122; use of autobiography in *Trial and Triumph*, 120, 132, 135, 139, 142, 144–145, 172. See also *Trial and Triumph* (1888–1889)
Henry George Assembly of the Knights of Labor (Philadelphia), 114
Hildreth, Richard, 55
Hopkins, Pauline, 95
Hughes, B. F., 40–41, 194n83, 194n86
Hurston, Zora Neale, 14, 177

Impey, Catherine, 113
Incidents in the Life of a Slave Girl (1861): and concept of "prematurely knowing" girl, 84; describes debt of a white owner to a black woman, 86; describes sexual exploitation of enslaved women and girls, 13, 87–89, 203n83, 204n98; and Linda Brent's creative use of cramped space, 15; literary techniques of, 84–85, 203n82, 203n83; presents an example of a black girl who makes deliberate plans to improve her situation, 88–89; presents an example of a youthful black girl, 61, 87–88; presents a model of development of nineteenth-century black girls, 10, 12, 14, 79. *See also* Jacobs, Harriet
indentured servitude: described, 80; in the Northeast, 27; whites present as beneficial for black girls, 46–47. *See also* black girls as servants; black child labor
independence: France E. W. Harper promotes for black communities, 141; Maria W. Stewart promotes for black communities, 75; as a republican value, 23–24, 72; as a route to black mobility, 30, 49–50
independent black women: Annette Harcourt (*Trial and Triumph*), 139, 142–145; discouraged in *Floyd's Flowers*, 158, 165; in the Douglass family, 110, 208n76; Frado (*Our Nig*), 83; Frances E. W. Harper as an example of, 122, 125, 139–141; Gertrude Bustill Mossell promotes, 106, 110, 114–116; Maria

W. Stewart encourages, 14; and prematurely knowing girlhood, 61; as a theme of black women's writing, 79
Indianapolis World, 98
"Industrial Education for the Negro" (1903), 150, 157, 214n25
industrial schools: Alexander Crummell advocates for girls, 7; in *Floyd's Flowers*, 153, 155; Institute for Colored Youth, 96, 107, 207n63; Lucy C. Laney and, 116; in *Trial and Triumph*, 28. *See also* Bordentown School; "Industrial Education for the Negro" (1903); Tuskegee Institute
Institute for Colored Youth (Philadelphia), 96, 107, 140, 207n63
integration of public schools, 125–127, 129
Interesting Narrative of the Life of Olaudah Equiano, The (1789), 27, 41. See also *Life and Adventures of Olaudah Equiano: Or Gustavas Vassa, the African, from an Account Written by Himself, The* (1829)
interiority: and black girls' development, 13; as a focus of black women's writing, 3, 10, 62, 178; male black authors do not focus on, 203n82; in "Theresa-A Haytien Tale," 39, 59; in *Trial and Triumph*, 120, 124, 130–131, 135, 172–173
interracial playdates: in "First Stage of Life," 76; in *Incidents in the Life of a Slave Girl*, 76
Iola Leroy (1892), 8

Jacobs, Harriet: discusses sexual violations during slavery, 13, 87–89, 203n83, 204n98; as example of black woman writer who writes about real girls, 59; introduces concept of "prematurely knowing" black girlhood, 10, 12, 84, 89–90; literary techniques of, 85, 203n84; presents a model of development for nineteenth-century black girls, 79, 183; presents an example of youthful girlhood, 61, 87–88; writes about money and debt, 86. See also *Incidents in the Life of a Slave Girl* (1861)
Jim Crow, 133, 148, 164, 172, 177
Johnson, Georgia Douglass, 173
Josie ("Of the Meaning of Progress," 1903), 146, 159
Juvenile Miscellany, 54, 214n27

Keckley, Elizabeth, 12–13
"Keeping School" (*Floyd's Flowers*), 166–168

Ladner, Joyce, 4
Larsen, Nella, 14, 177
Lewis, Edmonia, 116, 135
Liberator, The, 41; Philip Alexander Bell works on staff of, 47–48; publishes antilynching plays by black women, 173; publishes articles about black girls, 45–47; publishes early writings of Frances E. W. Harper, 210n19; publishes evidence that southern slaves read *Freedom's Journal*, 191n36; publishes poem "The Little Black Girl," 11; publishes work of Sarah Mapps Douglass and Sarah Forten, 195n101
libraries, 9–10, 30, 54, 101, 110, 158
Life and Adventures of Olaudah Equiano: Or Gustavas Vassa, the African, from an Account Written by Himself, The (1829), 41, 43. See also *Interesting Narrative of the Life of Olaudah Equiano, The* (1789)
Lipscomb, G. D., 173
literacy in black communities: and black press, 9, 54–55, 79, 99; linked to upward mobility, 10, 54, 58, 79, 83; and New Negro ideals, 169; in nineteenth-century North, 11, 26, 201n60, 209n4; in nineteenth-century South, 30; Sabbath schools and, 26; types of, 61, 91; and voter registration, 148. *See also* reading "aright"
"Little Black Girl, The" (1834), 45–47
"Little Black Girl, The" (1861), 68–70
Little Dansie's One Day at Sabbath School (1902), 100, 173–177
Little Keepsake: Or Easy Lessons in Words of One Syllable, The (1825), 66
"Loud Girl, The" (*Floyd's Flowers*), 161–163, 165
L'Ouverture, Touissant, 38–39
Lucy: Or, The Slave Girl of Kentucky (1858), 69–70

Madame Pauline ("Theresa-A Haytien Tale"), 37–39
Maine Temperance Gazette, 52
Manumission Society, 40, 42, 58
marriage: advice literature about, 85; black newspapers promote for black girls, 35–37; discussed in *Freedom's Journal*, 102, 192n59, 193n63; Frances E. W. Harper presents as one of several choices for professional women, 21, 120, 137, 141–142, 144–145; Gertrude Bustill Mossell advocates careful choice of partners, 95, 103–104, 108–109; Nella Larsen critiques in *Quicksand*, 14; Robert Charles O'Hara advocates singlehood over inadequate husbands, 152; Silas X. Floyd presents as ultimate goal for professional women, 9, 156–157

"Mary and Her Dolls" (*Floyd's Flowers*), 158–160
Matthews, Victoria Earle, 129
Maud Martha (1953), 14–15
Mercantile Library (Philadelphia), 101
Middle Passage, 43–46, 188n26
Mitchell, Joseph, 173
Moore, Abigail Mott, 41, 194n88
Morals and Manners (1904), 150
moral suasion, 25, 63, 91, 132–133, 135
Morrison, Toni, 15, 180
Mossell, Gertrude Bustill: advises black girls, 95, 104, 107–110, 112; advocates economic self-sufficiency in black community, 102–103; advocates founding of new school to educate black girls, 111–112; advocates thrift, 103–104, 109; difficulties resolving balance between black women's need to be full-time mothers and need to do waged work, 115–116; links undesirable behaviors in black community to history of slavery, 115; mentioned, 3, 8; optimism about economic opportunities for black girls and women, 102, 110–111, 115; personal history of, 96–98, 113, 208n86; presents independence as a choice for women, 110, 114–115; presents middle-class values to black readers, 93; work as newspaper columnist, 98–101, 116–117. See also *Little Dansie's One Day at Sabbath School* (1902); *The Work of Afro-American Women* (1894)
Mossell, Nathan, 97–98, 103, 111, 129, 205n20
Mossell family history, 97
motherless black girls: in "First Stage of Life," 74–75; Frances E. W. Harper, 121–122; Gertrude Bustill Mossell, 96; Maria W. Stewart, 74; in *Our Nig*, 80; in *The Tawny Girl*, 63; in *Trial and Triumph*, 121. *See also* absent mothers
mothers: advice to in black press, 49–50, 109; biracial unions of, 63, 127; critiqued as inadequate, 137, 153, 170; free black women as, 96; Gertrude Bustill Mossell's views on roles of, 115–116; as heroes, 37–39, 176; husbands unable to protect, 27; and moral suasion, 29, 200n38; presented as morally compromised, 120–121, 131; and rape, 12, 89, 128, 203; seek educational opportunities for their children, 41, 51; written out of stories, 159–160, 175. *See also* absent mothers; "The Colored Mother of New England"; "Enlightened Motherhood"; republican motherhood; surrogate mothers; surrogate parents
Mrs. Lasette (*Trial and Triumph*): biography of, 127, 131; nurturing of Annette, 120, 124, 132–133, 135, 137–139; role in community, 125, 129, 131, 137–138
Mulberry Street African Free School (New York), 41–43

National Association of Colored Women, 150
National Equal Rights League, 96, 129
National Negro Doll Company, 160
New Negro, 149–151, 155–156, 169, 172
New York Age, 98
New York Freeman, 3, 21, 94, 98–102, 117
Niagara Movement, 20, 15, 177

Obama, Malia, 181–182
Obama, Sasha, 181–182
obstacles to black employment: impact of on black families, 189n2; mentioned, 19–20; in mid-nineteenth century, 195–196n93; post-Reconstruction, 95, 104–105, 108, 134, 172; in *Trial and Triumph*, 128
"Only a Girl" (1886), 3–4
Our Nig (1859), 12, 19, 79–83, 212–202n62

Philadelphia, Pennsylvania: black abolitionist activity in, 20, 95–96, 113, 124, 205n16; black community institutions in, 30, 45, 96–98; black housing in, 125–127, 129; black labor activism in, 114; black literary societies in, 9–10; black professional women in, 99, 107, 129; black unemployment in, 104; black women's self-employment in, 110, 114, 208n76; Centennial Exposition at, 134; education of black children in, 25–26, 96–97, 107, 125, 129, 207n63; literacy rate of free black community of, 9; size of black community in, 29, 105, 125, 207n56
Philadelphia Echo, 97–98
Philadelphia Independent, 97
Philadelphia Society for Promoting the Abolition of Slavery, 43
Philadelphia Times, 98
Philadelphia Women's Medical College, 129
Philomethean Society, 48
photography and the New Negro, 169–170
playdates between white and black children, 66–68
Plymouth Committee for the Abolition of Slavery, 43
Poems: Moral and Religious, for Children and Youth (1821), 65
Post, Amy, 84
premature knowledge: of Middle Passage,

44–46; on need for self-reliance, 55; of slavery, 90; that whites will not protect black girls, 80, 82
prematurely knowing girls: defined, 10, 12–14, 60–61; in *Incidents in the Life of a Slave Girl*, 84–85, 88–89; in *Our Nig*, 80
Press Republican, 98
"Proper Training of Children, The" (1860), 74
Purvis, Robert, 113

Quakers, 41, 63, 96
Quicksand (1928), 14

rape: and advice about black girls' conduct, 162–165; in *Behind the Scenes*, 13; in *Freedom's Journal*, 37; in *Incidents of the Life of a Slave Girl*, 13, 84–85, 87; Jim Crow and, 148, 162; in *Trial and Triumph*, 127–128
Ray, Charles B., 47
reading "aright": and antebellum black newspapers, 59; defined, 8–9, 13, 15; *Floyd's Flowers*, 149, 173; and *Incidents in the Life of a Slave Girl*, 84–85; and *Little Dansie's One Day at Sabbath School*, 176; of Mossell's column on public deportment of black women and girls, 112–113
rebellious black girls: Elizabeth Keckley, 12; in *Freedom's Journal*, 31–32; Linda Brent, 12; in *Our Nig*, 79, 83; as a theme of black women's writing, 90. *See also* "Don't-Care Girl, The" (*Floyd's Flowers*); "Loud Girl, The" (*Floyd's Flowers*)
Reconstruction, 24, 94–95, 110, 134, 148
Red Record (1895), 172
Reformed Family, 52
"Remarks on the Slave Trade," 43–46
Repository of Religion and Literature, and of Science and Art (1858–1863), 71–74, 91, 94, 193n79, 199n25, 199n30
reprinting, 31–34, 36, 39, 44, 50–58, 61, 65, 100–102, 191n40, 191–192n49
republican motherhood: and challenges of for black mothers, 25, 58, 89–90; defined, 25; early black press promotes, 29; and training of children for citizenship, 135, 143; and use of moral suasion, 25; in writings of Martin Delaney, 6. *See also* "Enlightened Motherhood"
republican values, 23–25, 46, 141, 143
Rice, Rev. Raymond, 111

Sabbath schools: curriculum of, 26; mentioned, 13; and northern racial violence, 51; presented as route to upward mobility, 40. *See also* education of black girls; *Little Dansie's One Day at Sabbath School* (1902)
self-employment: and black independence in the antebellum North, 24–25; Bustill women and, 208n76; Gertrude Bustill Mossell encourages women to pursue, 114–115; Frances E. W. Harper and, 139–140; Mossell family and, 97, 103; in *Our Nig*, 83
self-governance: Booker T. Washington advocates, 157; in "The First Stage of Life," 78; in *Floyd's Flowers*, 155; Mariah W. Stewart advocates, 73; republican values and, 189n1
self-sacrifice: in *Floyd's Flowers*, 159; in *Little Dansie's One Day at Sabbath School*, 174–177; in "Of the Meaning of Progress," 146–147, 159
serialization: and black literacy, 118–119, 204n4; of "The First Stage of Life," 71–72; and greater attention to black girls in the black press, 17, 21, 62; and opportunities for black women writers, 45, 209n2; of "Theresa-A Haytien Tale," 37; of *Trial and Triumph* and, 2, 118–119
sexual vulnerability of black girls: black males' inability to prevent, 27, 31–33, 90; Elizabeth Keckley and, 12–13; in *Freedom's Journal*, 32–33; in *Incidents in the Life of a Slave Girl*, 12–13, 84–85, 88–90; in *The Interesting Narrative of the Life of Olaudah Equiano*, 28; in post-Reconstruction years, 162; in *Trial and Triumph*, 122, 136
Sigourney, Lydia H., 50
slave ledgers, 15–*16*
Slave's Friend, The (1836–1838), 67–68, 199n15
Smith, James McCune, 47
Socratic method, 132–133
Songs for My Children: With Memoirs with Numerous Illustrations (1861), 67
Souls of Black Folk, The (1903), 146
Stewart, Maria W.: advises black parents, 73, 78; autobiography in writings of, 59, 74–75, 79, 120; biography of, 13–14, 200n45; mentioned, 4, 8, 21, 39, 176, 178; speech to the New England Anti-Slavery Society, 5–6; urges black communities to be independent, 75; writing career of, 72–73, 91. *See also* "First Stage of Life, The" (1861)
Still, William, 121–123, 140–141, 209n11, 210n21
Stowe, Harriet Beecher, 63, 130
Sula (1973), 15
Sunday-School Monitor, 57
surrogate mothers: black, 110, 124, 127, 139, 209n4; white, 28, 46–47, 63, 182–183, 217n11
surrogate parents: in "The First Stage of Life,"

77; of Frances E. W. Harper, 209–210n11; of Gertrude Bustill Mossell, 110; in *The Tawny Girl*, 63; in *Trial and Triumph*, 124, 127–128, 133, 136; in white abolitionist literature, 28, 46–47, 62
Sylvia ("The Little Black Girl"), 45–47

Tawny Girl: Or the History of Margaret Russell, The (1823), 63–65
temperance: black press discusses need for in antebellum decades, 26, 28–29, 47–48, 54, 73; *Colored American* urges black girls to promote in their households, 52–53; Gertrude Bustill Mossell promotes, 95; Philip Alexander Bell promotes, 47–48
Terrell, Mary Church, 8
"Thanksgiving at Piney Grove" (*Floyd's Flowers*), 153–157, 169
Their Eyes Were Watching God (1937), 14
Theresa-A Haytien Tale" (1828): discussed, 37–39; read in conjunction with *Little Dansie's One Day at Sabbath School*, 176
Trial and Triumph (1888–1889), 2, 12, 21, 118–145
Tuskegee Institute, 153, 158, 215n38

Uncle Tom's Cabin (1852), 63
Underground Railroad, 96, 122, 205n9
University of Pennsylvania Medical School, 97, 129
uplift of the black race: and conduct advice to black girls, 147–148, 166, 215n42; Frances E. W. Harper advocates, 142–143; Gertrude Bustill Mossell's columns and, 95, 103; New Negroes and, 169–170; as a trope in black literature, 180; W. E. B. Du Bois praises women's work in, 214n24
upper tens, 136, 212n69

Vigilance Association, 96
Vigilance Committee, 96
violence against black girls: in the antebellum black press, 28, 31–32, 34, 37; and autobiography in black women's writing, 13; black women writers present responses to, 90, 173; and black writers' focus on proper conduct, 19, 57, 73, 94, 148, 162–165, 172, 177, 214n26; in "The First Stage of Life," 76; in *Our Nig*, 12, 80–83, 192n58; and prematurely knowing girls, 18–19, 61; in the slave South, 31–32, 87–88. *See also* sexual vulnerability of black girls

Walker, David, 27–28
Wallis, Quvenzhané, 183–184
Washington, Booker T.: lectures at Bordentown School, 111; mentioned, 1, 4, 156; views on education of black youth, 156–157, 214n25; views on racial uplift, 150–151, 215n38
Watkins Academy for Negro Youth (Baltimore), 25–26, 121
Wells, Ida B., 95, 164–165, 172
What a Young Girl Ought to Know (1897), 152
Wheatley, Phillis, 11, 185
Wilkins, Grace (*Floyd's Flowers*), 153–157
Willson, James, 9–10
Wilson, Harriet, 12, 78–79, 81–83, 120, 201n58. See also *Our Nig* (1859)
Women's Christian Temperance Union, 152
Wood, Samuel, 41, 45, 63–64, 198n3
Working with Your Hands (1905), 150
Work of Afro-American Women, The (1894), 94, 117

"Young Ladies Read!" (1860), 74
youthful girlhood: defined, 10–11, 60–61; in "First Stage of Life," 75–78; in *Incidents in the Life of a Slave Girl*), 86–88; in *Our Nig*, 80, 82; and responsibility for adults, 50, 53. *See also* childhood innocence
Youth's Companion, 54, 56

NAZERA SADIQ WRIGHT is an assistant professor of English at the University of Kentucky.

The University of Illinois Press
is a founding member of the
Association of American University Presses.

Cover designed by Faceout Studio, Kara Davison
Cover illustration © Shutterstock

University of Illinois Press
1325 South Oak Street
Champaign, IL 61820-6903
www.press.uillinois.edu